AN ANTHOLOGY OF KANSHI (CHINESE VERSE) BY JAPANESE POETS OF THE EDO PERIOD (1603-1868)

Translations of Selected Poems
with an Introduction and Commentaries
by
Timothy R. Bradstock
and
Judith N. Rabinovitch

Japanese Studies
Volume 3

The Edwin Mellen Press
Lewiston•Queenston•Lampeter

Library of Congress Cataloging-in-Publication Data

An anthology of Kanshi (Chinese verse) by Japanese poets of the Edo
  period (1603-1868) / translations of selected poems with an
  introduction and commentaries by Timothy R. Bradstock and Judith N.
  Rabinovitch.
      p. cm. -- (Japanese studies ; v. 3)
    Includes bibliographical references and index.
    ISBN 0-7734-8560-0
    1. Chinese poetry--Japan--Translations into English.
  I. Bradstock, Timothy Roland. II. Rabinovitch, Judith N.
  III. Series: Japanese studies (Lewiston, N.Y.) ; v. 3.
  PL3054.E5A65   1997
  895.1'.146080952--dc21   97-25575
                                                                     CIP

This is volume 3 in the continuing series
Japanese Studies
Volume 3 ISBN 0-7734-8560-0
JaS Series ISBN 0-88946-157-0

A CIP catalog record for this book is available from the British Library.

The Edwin Mellen Press   The Edwin Mellen Press
      Box 450   Box 67
Lewiston, New York   Queenston, Ontario
  USA 14092-0450   CANADA L0S 1L0

The Edwin Mellen Press, Ltd.
Lampeter, Ceredigion, Wales
UNITED KINGDOM SA48 8LT

Printed in the United States of America

To Our Parents

TABLE OF CONTENTS

Where titles are unknown or nonexistent, the first line of
the verse is given, in quotation marks.

LIST OF ILLUSTRATIONS

All of the following are in the authors' private collection.

1. An original document, dated 1852, written by Takahashi Yoshizumi
(unidentified) at age seventy-four, quoting the Kogaku scholar, Itō
Jinsai (1627-1705), as follows:

> Master Jinsai says, "Knowing the decree of Heaven means
> nothing more than being tranquil and having no doubts.
> Placed between life or death, survival or ruin, failure
> or success, and glory or dishonor, one remains calm and
> confident, and when the mists dissipate, leaving not a
> trace, one is not moved in the least. This is what we
> call knowing the decree of Heaven."

2. An original Japanese monochrome painting of a cowherd
astride an ox, probably from the late Edo or the Meiji period
(1868-1912), by an unidentified artist named Kakimata Hajime.

3. A handwritten piece of unknown provenance, probably early
nineteenth century, bearing an eight-line verse by Tachi Ryūwan
(1762-1844), titled "An Impromptu Poem Written on a Winter's
Night; Following the Rhymes of Another Verse" (poem 219 in
this anthology).

4. A holographic text of an untitled kanshi quatrain, written and signed
by Yanagawa Seigan (1789-1858). In translation it reads as follows:

> My wizened body is in essence just dust.
> Only after my hair turned white did I come
>   to understand truth.
> Since my youth, when I first began to study,
> I have spent fifty years by the lantern's blue flame.

For years we have read and admired the kanshi (poems in Chinese) composed by Japanese scholars, priests, and townsmen of the Edo period. The long-standing practice of writing poems and prose in Chinese is a reflection of the great prestige enjoyed by Chinese culture in Japan since earliest times. Most of the kanshi in this anthology have never been translated or otherwise read outside of Japan and are even inaccessible to the average Japanese, few of whom today can read classical Chinese. Since many of these poets are introduced to the Western reader here for the first time, our objective has been to offer a representative sampling of each individual's works rather than merely his or her best-known verses, the better to provide a balanced picture of Edo kanshi overall. By the same token we have included works by lesser poets, some of whom are better known as officials or military figures. Our choice of verses is to some degree a matter of individual taste; for any shortcomings in our selection of poems included herein, we ask for the understanding of the reader.

To preserve some semblance of the original poetic form, we have made each line in the English translations of these poems correspond with one line of the Chinese text. While trying to remain faithful to the original language we have, at the same time, aimed for a euphonic effect roughly imitative of the prosodic regularity of the Chinese poetic line. This has been accomplished by providing, as far as possible, an accented syllable in the English for every character per line in the original. Arthur Waley pioneered this technique, which has been used in more recent times by scholars such as David R. McCraw.[1] In conformity with the usual practice among modern translators of Chinese verse, we have not attempted to impose rhyme structure upon our translations, so as to avoid the

---

[1] See his *Du Fu's Laments from the South* (Honolulu: University of Hawaii Press, 1992).

virtually inevitable compromise of fidelity and possible creation of unharmonious auditory effects that can arise in the drive to achieve rhyme.

Some of the poems in this collection appear in our sources without a title, either because they never had one in the first place, or because the secondary collections failed to include the titles, and the original sources were unavailable to us for reference. Many of the collections cited in this anthology are known by multiple, often equivalent or roughly equivalent, titles. For example, the collection of Hayashi Razan's poems known as *Razan shishū* (The Collected Poems of Razan, 1662), seventy-five *maki* [volumes], is also known by at least four other similar titles: *Razan sensei shū*, *Razan sensei shibunshū*, *Razan Hayashi sensei shū*, and *Razan shū*.[2] To minimize confusion, we have adopted the practice of reproducing the title just as it appears in the modern source being cited, without listing variations. When citing the original source for a poem, we have not listed the author of that collection if the individual is also the author of the poem in question. Finally, an asterisk alongside a poet's name in the text after the introduction indicates that the anthology contains a biography and a selection of his or her verse.

In compiling the basic factual information on the lives and careers of the poets, we have in particular drawn extensively upon the following three excellent Japanese sources to which we acknowledge our debt:

(1) *Kangakusha denki oyobi chojutsu shūran*, edited by Ogawa Tsuramichi and published by Meicho Kankōkai, Tokyo, in 1977 (rpt. of orig. pub. 1925); (2) *Nihon kanbungaku daijiten*, compiled by Kondō Haruo and published by Meiji Shoin, Tokyo, in 1985; and (3) "The Appendix of Poets" in *Gozan bungaku shū Edo kanshi shū* [*Iwanami koten bungaku taikei*, vol. 89], pp. 480-502, edited and annotated by Yamagishi Tokuhei and published by Iwanami Shoten, Tokyo, in 1966.

---

[2] As these various titles collectively illustrate, the names of different editions of a given poetic collection typically include the term *shishū*, "poetic collection," *shibunshū*, "collection of prose and poetry," or simply *shū*, "collection." *Shishū* collections were in many cases originally part of a larger *shibunshū* but were later published as an independent work.

Without the textual, literary, and historical research of all who have gone before us—both in Japan and in the West—this anthology would not have been possible. In particular, we owe a scholastic debt to the renowned sinologist and kanshi specialist Professor Inoguchi Atsushi, whose research on the Edo poets presented in his monumental compilation of poems *Nihon kanshi* (Meiji Shoin, Tokyo, 1972), has been a constant source of enlightenment. Finally, we wish also to acknowledge the seminal translation and research in the field of kanshi done by Professor Burton Watson. Our earliest years as graduate students of Chinese and Japanese literature were shaped by his ground-breaking scholarship which was an inspiration to us as we prepared the present anthology.

ACKNOWLEDGEMENTS

We wish to thank the many devoted teachers and colleagues who have helped to guide us in our professional careers. In particular, we owe a debt of gratitude to Hamada Atsushi, Kajihara Masaaki, Minegishi Akira, the late Hiraga Noburu, Edwin A. Cranston, Donald H. Shively, Kang-i Sun Chang, Douglas Lancashire, Richard John Lynn, Paul Jiang, Alice Cheang, and Brian Victoria. During the preparation of our book, we also received much encouragement and support from Philip West, Director of the Maureen and Mike Mansfield Center at the University of Montana, as well as from Dennis O'Donnell, Martin Weinstein, and other esteemed colleagues in Asian Studies here at the University of Montana. We wish to acknowledge generous research grants from both the Mansfield Center and the College of Arts and Sciences under the stewardship of Dean James A. Flightner, whose support of this project was unfailing. We also gratefully acknowledge the assistance of Gerald Fetz and Maureen C. Curnow, present and former Chairs, respectively, of the Department of Foreign Languages and Literatures at the University of Montana. Their abiding interest in the anthology has spurred us on over the years. An expression of appreciation must also go to our son, Peter, who sat patiently at our side throughout the duration of this project, tolerating our seemingly endless preoccupation with the old texts and poets in our collection. Finally, we were buoyed by the enthusiasm of our parents and siblings who offered useful suggestions at various stages in the completion of this manuscript. To each and every person mentioned above and to all of our friends and colleagues around the world we offer our most sincere thanks. All deficiencies which remain, however, are entirely our own responsibility.

ABBREVIATIONS

Andō — [*Shintei*] *Nihon kanshi hyakusen*, comp. by Andō Hideo. Tokyo: Sōdōsha, 1983.

Fujikawa — *Edo kōki no shijintachi* [*Chikuma Shobō sōsho*, vol. 208], by Fujikawa Hideo. Tokyo: Mugi Shobō, 1973.

Iriya — *Nihonjin bunjin shisen*, comp. by Iriya Yoshitaka. Tokyo: Chūō Kōronsha, 1983.

Iwanami — *Gozan bungaku shū Edo kanshi shū* [*Iwanami koten bungaku taikei*, vol. 89], annot. by Yamagishi Tokuhei. Tokyo: Iwanami Shoten, 1966.

Ishikawa — *Kanshi no sekai*, by Ishikawa Tadahisa. Tokyo: Taishūkan Shoten, 1989.

Hirano — *Kanshi meishi hyōshaku shūsei*, comp. by Hirano Hikojirō, et al. Tokyo: Meichō Fukyūkai, 1936.

Inoguchi — *Nihon kanshi* [*Shinshaku kanbun taikei*, vols. 45 & 46; continuous pagination], comp. and annot. by Inoguchi Atsushi. Tokyo: Meiji Shoin, 1972.

NKD — *Nihon kanbungaku daijiten*, comp. by Kondō Haruo. Tokyo: Meiji Shoin, 1985.

Miner — *The Princeton Companion to Classical Japanese Literature*, comp. by Earl Miner, Hiroko Odagiri, and Robert E. Morrell. Princeton: Princeton University Press, 1985.

Miura — [*Shinsen*] *Senryū kyōshi shū*, comp. by Miura Osamu. Tokyo: Yūhōdō, 1914.

Nakamura — *Edo kanshi* [*Koten o yomu*, vol. 20], by Nakamura Shinichirō. Tokyo: Iwanami Shoten, 1985.

Roberts — *A Dictionary of Japanese Artists*, by Laurance P. Roberts. Tokyo: Weatherhill, 1976.

Sazan   *Kan Sazan* [*Nihon shijin sen*, vol. 30], by Fujikawa Hideo. Tokyo: Chikuma Shobō, 1981.

Sugano   *Nihon kanbun* [*Kanbun meisakusen*, vol. 5], by Sugano Hiroyuki and Kunikane Kaiji. Tokyo: Taishūkan Shoten, 1984.

Kudō   *Hirose Tansō, Hirose Kyokusō* [*Sōsho Nihon no shisōka*, vol.35], by Kudō Toyohiko. Tokyo: Meitoku Shuppansha, 1978.

Watson 1976   *Japanese Literature in Chinese*, vol. 2, trans. by Burton Watson. New York and London: Columbia University Press, 1976.

Watson 1990   *Kanshi: The Poetry of Ishikawa Jōzan and Other Edo-Period Poets*, trans. by Burton Watson. San Francisco: North Point Press, 1990.

WWW   *World Within Walls*, by Donald Keene. New York: Holt, Reinhart and Winston, 1976.

INTRODUCTION

"Nighttime Conversations in Mountain Homes"

A dog is barking in the woods, the night is wearing on.
East and west all talk has ceased; nothing more to discuss.
Vulgar stories, petty gossip—who would choose to listen?
Clouds block my brushwood gate, cold the mountain moonlight.

—Priest Gensei, 1623-1668

The writing of poetry and prose in Chinese played an important part in the lives of Japan's elite for well over a millennium, down to the early decades of the twentieth century. An immediate question which arises is how the Japanese came to appropriate the Chinese written language for their own use in the first place. In the absence of a native system, Japanese court scribes began to learn to write Chinese under Korean and Chinese tutelage from around the fifth century, some two centuries before a provisional system for writing Japanese was developed. Chinese thus emerged as the first official written language of the Japanese court. By the early seventh century, as the T'ang dynasty (618-907) was beginning in China, scholars, priests, and scribes in Japan were able to read and write Chinese with considerable skill. A century later, the Japanese were crafting kanshi with confidence, if not originality, and beginning to utilize the "modern style" regulated verse forms of the T'ang.

The first stage of Chinese studies in Japan peaked in the ninth century. After the termination of official missions to China in 894, composition in Chinese experienced a gradual decline in the Japanese court. Furthermore, from around this time, the Chinese language used in court records and documents, histories, and narratives began to incorporate significant new linguistic elements; specifically, characters of Japanese origin, Japanese words written with Chinese characters, and vernacular locutions written in a pseudo-Chinese orthography.

In this way, a form of Chinese known as *hentai kanbun* (variant Chinese) emerged as a distinct linguistic entity, reaching maturity as a hybrid prose form in the Heian period (794-1185).[1] During Heian times Chinese became firmly established as the formal literary language of the male literati, being used extensively in the court, in academe, and the Buddhist establishment. Although these early writers of Chinese were relatively few, they were nonetheless prolific and chose to write even their private diaries and records in some form of this language, while using Chinese as well as Japanese to write poetry.

By the Edo period (1603-1868), Chinese in its various forms had been in use for about a millennium, and Chinese versification had enjoyed an almost equally long tradition. Indeed, the Edo period represents the high-water mark for Chinese literary composition in Japan, kanshi versification becoming as central to the literary lives of Japanese intellectuals as the writing of native waka poetry had been among the aristocracy in earlier centuries.[2] This was a time of enforced national isolation from the rest of the world, the island of Dejima in Nagasaki being the only site where foreign trade was permitted. Knowledge about China—and its literary fashions—filtered into Japan largely through this single window to the outside world. Even though few literati had any direct contact with China, Chinese studies flourished nonetheless.

At the beginning of the Edo period, writing Chinese poetry was considered mainly as a means for the cultivation and transmission of Confucian values; in particular, decorum, self-discipline, filial piety, and obedience. It was also seen as a way of developing literary and aesthetic sensibilities. The poem by Priest Gensei, cited above, with its air of detachment from human concerns and its implicit appreciation for the icy beauty of moonlight viewed in solitude, is an

---

[1]For a detailed discussion of the evolution of variant Chinese, see Judith N. Rabinovitch, "An Introduction to *Hentai Kambun* [Variant Chinese], a Hybrid Sinico-Japanese Used by the Male Elite in Premodern Japan," in *Journal of Chinese Linguistics* 24 (Jan. 1996): 98-127.

[2]Waka, literally "Japanese poetry," includes all known vernacular verse forms. However, owing to the preeminence of the short five-line (31-syllable) tanka form from around the seventh century, the term waka in effect came to designate the tanka. In this study, we have used the term tanka where the short-verse form is specifically intended, reserving "waka" for verse in general written in Japanese.

archetypal expression of some of the essential aesthetic values of the Edo kanshi poet. The kanshi genre is also of significance for the insights the poems provide into popular culture and the social milieu of writers across a wide spectrum of society in Edo times. Edo popular culture has been studied extensively in the West and has become well-known even among general readers through the puppet theater, kabuki drama, haiku poetry, and other vernacular genres depicting the lively demimonde of the townsman, with its bathhouses, tea houses, inns, and theaters. Comparatively little research has been done on kanshi as a source of knowledge and insights into the lives of Confucian scholar-officials, priests, and educated members of the townsman class, whose literary endeavors included to a greater or lesser extent the composition of works in Chinese.

Very few kanshi of the many thousands written have been translated into English. The present anthology attempts to remedy this situation by collecting together and providing in translation some four hundred representative kanshi by one hundred Japanese poets, male and female, both famous and obscure, from the late-sixteenth century to the end of the Edo period. Our hope is that this anthology will bring kanshi more into the mainstream of Japanese literary and historical research and focus attention upon the many worthy but relatively unknown poets in this tradition. Biographical sketches are provided for each writer, and the translated poems are accompanied by notes illuminating their literary aesthetics and philosophical values and explaining any important historical or literary allusions present.

While the kanshi genre most closely resembles classical Chinese models, in some respects it exists in a middle realm between Chinese and Japanese traditions, since it draws cultural, literary, and aesthetic elements from both. This introduction will now turn to some general comparisons involving kanshi, Chinese poetry, and native waka. Though by no means an exhaustive treatment of the subject, this discussion is designed to orient the reader unfamiliar with the two poetic traditions, while identifying some of the important literary themes emerging in the anthology. Next, we will investigate the origins of Chinese composition in Japan and the development of the kanshi form down through the mid-nineteenth century, paying particular attention to the social, philosophical, and historical matrix in which the genre evolved during the Edo period. It will be shown that over time kanshi increasingly came to reflect Japanese concerns, displaying a greater degree of literary originality than its earlier, more derivative counterparts.

Japanese Kanshi and the Chinese *Shih*

The kanshi poets wrote on many of the same themes and subjects as their Chinese counterparts, adopting images, conventions, and rhetorical figures found in *shih* poetry.[3] Historical and literary allusions from the Chinese classics and poetic tradition abound in kanshi, and references to Chinese personages—such as emperors, concubines, and statesmen, as well as to famous places—are common, particularly in the verse written during the first half of the Edo period. As Donald Keene writes:

> When composing a kanshi it was not enough to write grammatically accurate and metrically correct Chinese, difficult though this was for a Japanese; the poet had to allude to Chinese poetry of the past and demonstrate also his knowledge of Chinese history.[4]

Indeed, most of the kanshi poets consciously strove to emulate the great poets of the T'ang and Sung, in a tradition that emphasized learning from and preserving the legacy of the Chinese masters.

However, significant generic and formal differences are nonetheless apparent when we compare the two traditions. Some of the genres of Chinese verse are

---

[3]The *shih* is one of five major Chinese poetic forms, the other four being the *sao* (elegiac verse), *fu* (the prose-poem), *tz'u* (lyrical songs), and *san-ch'ü* (the dramatic lyric). The *shih* genre includes (1) *ssu-yen shih* (four-character line verse), which arose ca. 800 B.C.; (2) the *yüeh-fu* (ballads), appearing ca. 120 B.C.; (3) *ku-shih* (ancient style poetry); and (4) the *chin-t'i shih* (modern or recent verse forms) of the T'ang (see below for details). Types (3) and (4) use five- or seven-character lines. See Kang-i Sun Chang, *The Evolution of Chinese Tz'u Poetry from Late T'ang to Northern Sung* (Princeton: Princeton University Press, 1980), pp. 210-212. The *shih* forms vary in length, but the four- or eight-line types are the most common. All of the poems in this anthology are formally classifiable as *shih*. The Japanese term kanshi means literally "Chinese *shih*."

[4]Donald Keene, *Seeds in the Heart: Japanese Literature from the Earliest Times to the Late Sixteenth Century* (New York: Henry Holt and Company, 1993), p. 76.

absent from Edo kanshi; for example, the Court poetry of the Han (206 B.C.-A.D.220), Six Dynasties (222-569), and early T'ang periods, with its grand descriptions of imperial ceremonies and palatial splendor. Moreover, kanshi poets wrote in certain *shih* forms but avoided others, favoring the T'ang "modern" regulated forms, which are further discussed below. There are also conspicuous thematic, aesthetic, and linguistic disparities, reflecting the different historical and cultural milieux in which the respective bodies of poetry developed, a subject to which we shall now turn.

The majority of the poems in this collection were written in times of relative political stability. The peace and prosperity that characterized most of the Edo period shaped the poets' outlook on life, their poetry on the whole reflecting a sense of contentment and well-being; relatively little of this verse displays real angst or deep suffering. By contrast, the lives of many of the leading Chinese poets were touched by civil war and political upheaval. Some of the most poignant poems by Tu Fu (712-770), for example, were inspired by the personal suffering and sense of dislocation he experienced during the An Lu-shan Rebellion of the late 750s. Another common source of distress for Chinese poets was the failure to gain or hold a post in the civil service. From early in its history, China was, in principle, a meritocracy, and even the lowliest individual, through his own efforts, could become a high official, a prime example being Kung-sun Hung (d. 121 B.C.), who rose from swineherd to become prime minister. Although the civil service examination system provided many opportunities for advancement in society, there was keen competition for the limited number of positions available, leading to disillusionment among those who were unsuccessful or who lost their posts through falling out of favor. Indeed, the despair and sense of injustice felt by the less fortunate among the ranks of China's scholars is at the heart of some of China's most moving and eloquent poetry.

Kanshi poets, on the other hand, show comparatively little interest in official service as a poetic subject, and we seldom see the kind of despair or sorrow discussed above. One reason may be that while Japan adopted many of China's institutions, a meritocratic civil service examination system was never among them. Instead, elite status in Japanese society was largely hereditary, with the scions of samurai families serving their respective daimyo from one generation to another in a system which offered far less room for raised—or dashed—expectations. Also, there existed respectable alternative careers for scholars besides official service, including lucrative posts in private teaching or school administration, which made obtaining a government appointment seem less of a life-or-death matter. Moreover, in spite of their high social status, scholar-officials were not necessarily well paid, living on fixed incomes and often falling into debt to their supposed social inferiors, the merchants. Thus, far from describing official service in glowing terms, Japanese poets, to the extent that they discuss it at all, tend to speak of it pejoratively, using terms such as "the world of dusty tassels."

Overall, however, the *shih* and kanshi share many of the same themes, artistic sensibilities, and philosophical attitudes. In both traditions we see a preoccupation with the celebration of natural beauty, which often entails the symbolic or figurative use of natural images to comment upon human affairs and emotions. All Japanese verse forms, kanshi included, have from earliest times emphasized the unity between the human and natural worlds, seeing Man as part of a greater whole rather than the center of the universe. The poets represented in the present volume never tire of recording their most minute observations of the scenery around them, in particular displaying an acute sensitivity to the seasonal changes manifested in nature. Of the four seasons, spring and autumn figure most prominently in both literary traditions. Spring, with its regenerative powers, brought hope and optimism, but autumn moved these poets even more, its transient, fading beauty reminding them of the sad evanescence of all life.

Despite their seeming predilection for writing descriptive nature verse, the Edo kanshi poets were motivated by more than just the desire to describe earthly beauty for its own sake. Communion with nature when combined with writing poetry was seen as conducive to spiritual inspiration and the attainment of enlightenment, which in turn could elevate the poet to a higher level of creative genius. By removing himself from human society, the poet was able to cast aside, even if only temporarily, the trappings of the mundane world, freeing his mind to meditate upon the transcendental principles of the universe. As Helen C. McCullough observes, this view of nature as a source of metaphysical and philosophical inspiration is traceable to the Chinese poets of the fourth century. At this time they began to "celebrate, rather than shrink from, the awe-inspiring qualities of the grand aspects of nature, and to invest them with mystical or philosophical significance."[5] Their sublime portrayals of nature and the joys of dwelling in rustic surroundings were far removed from earlier intimidating depictions of nature as an alien force, such as are seen in the *Ch'u-tz'u* (Songs of Ch'u, ca. third century B.C.-second century A.D.).[6]

Poetry on the theme of reclusion was popular in Japan as in China. Japanese poet-officials often express the notion that their "proper element" was not the Court or the city but rather the countryside, an ideal which originated in the Chinese tradition. T'ao Ch'ien (T'ao Yuan-ming, 365-427) was the first major eremitic poet, his verse becoming a model for countless later poets in both countries. The first of his two famous verses titled "On Returning to My Garden and Field" contains the following lines:

. . . .
Dogs bark somewhere in deep lanes,
Cocks crow atop the mulberry trees.
My home is free from dust and care,
In a bare room there is leisure to spare.
Long a prisoner in a cage,
I am now able to come back to nature.[7]

This and similar verses by Chinese poets extolling the pleasures of life in quiet seclusion far from the pressures of the mundane workaday world were a source of inspiration for kanshi poets like Ishikawa Jōzan (1583-1672) and Muro Kyūsō (1658-1734). An eighteen-line verse by Kyūsō titled "Returning to My

---

[5]Helen Craig McCullough, *Brocade by Night: 'Kokin Wakashu' and the Court Style in Japanese Classical Poetry* (Stanford: Stanford University Press, 1985), p. 44.

[6]Ibid.

[7]Trans. by Wu-chi Liu in *Sunflower Splendor: Three Thousand Years of Chinese Poetry*, Wu-chi Liu and Irving Yucheng Lo, eds. (Bloomington and Indianapolis: Indiana University Press, 1990; orig. pub. Doubleday, 1975), p. 52.

Fields" (poem 65) is clearly reminiscent of the T'ao Ch'ien tradition. The final nine lines read:

> ...I keep my distance, here among the clouds.
> In the morning I go out once the others have left;
> In the evening I come back before they return.
> Thick trees surround a distant village;
> Thin, dark smoke rises from a nearby town.
> The cows and sheep return at dusk
> When the mountain peaks are bathed in evening light.
> Drunk, I lie beneath the eastern eaves;
> Happiness is found in being true to one's nature.

Although some eremitic poets merely wrote in the persona of the hermit, most such poets in both traditions truly lived the life they described. Either they were forced into this position by political and economic circumstances, like Tu Fu and Su Shih, or else they chose the reclusive lifestyle for philosophical reasons. As Burton Watson explains,

> For Confucians, reclusion was essentially a form of political protest, to be carried out when one felt that conditions in the government were so unsavory that there was no longer any hope of reform....For the Taoists, the hermit is a man who has retired from society...to remove himself from the corrupting influence of civilization and further his own chances for safety and survival.[8]

Kanshi poets writing in this mode were mostly living in retirement by choice, for aesthetic reasons, and seldom because they were escaping political turmoil or had lost favor at court, as was often the case with Chinese poets. Absence of company rarely occasioned loneliness, instead being perceived as an opportunity to develop emotional self-sufficiency and tranquility, a process aided by music, wine, and writing verse. Ensconced in the solitude and privacy of their rough cottages set among pines and bamboo, they sought nothing more than to divest their minds of worldly concerns and, like T'ao Ch'ien, become at one with nature. The Taoist notion of *wu-wei* or "non-striving," in other words, following

---

[8]Burton Watson, *Chinese Lyricism: Shih Poetry from the Second to the Twelfth Century* (New York and London: Columbia University Press, 1971), p. 73.

one's natural inclinations instead of pursuing high office and fame, was their highest ideal.

Poets living in rural Japan were never far from familiar surroundings, unlike so many of the Chinese scholar-officials, who, if in government service or exile, typically found themselves in some remote corner of the empire and far from any large city. The enormously varied physical environment of China, with terrain ranging from the deserts of the north to the lush tropical forests and craggy peaks of the southwest, often engendered wonderment and fascination in the poet and at times a compelling sense of alienation and loneliness rarely seen in Japanese kanshi. No matter where the Japanese poet went, he was unlikely to experience the extreme cultural and geographic differences between places like Ch'ang-an and Kueichow. Overall, the rugged imagery of the often inhospitable Chinese landscape is seldom seen in Japanese verse, which for its part tends to reflect a gentler, more benign natural environment.

In both *shih* and kanshi, life is seen as an inexorable and ceaseless process of change, decline, and reversals of fortune, this in accordance with the basic Buddhist notion that impermanence and suffering are the only constants of existence. The ravages of old age and the inevitability of death are thus a major preoccupation. Such matters are typically treated using the autumnal images of withering plants, fallen leaves, vanishing dew, and the forlorn cries of cicadas, natural images commonly encountered in Japanese waka as well.[9] Observation of nature is invariably tinged with sorrow; the knowledge that today's blossoms will tomorrow be trodden into the soil evokes a sense of sympathy and serves as a bitter reminder that a similar end awaits us all.

Related to these mortal concerns is the *sic transit gloria mundi* theme which again figures prominently in both traditions, a reflection of the importance they attached to antiquity. David R. McCraw writes in his discussion of the centrality of the past in T'ang poetry, "It is not unreasonable to envision Chinese literati focused on the past in front of them, walking backward into the future....It was common practice for Tang poets to visit historical sites and write down their

---

[9]McCullough, pp. 21-22.

feelings and meditations on antiquity."[10]   The Edo poets similarly recalled
bygone eras whenever they paid visits to ruins, ancient sites, and cities whose
appearance had changed over time.   These were a sharp reminder of human
mortality and the transience of glory, made all the more poignant by the
regenerative powers of nature.   "Recalling the Past while at Nara" (poem 93) by
Dazai Shundai (1680-1747) is a representative example of such verse:

> In the boundless lands south of Kyoto the ancient capital lies:
> Third Avenue, Ninth Avenue—these roads still cross the city.
> Wheat ripens in the old royal paddies as peasants wander by.
> Mugwort grows on the imperial road as peddlers travel past.
> Slender willows droop down low, ever evoking sadness.
> Tranquil blossoms lie scattered about, showing no emotion.
> The temples now are all that remain from a thousand years ago,
> And the belling of wild deer is heard in the light of the setting sun.

This theme is a popular one in the waka tradition as well, as illustrated by the
following tanka (*Shinkokinshū*, poem 420) which the priest Saigyō wrote upon
visiting the former capital at Naniwa:

> Only a dream!
> The bygone glories of the spring
> At Naniwa in Tsu—
> Everywhere the rough wind rustles over
> The frost-withered leaves of reeds.[11]

Kanshi and the Vernacular Waka Tradition

While the kanshi genre differs both in form and language from waka, there are
striking thematic and aesthetic similarities, a reflection of the fact that many
kanshi poets also wrote waka and moved easily between the two traditions.
Compare the following poems on evening fireflies, the first a four-line kanshi by
Oka Chōshū (d. 1766), titled "Returning by Night along the River" (poem 102),
and the second, a tanka by Priest Keichū (1640-1701), both combining images of

---

[10]David R. McCraw, *Du Fu's Laments from the South* (Honolulu: University of Hawaii
Press, 1992), p. 180.

[11]Robert Brower and Earl Miner, trans., in *Japanese Court Poetry* (Stanford: Stanford
University Press, 1961), p. 276.

flowing water, fireflies, and the evening cool to produce a similar aesthetic atmosphere:

Fireflies flit about beside the river;
Few the travellers on the road tonight.
Along the way, the night cool as water.
Singing loudly, I walk home in the moonlight.

The color of the sky
Is clearer than water;
How cool is this night
When fireflies are flowing
Down the River of Heaven.[12]

From the medieval period, waka and kanshi poets, besides sharing a common preoccupation with nature, show a predilection for presenting natural images without authorial comment or elaboration, often utilizing the poetic style that Brower and Miner have termed "descriptive symbolism." As they observe, "[I]t often seems as if the [waka] poet himself has retired from the [poetic] scene and the objective world exists as a thing in itself,"[13] with nature serving as a commentary upon human affairs, one replete with symbolic or emotional value. The following verse by Hara Sōkei (1718-1767), titled "A Grave By the Roadside" (poem 122), illustrates the use of this technique in kanshi:

Forlorn the grave mound in the field,
Its headstone overgrown with moss.
The autumn grass has buried all footprints.
The mournful wind comes and goes at will.

Here, the images of the grave overgrown with moss and the buried footprints are suggestive of human impermanence. These elements are made doubly poignant by the implicit contrast with nature's constancy, represented here by the autumn grass and the wind which blows with seeming indifference to the fate of man.

The sense of forlorn solitude so palpable in Sōkei's verse is an expression of an aesthetic ideal known as *sabi* (loneliness or lyric melancholy) common in both

---

[12]Translated by Donald Keene, *WWW*, p. 309.

[13]Brower and Miner, p. 30.

kanshi and waka. Deriving from the Chinese literary tradition, *sabi* may be described in poetic terms as a melancholy tone associated with rustic isolation in a bleak setting of understated, withered beauty. The following kanshi, titled "A Deserted Military Camp in the Moonlight" (poem 55), by Hayashi Baidō (1643-1666), also embodies this quality:

> A deserted camp in a meadow of weeds; I gaze up at the moon.
> Coming to this spot has stirred my emotions, my hood is wet with tears.
> The moon comes and goes as in ancient times, following its natural course.
> Nothing to see but cawing crows, nary a soul in sight.

As this verse also demonstrates, *sabi* is sometimes found in conjunction with an aesthetic concept known as *mono no aware*, "the pathos of things," which arose from the Buddhist awareness of the impermanence of all life and which has parallels in the classical Chinese tradition. Both the rustic melancholy of *sabi* and the bittersweet pathos of *mono no aware* are pervasive elements in the verse of the present anthology as well as in Japanese court literature as a whole, where perishability and beauty are seen as inextricably linked.

Despite the abundance of similarities between the kanshi and waka genres, certain formal and thematic differences exist as well. First, kanshi were not subject to restrictions in length, ranging from four lines to—in some cases—hundreds, the genre permitting extensive description or narration not feasible in the tanka or other even shorter Japanese verse forms.[14] Kanshi tend to be imagistically denser in texture, containing more descriptive elements than do tanka, reflecting the fact that Chinese is an ideographic rather than a syllabic script. A Chinese poem typically contains five or seven complete words per line; in tanka, by contrast, a single word can occupy an entire line, being as long as seven syllables when phonetically written. Thus, in two poems of seemingly

---

[14]Watson 1976, p. 12. Watson writes that "...Dazai Shundai's (1680-1747) verses on currency and rice prices, Yokoi Shōnan's (1809-1869) attacks on the principle of hereditary rule, or Hirose Kyokusō's (1807-1863) 290-line description of a smallpox epidemic, are all representative of poems that could not possibly have been encompassed in the Japanese verse of the time" (ibid.). The long Japanese chōka form was revived by Kokugaku scholars ca. 1750, after a hiatus of about 750 years, but these verses possess little literary or historical interest, being largely imitative of the eighth-century Japanese poetry anthology *Man'yōshū*.

comparable length, we typically find fewer distinct images in the waka than in its kanshi counterpart, as may be observed, for example, in comparing the following two verses on the theme of viewing plum blossoms on a moonlit night. The first is a four-line, twenty-eight character kanshi by Ema Saikō (poem 299), the second, a five-line tanka in thirty-one syllables by Priest Ryōkan:

> Moonlit plum trees enchantingly lovely—how should I spend this evening?
> Softly chanting verse, I wander through the crisscrossing shadows
>   of the trees.
> My body is dappled with patterns of light as distinct as water is clear.
> I can only perceive the subtle fragrance and cannot see the blossoms.

> A moonlit evening
> In this village in the mountains,
> So weary to cross—
> What I faintly discern
> Are plum blossoms, I am sure![15]

In kanshi we also find a greater range of topoi than in traditional tanka. This is partly due to the changing demographics of kanshi writing, for, as the Edo period progressed, kanshi came to be composed by poets from a wider range of social classes, who incorporated new, more plebeian and contemporary subjects into their verse: low-brow references to sexual matters, drunkenness, and the lives of beggars and geisha, for example. Such subjects were generally considered coarse by mainstream tanka poets writing in a tradition heavily influenced by the courtly past. As Donald Keene observes, "...[P]oetic decorum forbade the [tanka] poets of 1800 to describe what were actually the dramatic pleasures of their lives—sex, liquor, a good dinner, a promotion...."[16] Indeed, tanka poets seldom transcended traditional values and courtly propriety, mostly confining themselves to elegant, conventional themes. While it is true that certain experimental poets like Ōkuma Kotomichi (1798-1868) and Tachibana Akemi (1812-1868) wrote unorthodox verse dealing with such "unpoetic" subjects as

---

[15]*WWW*, p. 495; translated by Donald Keene.

[16]Ibid., p. 480.

14

mice and snails, these could hardly have been considered the norm in Edo tanka and were more usually found in comic vernacular forms.[17]

Kanshi, while admitting even the earthiest of subjects, sometimes by contrast manifest moral, even political, didacticism seldom seen in vernacular poetry of the same period. This didactic bent is exemplified by a poem written by the conservative Confucian scholar Bitō Jishū (1745-1813) titled "To My Students" (poem 151), which expounds on the pitfalls that young scholars must avoid in life and the "correct" way for them to behave:

If you wish to become a gentleman,
First you must become a man.
Men value firmness of principle:
Such is the Way of Manliness.
Why is it that today's men
All behave like young girls,
Striving to be like them in speech and appearance,
And feeling ashamed if they aren't?
Men must behave in the proper manner—
Where is the shame in this?
. . . .

A further area where the two genres differ is the Edo kanshi poet's relative disinterest in the subject of romantic love, an attitude which may be traced to Confucian morality and the priority it placed upon the bonds between friends and among kin over romantic relationships.[18] Where the theme of love between the sexes is present in kanshi we find restraint and little of the deep passion and psychological complexity seen in waka. The following kanshi by the female poet Ema Saikō, titled "Picking Lotus Seeds and Throwing Them at the Mandarin Ducks" (poem 301), is one of the more evocative love poems in this anthology:

The two of you floating and swimming there, on the green
    and rippling waters,
Unaware that in the human world there is parting and separation.
For fun I take some lotus seeds and throw them into the pond.
"As you both fly off in opposite directions, may you feel a
    moment of longing!"

---

[17]See *WWW*, pp. 497-506 for examples of poems by these two poets.

[18]McCullough, p. 39.

Eroticism and allusions to sexual activity, however, are present in later Edo kanshi, especially in private verse, although often depersonalized by the use of anonymous third-person characters, as seen in this verse (poem 250) by Hitta Shōtō (1779-1833):

Wispy tresses disheveled and in wild disarray;
Jewelled hairpins lying on the floor, pearls scattered about.
With skin so soft, nothing should come between them.
Her fancy clothes, now flung aside, dangle from a screen.

While sexual intimacy itself is rarely described in waka, the theme of love, disappointed or unrequited love in particular, constitutes a major motif, one that is handled with a sensitivity and depth of psychological insight not typical of kanshi. The following two poems by ex-Empress Eifuku (1271-1342) exhibit an intense interest in the workings of love and show remarkable analytical complexity:

Is it the case
That you today have given me
Some passing thought,
That I, even more than usual,
Long for you with such intensity?[19]

Is it that your feelings
Have begun to change into indifference,
Or that now I need you more
Which makes the most trivial occurrence
An unfailing omen of wretchedness to come?[20]

We have outlined some of the conspicuous similarities and differences in theme and imagery between the kanshi and waka genres and earlier, between the kanshi and the *shih*. It is to this latter comparison that we shall now return. It is important to emphasize the vast backdrop of shared philosophical traditions and literary conventions between kanshi and *shih*. These areas of affinity also include shared formal standards of versification, which will be our next subject for

---

[19]Brower and Miner, trans., p. 373.

[20]Ibid., p. 340.

discussion. Kanshi poets not only adopted and attempted to use (albeit not always successfully or rigorously) Chinese rules governing rhyme and tone, they also imported wholesale classical Chinese rules for metrical prosody and lineation. The net effect of this formal borrowing in combination with the other more literary and philosophical aspects of Japanese indebtedness was the creation of a genre remarkably similar to its classical *shih* models. This was particularly the case during the first two centuries of the Edo period; later, as kanshi composition filtered down through the population and adapted further to the native cultural and linguistic environment, we see a greater degree of divergence from Chinese syntactical and grammatical requirements as well as a growing tendency to include Japanese vocabulary and decidedly Japanese subjects in kanshi. But the varieties of kanshi—their metrical prosody and lineation—did not substantially change during the Edo period, nor did Japanese poets attempt to create new Chinese poetic genres, choosing to remain within the traditional formal boundaries.

A Brief Survey of the Poetic Genres in Edo Kanshi

As already noted, kanshi always followed Chinese models where form is concerned. The poetic sub-genres represented in the kanshi tradition are without exception varieties of *shih*, a reflection no doubt of the poets' desire to adhere to time-honored models for the sake of legitimacy. In the Edo period, the *chin-t'i shih* (J. *kindaishi*) or modern regulated forms of verse were preeminent, accounting for the vast majority of kanshi written. Modern regulated verse forms include (1) the eight-line *lü-shih* (regulated verse, J. *risshi*), either five or seven characters per line and (2) the four-line *chüeh-chü* (quatrain, J. *zekku*, literally, "broken-off lines"), also five or seven characters per line. Among the regulated forms, five- and seven-character *risshi* and seven-character *zekku* were held in particularly high favor, being promoted as the so-called *santaishi* (three poetic forms [of choice]) by such leading figures as Hayashi Razan (1583-1657), Hattori

Nankaku (1683-1759), and Gotō Shizan (1721-1782).[21] Both *risshi* and *zekku* are characterized by rigidly prescribed patterns of tone and rhyme. These tonal and rhyme requirements were by and large observed by the kanshi writers, many of whom, when memory failed them, relied upon their trusty pocket manuals which gave the rhyme and tonal categories of characters. But when a verse was read aloud to a Japanese audience, it was invariably rendered on the spot into a special kind of literary translationese. Thus, the resulting Japanized poem, while giving the literal meaning of the verse, entirely lacked the aural qualities of rhyme, tonal alternation, and linear uniformity which the poet had in the first instance labored to produce. In other words, it was more to the eye than to the ear that the poem bore any formal resemblance to Chinese verse.

The *lü-shih* form, whose rules were codified in the late-seventh century, utilized a rigidly fixed rhyme-scheme: rhyming characters had to be in the level tone, and the same rhyme sound was sustained throughout. In the five-character type, end-rhyme was placed in lines 2, 4, 6, and 8, but in the seven-character variety, the first line was included in the rhyme-scheme as well.[22] Patterns of alternating (that is, level vs. deflected) tone-sequences were incorporated in fixed positions throughout the poem, with strict verbal parallelism as well in the middle two couplets (lines 3 through 6) so as to form "antithetical couplets."[23] The net effect of these patterns of variation was to produce a euphonic contrast and repetition of tones not only within each line but also between key correlated words in a couplet.

Similar rules of tonal parallelism (with some loosening of the rules of verbal parallelism) applied to the shorter, highly economical *chüeh-chü*. This was basically half of a *lü-shih* in length and prosodic form. But the form was nonetheless artistically complete in itself and became, in the words of James R.

---

[21]*NKD*, p. 274.

[22]James R. Hightower, *Topics in Chinese Literature: Outlines and Bibliographies* [*Harvard-Yenching Institute Studies*, vol. 3] (Cambridge: Harvard University Press, 1966), pp. 65-66.

[23]James J.Y. Liu, *The Art of Chinese Poetry* (Chicago: University of Chicago Press, 1962), p. 26; 1966 paperback ed. consulted here.

Hightower, "the most sophisticated and exigent of all Chinese verse forms,"[24] bound by some of the rules for regulated verse. As Hightower further observes, "The twenty words of the five-word [per line] *chüeh-chü* were expected to carry the matter and weight of a *lü-shih* verse twice its length," with "conciseness and concentration [being] achieved by reliance on connotation and allusion."[25] End rhyme occurred in even lines in the five-character-line type; the first line could also contain a rhyme-word (using the deflected tone) in the seven-character-line variety. Six-character verses are only rarely encountered. All rhymes had to be in the same tonal category, as in *lü-shih*, and similar rules of tonal prosody had to be followed as well.

In the late-Edo period, the *zekku* emerged as the most popular kanshi sub-genre. In Watson's view, its popularity was probably linked to the ascendancy of the haiku.[26] However, a decided preference for shorter verse forms is characteristic of Japanese poetry as a whole and may help to explain why kanshi poets gravitated toward *zekku* rather than to more complicated, longer *shih* forms.

A third form of regulated verse, seen only occasionally in Edo kanshi, is the *p'ai-lü* (lined up [i.e., extended] regulated verse, J. *hairitsu*). This form resembled the *lü-shih* in its tonal requirements and utilized parallelism in all but the opening and final couplets.[27] However, it had no set length, being more than ten lines long and most typically twelve in Japan, although verses even three times this length are not unknown. Five- and, far less often, seven-character lines are common, six-character lines relatively rare. The poet was permitted to vary the rhyme-word, making this form somewhat freer than the *lü-shih*, which it otherwise resembled.

[24]Hightower, p. 69.

[25]Ibid.

[26]Watson 1990, p. xv.

[27]Kobayashi Nobuaki, Ichiki Takeo, et al., eds., *Kanbun binran* (Tokyo: Hyōronsha, 1973), p. 105.

Somewhat more common than the *p'ai-lü* in Edo kanshi is the *ku-shih* (ancient verse form, J. *koshi*) form, which emerged in China during the Han dynasty but was only called "ancient" after the introduction of "modern" regulated verse in the early T'ang period. The number of lines in the *ku-shih* was not specified, and even-numbered lines rhymed, although more than one rhyme sound could be used if the poet so desired. *Ku-shih* most often had five or seven characters per line, but occasional deviation from this formula was tolerated.[28] A final sub-genre of kanshi is the *tsa-t'i* (J. *zattai*), the "mixed form," characterized by lines of irregular or unequal length. Poem 193, titled "A Poem in Three-, Five-, and Seven-Character Lines," by Ryū Kinkei (1752-1824), is one example, another being poem 283, "Waiting Upon Mother In Her Litter" by Rai San'yō (1780-1832).

It should be noted that these last three forms, *hairitsu*, *koshi*, and *zattai*, were relatively seldom used in Edo times and were also uncommon in the poetry of the preceding medieval period. From the late-thirteenth century onward, with the rise of the Gozan Zen priest-poet tradition of kanshi writing, the *santaishi* regulated forms predominated. It is to this medieval phase of the kanshi tradition that we shall now turn.

The Kanshi Tradition in the Medieval Age

As stated earlier, the Heian age is considered the first great epoch in Chinese literary writing in Japan, and the growth of Chinese studies in this period was fostered by scholarly and official exchanges with China. These exchanges were terminated at the end of the ninth century, after which time interest in China declined somewhat. The last two centuries of the Heian saw cultural retrenchment and further assimilation of the Chinese literary traditions introduced thus far. Between the thirteenth and fifteenth centuries, Japan's early feudal period, a second great flowering of Chinese literary activity occurred. The Kamakura shogunate promoted secular Chinese learning, especially Confucianism

---

[28]Ibid., p. 24.

and Chinese history and philosophy, establishing the important Kanazawa Bunko library and Ashikaga Gakkō, a school staffed by Zen priests.[29] Trade and scholarly exchange with China were renewed in the fourteenth century, providing an additional stimulus to the development of sinology in Japan after a hiatus of roughly four centuries. The fruition of Chinese studies in this period is best represented by the literary tradition known as *gozan bungaku* or "Five Mountains Literature," associated with the Zen priesthood.[30]

The Gozan priests, starting with the first eminent poet in this tradition, Sesson Yūbai (1290-1346), wrote religious, philosophical, and secular poetry. The secular poems in particular are marked by refreshingly inelegant imagery and individualistic descriptions of everyday life in Japan, setting the stage for the further development of Japanese realism in the kanshi genre later in the Edo period. The following verse, titled "Fish-Oil Lamp at a Roadside Inn," by Banri Shūkyū (1428-1502), is jarringly earthy in its language and imagery and amply demonstrates this unaffected eccentricity:

Oil squeezed from fish guts makes the lamp burn strange,
A hazy light in a dim room reeking of fish.
Midnight, can't sleep, try to trim the lamp—
And the tiny glow is buried in a real fog.[31]

Many Gozan poet-priests ventured forth to China where they advanced their education in sinology and perfected their language skills, returning to Japan with knowledge of both Zen Buddhism and Sung dynasty (960-1279) Neo-Confucianism, which became fully assimilated into the Japanese cultural milieu

---

[29]Keene, *Seeds in the Heart*, p. 1062.

[30]"Five Mountains" refers to two sets of five officially-designated Zen temples in Kyoto and Kamakura (a sixth is often added to the list in the case of Kyoto), where this Chinese literary activity was centered. Strictly speaking, "five" originally referred not to the number of the temples themselves but to the numbers in the ranking system, first rank through the fifth rank, under which the temples were classified, following the Chinese Southern Sung model. See Marian Ury, *Poems of the Five Mountains* (Tokyo: Mushinsha, 1977), p. xii. The ranking, number, and even the selection of temples designated as Gozan institutions varied from time to time in accordance with the preferences of the Shogun or the priesthood itself.

[31]Trans. by Donald Keene, *Seeds in the Heart*, pp. 1076-1077.

by the end of the sixteenth century. Current knowledge about Chinese poetics was also acquired by the priests while they lived and worked in China. Zekkai Chūshin (1336-1405), who spent some nine years there, is considered today to be the preeminent poet in the Gozan tradition. However, Konishi Jin'ichi avers that he was probably not considered a first- or even second-rank poet by standards upheld in China, as he lacked sufficient "thematic weight."[32]

Another outstanding poet, though not a Gozan priest himself, was the endearingly quirky Priest Ikkyū (1394-1481), a son of Emperor Go-Komatsu (1377-1433). Konishi writes that he "lived like an outlaw," choosing a lifestyle that was "the very antithesis of that of a conscientious Zen monk," one that evidently included visits to bars and brothels.[33] We find his verse particularly captivating for its ingenuousness, spontaneity, and apparent disregard for the conventions of the Chinese masters. The following humorous verse, "The Flea," well illustrates his style:

Could it be dirt? Or is it dust? Just what is this thing?
All my life I've thought of you as just a worthless wretch.
Feeding off the blood of others made you very fat,
But now this skinny priest has crushed you, snuffing out your life![34]

From the mid-fifteenth century to the end of the sixteenth century, a time of almost constant warfare and anarchy, the political and cultural influence of the Gozan priesthood effectively came to an end. Many of the great temples were destroyed in the wars of the sixteenth century as armies raised by the chief priests did battle in the manner of feudal daimyo. Some monks, the above-mentioned Banri Shūkyū being a case in point, abandoned the priesthood altogether, fleeing into the countryside in search of refuge, no doubt viewing the wars as the anticipated final stage in the collapse of Buddhist law in the dark Mappō (The Latter Age of the Buddhist Law) period.

---

[32]Konishi Jin'ichi, trans. by Aileen Gatten and Mark Harbison, *A History of Japanese Literature*, vol. 3 (Princeton: Princeton University Press, 1991), p. 367.

[33]Ibid., pp. 380-381.

[34]Iwanami, p. 371.

Reunification and the Rise of Neo-Confucian Studies:
A Short Survey of Kanshi Composition in the Edo (Tokugawa) Period

With the rise of the great daimyo warlord Oda Nobunaga (1534-1582) and the beginning of the reunification movement came a new and salutary emphasis upon the promotion of Confucian studies. A directive was issued in 1573 to the Kyoto citizenry, advising that favorable treatment would be given to persons who devoted themselves to Confucianism. The rationale for this policy was that Confucian principles could be utilized to create a structured social hierarchy conducive to restoring order and maintaining the new status quo after generations of internecine war. Neo-Confucian doctrines thus came to enjoy a high level of official acceptance approaching that of state orthodoxy during the seventeenth century, though Buddhism and Shinto still played an important part in the legitimization and consolidation of shogunal authority.[35] Needless to say, Buddhism and Shinto remained the dominant popular religions throughout the Tokugawa period and were by no means supplanted by Confucianism.

By the early seventeenth century, Tokugawa Ieyasu had reunified the nation, ending centuries of military strife and ushering in a social revolution. Laws freezing the social classes were enacted, establishing rigid hereditary divisions among the classes. There were also new laws designed to ensure universal obedience to the shogunate. The warring daimyo, while retaining relative autonomy in their respective feudal domains, were placed squarely under the shogun's laws, with even their marriages being subject to approval. Ieyasu also proscribed Christianity, viewing it as a potentially subversive foreign doctrine and persecuting Christians with even greater harshness and tenacity than had his predecessor, Toyotomi Hideyoshi, the first to ban missionaries from Japan. Furthermore, the emperor's role was legally redefined at this time, imperial duties now being limited to the performance of ceremonial functions and literary pursuits.

---

[35]Peter Nosco, "Introduction: Neo-Confucianism and Tokugawa Discourse," in Peter Nosco, ed., *Confucianism and Tokugawa Culture* (Princeton: Princeton University Press, 1984), pp. 8-10.

With the restoration of political order and social stability, a proper climate for serious scholarly research and creative activity was reestablished. In fact, the shogunate encouraged learning as never before and continued to do so throughout the Edo period. There was a boom in the teaching of Confucian doctrine and Chinese letters marked by a rapid growth in the number of domainal and private teachers and schools, particularly toward the end of the seventeenth century. The famous Thirteen Clauses in Ieyasu's Buke Shohatto (Laws for the Military Houses), a set of laws promulgated in 1615, exhorted the entire military class to study literature (*bun*) as well as practice the military arts (*bu*): "On the left hand learning, on the right hand the use of weapons," states the first of these clauses.[36] Accordingly, the samurai in the Edo period were gradually converted into a class of stipendiary civil servants and writers, living by the pen rather than the sword.

Edo Kanshi: The First Stage, circa 1600-1700

The shogunate's promotion of scholarship ushered in what may be considered the first stage of Edo kanshi development, corresponding roughly with the seventeenth century. The writing of poetry in Chinese—and the teaching thereof—became a popular activity among priests, scholars, and officials alike. This first period also saw a decline in the political influence of Buddhism relative to Neo-Confucianism. In an official climate which now promoted Confucian learning and textual research at all levels, some priests returned to the laity and became Confucianists, a prime example being Fujiwara Seika (1561-1619), who is credited with establishing the academic foundation for Neo-Confucian studies in Japan. While Seika also wrote poetry, he did not consider himself a professional poet in any sense, and, in line with Confucian teachings, attached little importance to poetic activity as a purely aesthetic pursuit. Indeed, most of the early Edo kanshi poets considered poetry at best to be primarily an intellectual diversion or else viewed it didactically as a means of conveying Confucian principles.

---

[36]George Sansom, *A History of Japan, 1615-1867* (Stanford: Stanford University Press, 1963), p. 7.

It follows that few early Edo kanshi poets broke new ground, particularly as compared to the Gozan poets. Most of the poetry was inferior to Five Mountains verse, in part, no doubt, because of the damper Confucianism placed upon lyrical expressiveness. There were also few full-time kanshi poets during this first phase. Ishikawa Jōzan was a notable exception, devoting much of his later life to writing poetry and prose in Chinese, as few Edo poets before him had done. Apart from the works of the better poets like Jōzan and Itō Tōgai (1670-1736), most of the verse from this first century is derivative in nature, containing frequent references to Chinese places and historical events, and allusions to the Chinese classics. A more serious shortcoming, however, is its failure to reflect the individuality and times of the poets, depriving it of authenticity as a representation of contemporary Japanese life and the minds of native writers. The rise of lyrical, distinctively Japanese styles of kanshi awaited later poets such as Kan Sazan (1748-1827), Murakami Butsuzan (1810-1879), and the aforementioned Rai San'yō. The following verse by Seika, titled "A Winter's Night" (poem 1), is typical of early Edo kanshi, with its lack of personalism and its appealing but conventional description:

> The skies are clear as far as the horizon, vast the heavens of blue.
> I sit writing verse in praise of the moon, deep into the night.
> Now that the autumn leaves have fallen on the peak beyond
>   my windows and eaves,
> The clear moonlight and the fallen snow fill my garden with cold.

The Second Stage: circa 1700-1760

During this second period, kanshi writing came under the influence of the formalist (ko-t'iao, J. kakuchō) poetic school. The principles of ko-t'iao were developed in China during the sixteenth century and, as noted by Burton Watson, "emphasized diction and formal elements of poetry over content or originality and advocated careful imitation of the works of the past...."[37] In particular, this school advocated emulation of the High T'ang masters of the eighth century, especially Li Po and Tu Fu, eschewing late T'ang (ca. 836-907) and Sung styles.

---

[37]Watson 1990, p. x.

Ishikawa Jōzan was an early admirer of the T'ang poets and may be considered an important forerunner of the *kakuchō* style, even though he lived well before the period when this style became dominant. Jōzan believed strongly in the artistic validity of poetry for its own sake, seeing it as far more than a mere vehicle for the expression of religious and philosophical ideals.[38] The following verse, "Passing Thoughts" (poem 22), was one of many he wrote on the pleasures of quiet retirement:

> Retiring from the world was once far from my mind;
> Now I spend my last years in constant tranquility.
> I pick flowers along the woodcutter's path
> And plant sweet potatoes here at my retreat.
> This robe of coarse cloth displeases me not;
> My sash of light gauze has length to spare.
> The spring days are a perennial source of joy,
> As I open and close my scattered books.

The preeminent poet of the formalist phase in Edo kanshi was Ogyū Sorai (1666-1728), the founder of the Kobunjigaku school of classical philology and a towering figure in the development of Japanese Neo-Confucianism. Sorai championed the elevation of the Chinese classics to a position of intellectual and literary primacy, promoting the works of the mid-T'ang poets as well. He rejected the "modern" literary styles of the Sung dynasty, disapproving of the emphasis Sung scholars placed upon "content over form," that is, their tendency to value the exposition of meaning above all and to eschew the propagation of classical styles, diction, and figures of speech.[39]

Sorai, like Jōzan, held that mastering the classics and writing in classical Chinese provided the key to understanding the Way of the Sages and constituted the starting point for the cultivation of individual human virtue. To use the words of Samuel Yamashita, "[H]uman nature could not be accepted as it was but had

---

[38]Ōsone Shōsuke, et al., eds., *Kanshi, Kanbun, Hyōron* [*Kenkyū shiryō Nihon koten bungaku*, vol. 11] (Tokyo: Meiji Shoin, 1984), p. 74.

[39]See "Nature and Artifice in the Writings of Ogyū Sorai (1666-1728)" by Samuel Hideo Yamashita, in Nosco, pp. 138-145.

to be refined...."[40] This stood in sharp contrast to the position of the Chu Hsi (J. Shushi) school, which held that since all people possessed an innate goodness and a universal moral mind, everyone could, through proper self-cultivation, achieve perfection. That is to say, sagehood was to be attained by looking within oneself rather than by internalizing and emulating the ancient examples of virtue enshrined in the classical canon.

Despite his emphasis upon self-improvement through study of the classics, Sorai felt that versification was a private affair and should not be used as a tool for inculcating political or moral principles. Poetry was "not meant to expound the Way, to discipline oneself, and to govern others." Nor was poetry intended, in Sorai's words, "to show how to maintain order in the state and peace in the world."[41] But as Maruyama points out, Sorai believed that poetry could nonetheless provide certain tangible "benefits" to the reader: "...[I]t has the power to develop one's heart and reasoning faculties naturally...[and] enables one's heart to experience human feelings extensively...."[42]

Sorai's ideas influenced generations of poets to come, among them his own disciple Hattori Nankaku (1683-1759). Nankaku, too, was skilled at imitating the T'ang masters, albeit at the expense of originality and domestic color. In the following *zekku*, titled "Border Song," we see the incorporation of alien Chinese images ("the mighty barbarians"), as well as a Chinese frontier setting never actually seen by the poet (one of the "stiltedly sinicized landscapes" of the *kakuchō* poets referred to by Burton Watson[43]), giving this somewhat banal verse an added ring of inauthenticity:

---

[40]Ibid., p. 154.

[41]Maruyama Masao, trans. by Mikiso Hane, *Studies in the Intellectual History of Tokugawa Japan* (Tokyo: University of Tokyo Press, 1974), p. 109 (citing Sorai's *Keijishi yōran*, vol. 1).

[42]Ibid., p. 168.

[43]Watson 1976, p. 10.

Last night we pursued the mighty barbarians,
Then rested our horses on the mountain's north side.
The myriad horses were about to neigh,
When a wind from the north descended upon the plains.[44]

Gion Nankai (1677-1751) was another well-known practitioner of the *kakuchō* style and himself an admirer of the T'ang poet Li Po. Like so many *kakuchō* poets of his time, his verse, as Andō Hideo points out, tends to display a mannered ornamentalism, often lacking a sense of immediacy, emotional honesty, and a distinctively Japanese aesthetic character.[45] Similar shortcomings are evident in the following *risshi*, titled "Ruined Mansion," by Nankai's contemporary Itō Tōgai, who is nonetheless considered one of the better poets of his age:

I recall that long ago a jewelled hairpin was lost here,
But now water oats and rushes cover the river banks.
Building this mansion cost a fortune;
It is now but a dream, and we lament its lost magnificence.
In the midday sunlight fly the swallows of ancient times.
In the spring breezes grow the flowers that have bloomed
     so many times before.
People wandering past sigh in vain,
For no one knows whose home this was.[46]

Despite these reservations about the formalist style, one must grant that some poets, at least, succeeded in capturing the beauty of the Japanese landscape and expressing native lyrical sentiment, even while relying too heavily upon many of the images and conventions of Chinese verse. Although Watson is generally correct in characterizing *kakuchō* poetry as "doubly derivative and barren" and based upon Ming imitations of T'ang verse that were "dull affairs at best,"[47] it is perhaps unfair to dismiss kanshi from this period as lacking in originality and

---

[44]Inoguchi, p. 165; our translation.

[45]Andō, p. 246.

[46]Hirano, p. 192; our translation.

[47]Watson 1976, p. 7.

literary merit. Undoubtedly Dazai Shundai's evocative verse, "Recalling the Past while at Nara" (poem 93, cited earlier), is one of the more successful creations.

The Third Stage: circa 1750-1800

The latter half of the eighteenth century may be considered a third distinct period in the development of Edo kanshi. A time of great intellectual ferment reminiscent of late-Ming China, these decades saw the gradual decline of Sorai-style formalism. As if to set the stage for the events to follow, the ban on foreign books was lifted in 1720. Thereafter, current knowledge about China and the Western nations filtered into Japan at an unprecedented rate. By the middle of the century, the orthodox Chu Hsi school (the Shushi or Teishugaku school) had passed its prime, and its influence upon kanshi poets was waning, which helped to liberate poetry from didactic concerns. Moreover, new heterodox Setchūgaku (Syncretic) schools, which blended Shushi doctrine with Kogaku and Yōmeigaku,[48] began to emerge in the later decades of this century, becoming the new trend in Edo Confucianism. The popularity of these schools contributed to the decline of the Sorai school, whose influence was already dwindling due to the death of Sorai's leading successors, Dazai Shundai and Hattori Nankaku, in 1747 and 1759, respectively. As Maruyama Masao has observed, the weakening of the school in the 1760s had progressed to intellectual decay and aesthetic decadence by the 1780s, made all the worse by the growing factionalism in the school that set in following Sorai's death.[49]

Around the time when the Sorai school started to wane, the National Learning (Kokugaku) movement was beginning to challenge the primacy of Confucian studies. This essentially apolitical movement brought about a revival of pristine Shinto and led to new research into the ancient Japanese classics, rejecting Confucian and Buddhist influences at the same time. Kokugaku scholars viewed the awakening of human emotions and the realistic depiction of the innermost life

---

[48]Kogaku and Yōmeigaku are defined in the biographies of Itō Jinsai and Nakae Tōju, respectively, below. On the Syncretic schools, see also the biography of Hosoi Heishū.

[49]Maruyama, pp. 138-141.

of man as lying at the very heart of literature, which they believed should be the repository of native sentiments, untainted by Chinese or other "foreign" civilizations. In this way, Kokugaku played a role in the gradual aesthetic distancing of kanshi from Chinese traditions.

Another important trend during this period was the widening of the social spectrum of kanshi poets to include members of the peasant, artisan, and merchant classes. This was linked to the growing affluence and leisure enjoyed by these people and to the spread of literacy downward through society. The poet Hirose Tansō (1782-1856), for example, came from a merchant-class background, and Kan Sazan was from peasant stock, yet both were ranked among the most popular poets and teachers of their day. These writers, perhaps by virtue of their humbler origins, seem to have been less preoccupied with Chinese conventions, and their kanshi on the whole display themes and language more clearly reflective of everyday Japanese life. Also, the rise in popularity of free-wheeling vernacular verse forms such as haikai (comic linked verse) and senryū (comic seventeen-syllable verse) helped to expand the range of subjects in kanshi to include topoi of a more plebeian nature. Kyōshi, a variety of humorous and often vulgar Chinese verse, came to the fore during the latter half of Edo, while erotic poetry set in the urban pleasure quarters similarly flourished as another sub-genre of kanshi at this time.

Paralleling these social changes and the overall weakening of Confucian influence was the emergence of yet another new style of kanshi composition associated with the *seirei* (Spiritualist or Native Sensibility) school,[50] which produced some of the finest poets of the Edo period. The Spiritualist poets rejected the archaizing, formalist tendencies of earlier times, advocating instead the cultivation of natural sensibility and spiritual depth. This style emphasized the expression of the poet's innermost emotions and the depiction of everyday surroundings to create a more naturalistic and personal poetry. *Seirei* was inspired by the Sung *hsing-ling* style, whose leading exponent in China at this

---

[50]"Native sensibility" is James J.Y. Liu's term, borrowed from the writings of Yuan Mei. See Liu, p. 74.

time was the poet Yuan Mei (1716-1798). In the following excerpt from the *Sui-yuan shih-hua* (Poetry Talks from the Sui Garden), Yuan Mei sets forth his views on poetry, which he believed should reveal human emotions, regardless of their moral validity:

> Poetry is what expresses one's nature and emotion. It is enough to look no further than one's self (for the material of poetry). If its words move the heart, its colours catch the eye, its taste pleases the mouth, and its sound delights the ear, then it is good poetry.[51]

Perhaps the first Japanese *seirei* poet was Priest Gensei (d. 1668), a literary figure far ahead of his time who incorporated this spirit into his philosophy of poetry a century before it became fashionable. For Gensei, poetry was a natural part of daily life, an act of spontaneous creation that revealed one's innermost feelings. In his collection of poetry entitled *Sōzan shū*, he wrote, "I follow my heart, expressing my feelings, and when I write verse I am not fettered by rules."[52] The principal exponents of the Spiritualist style later in the Edo period were Rikunyo (1734-1801), Yamamoto Hokuzan (1752-1812), and Kan Sazan. Rikunyo excelled in depicting homey, plebeian scenes but was less lyrical than many other *seirei* poets. Concerning Rikunyo's poetry, Hirose Tansō remarked: "It has much scenery but little sentiment and is much too dense. You like it at first but easily tire of it later."[53] Although Tansō places Kan Sazan's verse in the Rikunyo tradition, he is somewhat more complimentary, characterizing it as "a combination of scenery and sentiment, poetry that finds the middle ground between dense and thin, retaining its appeal over time."[54] Kan Sazan himself had the following to say about the importance of emotional truth and realism in poetry:

---

[51]Ibid., p. 73.

[52]Ōsone, p. 74; our translation.

[53]Ibid., p. 104.

[54]Ibid.

If you state the facts and write about reality, without slavishly imitating earlier poets or trying to "dress yourself up" in the superficial garb of your time, then, and only then, will you avoid becoming a writer of inauthentic verse.[55]

Yamamoto Hokuzan, one of the leading *seirei* theorists of his day, struck a similar chord, calling the *kakuchō* poets Sorai and Nankaku creators of "fake T'ang poetry" and championing the use of novel, direct and simple language.[56] Among Hokuzan's followers were Ichikawa Kansai (1749-1820) and Ōkubo Shibutsu (1767-1837), two of the most accomplished poets of their day. The following poem by Kansai, "A Word to My Child" (poem 189), exhibits an unaffected, homey quality characteristic of the style:

Sunlight bakes my window; spring is in the air.
Reading makes me sleepy and I yawn and stretch.
Don't shout at the maid just because lunch is late!
Last night the firewood was badly soaked by rain.

Both Kansai and Shibutsu belonged to a popular literary coterie known as Kōkosha (The River and Lake Poetry Society), which flourished in the 1790s. As with other contemporaneous literary societies, its function was to instruct its members in the proper styles and forms of kanshi and to provide a social forum for versification. Poetry societies had begun to flourish all around the country from the 1750s, a reflection of the burgeoning popularity of Chinese poetry composition among an ever-widening cross section of society.

Kōkosha met regularly in Edo's old Kanda-Otamagaike district and included among its members such rising stars as Kashiwagi Jotei (1763-1819) and Kikuchi Gozan (1772-1855). The coterie had a particular interest in urban popular life, including its seamier side, and stood in the forefront of poetic change. Its members tended to prefer the more plebeian—and increasingly fashionable—Sung styles and aimed for a realistic effect in their verse, using the simpler, less ornate language and the more subdued colors associated with Sung poets. Jotei and his

---

[55]Ibid.

[56]Andō, p. 247.

colleagues often made their immediate (and typically humble) surroundings the subject of their verse, delighting in treating even the most lowly and undignified of topics. The following verse by Jotei (poem 227), set in the geisha quarters of Yoshiwara in Edo, is representative of the poetry associated with this group:

> Over and over the clappers are struck; still the night is young.
> The young man and the young lady with him are facing one another.
> Their emotions so deep they do not speak, for they're shy in each
>   other's presence.
> The incense stick beside the pillow has burned completely down.

A second poetry coterie, founded by Katayama Hokkai in Osaka in 1765, was also highly influential in the last decades of the eighteenth century, counting among its members the eminent poets Shibano Ritsuzan (1736-1807), Rai Shunsui (1746-1816), and the aforementioned Bitō Jishū. Calling itself Kontonsha (The Chaos Poetry Society), it was distinctive for the diversity of its membership, which included not only former samurai and Confucian scholars but also doctors and shopkeepers. Kontonsha's members generally favored the more conservative poetic styles, showing the lingering influence of the Sorai school. The group met monthly on the evening of the sixteenth day and assigned topics for extemporaneous kanshi composition. Between cups of sake, members wrote verse and critiqued one another's poems in a relaxed and convivial atmosphere marred only by the occasional drunken outburst.[57] Poetic accounts of the activities of this group sometimes mention the poet Katsu Shikin (1738-1784), who could write perfect regulated verse without the use of a rhyming dictionary.[58] Kontonsha passed out of existence around the time of the death of Katayama Hokkai, in 1790.

Certain leading Kontonsha members participated in the drafting of anti-heterodoxy legislation commonly referred to as Igaku no Kin (The Prohibition of Heterodox Studies). These laws, promulgated in 1790 and opposed by many of the members of the rival Kōkosha society, were enacted in an attempt to combat

---

[57]Ibid., p. 248.

[58]Ibid., p. 249.

political and social disturbances, as well as to halt the erosion of strict class distinctions and the supposed moral decay of the times. The political elite were convinced that such problems could only be remedied by rescuing the Chu Hsi school from the decline it had experienced since the death of the leading shogunal Confucianist Hayashi Hōkō in 1733. Efforts to bolster the Chu Hsi school entailed what Maruyama calls "general thought control," meaning the reduction of the influence of competing philosophies. This was to be achieved by banning instruction in these doctrines in officially-sponsored schools and prohibiting the employment of non-Chu Hsi scholars in government posts.[59]

The anti-heterodoxy laws were less rigidly enforced than is commonly imagined, and the lines between orthodox and heterodox Neo-Confucian teachings gradually became further blurred.[60] Although it is true that Teishugaku was reinstated as the core subject in the official curriculum, it never entirely displaced other subjects in the shogunal college, and even Nativist studies were incorporated in time.[61] Be that as it may, the legislation had the general effect of undermining the prestige of textual scholars and served to inhibit philosophical discourse among the more marginalized Confucianists in particular. Some academicians turned away from the classics, gravitating instead toward the writing of Chinese poetry, which came to be seen as a more reliable means of making a name for oneself.[62]

But as certain intellectuals distanced themselves from study of the classics, members of the lower classes were, at the same time, availing themselves of new opportunities to enter Shōheikō, the venerable shogunal college for Chu Hsi

---

[59]Maruyama, p. 280.

[60]Takehiko Okada, "Neo-Confucian Thinkers in Nineteenth Century Japan," in Nosco, pp. 217-218.

[61]Yukichi Sakai, "The Constitutionalism of Inoue Kowashi," trans. from the Japanese by Thomas M. Huber, in Tetsuo Najita and Irwin Scheiner, eds., *Japanese Thought in the Tokugawa Period, 1600-1868: Methods and Metaphors* (Chicago and London: The University of Chicago, 1978), p. 166.

[62]Inoguchi, p. 38; Andō, p. 248.

learning established a century earlier. Changes in the admissions policy meant
that townsmen and peasants could now attend this academy and upon graduation
be eligible for domain employment as Confucian scholar-officials.[63] This
democratization served to expand the intellectual class and broaden the ranks of
kanshi poets as well. The case of Matsuzaki Kōdō (1771-1844), who came from
a farming background, is a good example of such upward mobility, for he not
only graduated from the academy but also became a teacher in one of the
orthodox Hayashi private schools in Edo and served a succession of daimyo in the
Kakegawa domain. Yanagawa Seigan (1789-1858), the son of a prosperous
farmer, was another such product of these changing times.

Besides rising in the social hierarchy, this new breed of scholar-official also
came to enjoy horizontal occupational mobility as lifelong allegiance to a single
daimyo gradually ceased to be the rule. Moreover, having advanced in life often
through their own merits, these men became more independent of the direct
control of their families, which were less able to dictate their choice of marriage
partner, for example. Matsuzaki Kōdō exemplified this spirit of independence,
taking the normally unthinkable step of marrying an Edo courtesan who had
helped pay for his education.[64] This growing social freedom fostered a degree
of intellectual liberation reflected in some of the more individualistic kanshi
written at this time.

The Fourth Stage: 1800-1868

Kanshi versification became further popularized throughout society during the
first half of the nineteenth century, a process aided by rampant growth in the
publishing industry. This growth led to the greater accessibility of printed texts,
which were devoured by an increasingly literate population. Many kanshi written
in this period show the moral influence of the late-eighteenth century Chu Hsi
revival. Their themes also reflect the rise of nationalism among the elite and the
uneasiness felt over the growing foreign interest in their country. Among the key

---

[63]Nakamura, pp. 10-14.

[64]Ibid., pp. 12-13.

political concerns which emerged in poetry, and in intellectual discourse in general during these decades, were the relationship between ruler and ruled, national defense, and the protection of the emperor. Kanshi in short assumed a new role as a vehicle for the articulation of political views, providing us with useful insights into these tempestuous times. The poem "Hearing that the Port of Shimoda Had Been Opened" (poem 383), written by the imperial loyalist Priest Gesshō (1817-1858), displays this political consciousness as well as a xenophobic tone often seen in the poetry of the nineteenth century:

> The mountains and rivers of Shichiri were handed over to those dogs
>   and goats.
> After the earthquake the spring landscape was a scene of desolation.
> The cherry blossoms don't bear the taint of that rancid, frowzy odor:
> Alone they shine in the morning sun, their scent our nation's finest!

This verse was written a year after the ports of Shimoda and Hakodate were opened to American commerce on the third day of the Third Month of 1854, a development violently opposed by many among the elite who wanted their nation to remain closed to the outside world.

The next poem, composed by the female poet Yanagawa Kōran (1804-1879) and titled "On Hearing of the Chōshū Campaign," further illustrates this growing interest in national affairs:

> I've heard that battle dust's been raised by the Western Sea.
> Who are loyal among the court officials?
> I weep with emotion, but do not laugh at me.
> The ruler of England is a woman, too.[65]

---

[65]From Inoguchi Atsushi, *Josei to kanshi: wakan joryū shi shi* [*Kazama sensho*, vol. 103] (Tokyo: Kasama Shoin, 1978), pp. 320-321; our translation.

The Chōshū Wars lasted from 1864 to 1866. The Chōshū domain wanted to restore rule by the emperor and expel the foreigners in Japan, thus launching an attack on Kyoto in 1864. The shogunate sent a large army against Chōshū in response. However, this and subsequent attempts to subdue the domain were unsuccessful, and the shogunate was compelled to negotiate for peace. The shogunate eventually fell, and the united domains of Chōshū and Satsuma soon took control of the entire country, ushering in the Meiji Restoration of 1868. The Restoration was to change the course of Japanese history, ending feudalism and bringing Japan into the modern age.

Kōran felt compelled to cite the example of "the ruler of England" (Queen Victoria), in order to justify her interest in political affairs, which were not considered the province of women.

Late-Edo kanshi also saw broad experimentalism in the choice of poetic subject and a shift toward a decidedly Japanese focus and feeling. Kōran's verse about the Chōshū campaign is a good example; the next verse, by Saitō Chikudō (1815-1852), which deals with the Ainu of northern Japan, further exemplifies the fresh, native subject matter featured in many of these poems:

> Shaved eyebrows, like blue-green tattoos, never drawn in.
> Rearing cranes, raising bears on human milk: such is their life.
> In thatched huts they lead healthy lives, and at the third watch,
>   when the moon is out,
> They weave tree bark by its abundant light.[66]

The most distinguished kanshi poet of this period was Rai San'yō (1780-1832), one of the luminaries of Edo historiography as well. Like Kōran, he wrote a number of poems on historical subjects, particularly in his later years, and often expressed strongly nationalistic views therein. His kanshi titled "The Mongols Are Coming," from a series of sixty-six *yüeh-fu*-style verses describing events in Japanese history through the ages, is representative of this segment of his corpus.[67] A member of a distinguished family of kanshi poets, San'yō was a brilliantly eccentric but troubled man who suffered most of his life from chronic depression and epilepsy and was given to fits of unpredictable behavior. He nonetheless became the most popular kanshi poet Japan had ever seen. His works were constantly reprinted, and each new collection became a best seller, apparently even outselling the works of the highly renowned Kan Sazan.[68] The following verse, "A Short Poem Written on the Road while Escorting My Mother" (poem 282), is typical of the unadorned personalism we associate with San'yō:

---

[66]Fujikawa, p. 341; our translation.

[67]This poem is translated by Donald Keene in *WWW*, p. 553.

[68]Andō, p. 256.

The east wind greeted my mother when she arrived.
The north wind farewelled her when she returned.
When she came, the roadside plants were fragrant,
But soon they were frozen by the frost and snow.
When I heard the cock crow, I wrapped my feet,
Then hobbled along behind her litter,
Never complaining that my feet were sore,
Only concerned that she journey in comfort.
I offered my mother a cup of tea, then drank a cup myself.
The teashop was filled with the sunlight of dawn,
    the frost had disappeared.
For a son of fifty to have a mother seventy years of age—
Fortune like this is rarely seen in this world of ours!
People were travelling north and south, like the threads of silk on a loom;
Yet who among them could possibly be as happy as this mother and son?

Another influential poet from this period is Yanagawa Seigan (1789-1858), a prolific and eclectic writer who experimented with different poetic styles. His corpus includes some five thousand poems, and he was in many ways the quintessential nineteenth-century kanshi poet: patriotic, socially aware, and wide-ranging in his choice of subjects. In his earlier years, Seigan took the Sung poets as his models, preferring the *seirei* style. He was, to quote one source, "a romantic poet in a world at peace," a writer whose poetry was "pure and elegant."[69] Later, as Japan became less politically stable, Seigan's verse grew increasingly nationalistic, often expressing strong political and moral sentiments, as revealed in the following poem (from a series of twenty-five) showing contempt for the shogun:

Back then your ancestors, spirited and powerful,
Bellowed at the wind and skies as they swept across the land.
But now you cannot repel the foreign menace.
Those words, "Conqueror of Barbarians"—so meaningless a title![70]

Seigan and San'yō were among the most innovative poets of this fourth phase of kanshi composition. It should be remembered, however, that poems on more

---

[69]Ōsone, p. 112.

[70]Inoguchi, p. 328; our translation.

traditional themes, using conventional imagery and diction, continued to be composed in great numbers and doubtless still constituted the mainstream at this time. As in earlier ages, most literati tended to be followers rather than innovators; this was especially true of literature written in Chinese, where the inherent foreignness of the language may have inhibited writers from breaking new ground. We need also to recognize the existence of a middle road between conventionality and the cutting edge in kanshi writing. In the poetry of Hirose Tansō, for example, we find a balance between the old formalism and the new emphasis upon personal sentiment and native spirit. Tansō discusses what he calls the "middle ground" in his *Tansō shiwa* (Tansō Talks about Poetry), as follows:

> Poetry from the Shōtoku period (1711-1716) and the Kyōhō period (1716-1736) is in the *kakuchō* style and has no personal sentiment. Poetry written during and after the Tenmei period (1781-1789) emphasizes personal sentiment and is devoid of *kakuchō* formalism. Each of these tendencies represents one extreme; the middle ground is excluded. What I prefer is to make personalism my mainstay while not rejecting formalism. Thus, I take the middle road. During Kyōhō, kanshi poets followed Ming styles, and during the Tenmei period they followed Sung styles. I mainly follow T'ang styles but I also incorporate Sung and Ming elements as well.[71]

The following Tansō verse, "A Poem for Master Gofū Who Entertained Me with Wine near the Naka River" (poem 295), combines local color and Japanese atmosphere with the formalism and quiet detachment of earlier Edo poetry:

> Fragrant plants are now appearing before the Sumiyoshi Shrine.
> Beside the riverbed, hand in hand, we slowly strolled along.
> With pride I'll tell the village folk after I return
> Of the noodle-fish we cooked and ate in the shade of the willow trees.

In the preceding pages, we have identified and discussed some of the main trends in kanshi composition during the Edo period. Most significant among these developments was the naturalization of kanshi, a process which is most evident in the latter half of the period, especially after about 1800. The more

---

[71]Andō, p. 257; our translation.

innovative poets of this age moved beyond mere imitation of Chinese models and successfully incorporated imagery, vocabulary, and themes representative of the native environment and Japanese society, bringing a robust vitality and sense of confidence to their verse. In this way, the kanshi poets stepped out of the tall shadows of the great Chinese masters, creating a body of poetry the best of which retained the formal beauty of the original models while possessing honesty and authenticity as a Japanese literary form.

POETRY

Fujiwara Seika, 1561-1619

Fujiwara Seika's name is synonymous with Confucian studies, as he is credited with establishing Sung dynasty Neo-Confucianism in Japan during the Edo period. A native of Harima in modern Hyōgo prefecture, Seika was a twelfth-generation descendant of the great court poet and arbiter of poetic taste, Fujiwara no Teika (d. 1241). Like many of his peers, Seika had a reputation as a young boy for being a child prodigy. He took orders as a Buddhist priest at Shōkokuji temple in Kyoto, but left the priesthood at the age of twenty-eight when his interests turned to Confucianism.

Seika went to Kagoshima in the Sixth Month of 1596, intending to cross to China for the purpose of acquainting himself with Confucianism, as there seemed to be no expert teacher in Japan. Various delays and bad weather foiled his plans, and Seika, in fact, never managed to get further than Kikaigashima (Iōjima) off the coast of southern Kyushu. However, while in nearby Yamagawa, where he was awaiting a second ship bound for China, Seika happened to meet a local priest in the Shōryūji temple who was lecturing with an annotated set of *The Four Books* prepared by his contemporary *Priest Bunshi Genshō. Inspired by Genshō's scholarship, Seika decided then and there to abandon the idea of going to China, realizing that he could learn what had to be learned in Japan. Thus, he returned to Kyoto, bearing a handwritten set of these works, and embarked upon the task of mastering Confucian doctrine.[1]

Seika's most famous disciple was *Hayashi Razan, who, on Seika's recommendation, later became an advisor to Ieyasu and to three subsequent shoguns. Other notable students included *Matsunaga Sekigo, *Hori Kyōan, and *Naba Kassho, who, together with Razan, were collectively known as the "Four Kings" of the Seika school. Seika lectured Ieyasu on the classics, and his works

---

[1]Iwanami, p. 28.

clarified the Confucian canon for many generations to come, drawing not only from ancient Confucian doctrine and Sung Neo-Confucian teachings, but also from the teachings of Wang Yang-ming and the ideals of Zen Buddhism.[2] His own writings reflect a tendency toward quiet reflection and self-cultivation rather than the pragmatic emphasis upon public matters typical of some of the later Neo-Confucian thinkers.[3] He received numerous invitations to serve and lecture in various domains, but declined all of them, preferring to live quietly in seclusion at his retreat in Ichihara, north of Kyoto, well away from the mundane world of political affairs.

Where literature was concerned, Seika took the traditional Confucian view that it was the honey by means of which the bitter medicine of philosophical principles could be taken. Thus, it was not considered valuable in itself as a medium for the expression of individual sentiment.[4] Keene describes Seika's poetic reputation as "dismal,"[5] a judgment which seems unreasonably dismissive. Granted, his poetry is far less individualistic and personal than that of many later Edo poets, but it nonetheless has an appeal of its own. Some among the verses selected below are striking for their crystalline brightness and silvery hibernal beauty, while others possess a refreshing pellucid quality and contain seasonal imagery that transports the reader into the very scene itself. The image of cold moonlight is particularly striking and constitutes a classic example of the Japanese use of synaesthesia (transference of the senses), which involves the tactile or olfactory representation of color, light, and other natural phenomena: for example, the use of the color white to describe ambient coldness. A technique which occurs in both waka and kanshi, synaesthesia is especially prevalent in the haiku of Bashō, an example being his verse which reads, "The sea darkens:/The

---

[2]On the teachings of Wang Yang-ming, see the biography of Nakae Tōju, below.

[3]*Kodansha Encyclopedia of Japan* [hereafter, *KEJ*] (Tokyo and New York: Kodansha, 1983), vol. 2 of 9 vols., p. 358.

[4]*WWW*, p. 537.

[5]Ibid.

voices of the wild ducks/Are faintly white."[6]   As Ōoka Makoto observes, "...Japanese seldom perceive colors in an exclusively visual way.   Their perception of color is more tactile, or filtered through some tactile impression."[7] Synaesthesia was to remain a common literary device in kanshi throughout the Edo period.

◉ 1 A Winter's Night

The skies are clear as far as the horizon, vast the heavens of blue.
I sit writing verse in praise of the moon, deep into the night.
Now that the leaves have fallen on the peak beyond my window and eaves,
The clear moonlight and the fallen snow fill my garden with cold.

Iwanami, p. 170.   From *Seika sensei bunshū* (The Collected Works of Master Seika), 1627

◉ 2 Leaves Falling with the Rain

Autumn winds awake me from my dreams at the inn where phoenix trees grow.
A shower of rain brushes the mountain tops, sweeping across the village.
The pit-a-pat of falling leaves seems to go on all night.
Away in the distance beyond the railing—a sliver of a moon!

Iwanami, p. 169.   From *Seika sensei bunshū*, 1627

Line one: The phoenix tree (*Firmiana plantanifolia* or *Sterculia plantanifolia*), alternately known as the Chinese parasol or dryandra, *wu-t'ung* in Chinese. Considered the national tree of China, it is a large deciduous tree with huge leaves and deep green bark. According to legend, this was the only tree upon which a phoenix would roost.

---

[6]Donald Keene, trans. in ibid., p. 86.

[7]See Ōoka Makoto, trans. by Takako U. Lento and Thomas V. Lento, *The Colors of Poetry* [*Reflections series*] (Rochester, Michigan: Katydid Books, 1991), p. 41.

🌙 3 The Cold Moon

The clear, cold light of the moon appeals to the poet in me.
Never say that the autumn moon is surpassed in any other season.
All at once the treetop leaves have fallen off in the frost,
And through the wisps of twilight clouds, an eyebrow of a moon!

Iwanami, p. 169. From *Seika sensei bunshū*, 1627

🌙 4 Visiting Wakanoura

Sightseers all, we've come to visit this castle beside the sea.
Sparkling waters of billowing waves merge with the heavens of blue;
Fish leap from nets and flap about, all so lively and fresh.
The sound of a sea-shanty sung by a fisherman trails away into the sunset.

Iwanami, p. 170. From *Seika sensei bunshū*, 1627

🌙 5 The Mountain Dwelling

Blue mountains towering high, soaring into the clouds.
The faint song of a distant woodsman; I forget all worldly ties.
Content, I feel no need at all for the music of bamboo and strings.
Secluded birds rest sound asleep beside the azure cliffs.

Iwanami, pp. 170-171; Andō, p. 42. From *Seika sensei bunshū*, 1627

Date Masamune [Teizan], 1567-1636

Date Masamune was from Yonezawa, where his father Terumune was the lord of Yonezawa Castle in modern Yamagata prefecture, northeastern Japan. Though a great warrior, he is mainly remembered today for his political opportunism and cruelty to Christians in his later years. Masamune was called "The One-Eyed Dragon," because he had lost his right eye to smallpox when he was young. In his genealogical work titled *Hankanpu* (1702), *Arai Hakuseki describes Masamune as being extremely strange in appearance, with just one eye and closely cropped hair.[1]

At nineteen, Masamune succeeded his father as daimyo of Yonezawa after the latter died in battle at the hands of the Nihonmatsu daimyo, Hatakeyama Yoshitsugu, while Masamune was away hunting. Masamune immediately set off to avenge his father's death, attacking Nihonmatsu Castle and killing Yoshitsugu, whose corpse he dumped on the beach at Obama.[2] He then led successful military campaigns against various neighboring domains, enlarging his own base by annexing seventeen districts of the provinces of Mutsu and Dewa in the north. In 1589, he defeated the Ashina family who controlled Aizu and then moved to Kurokawa Castle (in modern Fukushima). However, Toyotomi Hideyoshi, suspicious of his dilatoriness in joining the campaign against Odawara Castle in 1590, forced him the following year give up this new residence and the three districts in Aizu over which he had assumed control and made him return to his native Yonezawa.

Masamune managed to convince Hideyoshi that his intentions in Odawara had been honorable and regained his good favor. Then, after putting down some small revolts back in his own domain, he set forth to accompany the military

---

[1] As related in Kato Shuichi, *A History of Japanese Literature*, vol. 2 (New York: Kodansha International, 1990) [paperback ed.], p. 79.

[2] Inoguchi, p. 115.

leader Asano Nagamasa (Hideyoshi's brother-in-law) to Korea, where he served with distinction from 1592 to 1596. As a supporter of Hideyoshi and later Tokugawa Ieyasu, the third of the great unifiers of early Edo Japan, Masamune fought at the Battle of Sekigahara in 1600 and captured the Shiroishi Castle belonging to the daimyo Uesugi Kagekatsu in the Karita district of Mutsu. For this accomplishment he was given Karita as a reward. Shortly after the battle, he built the Aoba Castle in Sendai (in old Mutsu, modern Miyagi prefecture), a fortress which had an assessed yield of 623,000 *koku*.[3] After moving to Sendai in 1603, he did much to improve the local economy, building a salt industry, breeding horses, opening gold and silver mines, and establishing lacquer and mulberry plantations.[4] During the Siege of Osaka, in the winter of 1614, Masamune led eighteen thousand troops on the side of Ieyasu. He renewed his attack on Osaka the following year and succeeded in destroying Toyotomi Hideyori and his supporters.

Masamune had originally been sympathetic to the activities of Christian missionaries. He allowed them to proselytize in his domain and even planned the building of a cathedral. Further, he helped win the freedom of the Spanish Franciscan Father Luis Sotelo, who had been arrested during Shogun Hidetada's persecution of Christians in 1613, and even commissioned Sotelo to accompany an embassy to the Pontiff Pope Paul V in Rome, via Spain. This mission, headed by Hasekura Tsunenaga (1571-1622), left Japan in 1613 and returned in 1620, by which time the shogunate had meanwhile proscribed Christianity in Japan. All further visits by Westerners were restricted to Dejima in Nagasaki and the port of Hirado. Fearing the suspicion of the shogun, Masamune changed sides and became a ruthless persecutor of Christians himself.

His martial propensities notwithstanding, Masamune was an influential patron of the arts and a skillful waka and kanshi poet. He also practiced the tea ceremony, calligraphy, and the art of incense preparation. On his deathbed,

---

[3]It should be noted that a mere five *koku* ("piculs") of rice, a total of about twenty-five bushels dry measure, was considered a volume sufficient to feed one man for a year.

[4]*KEJ*, vol. 2, p. 78.

Masamune is said to have asked that any paintings done of him following his death should depict him with both eyes intact.[5]

The first of the following poems displays the martial temper of this famous warrior, while the second affords us a glimpse of his patriotism. The final verse shows the more contemplative and sensitive side of a man who had led the arduous life of a military leader. Reading these poems remind us that the members of samurai class were expected to display not only military prowess but artistic refinement as well, the qualities of *bu* and *bun*, respectively.

◙ 6 A Poem Expressing the Wish to Mount a Punitive Expedition against the Southern Barbarians

Evil doctrines delude the land; the clamor never ends.
I long to conquer their barbarian realm but have yet to achieve my goal.
When will the roc that is southward bound begin to flap its wings?
Long have I waited for the typhoon to bear me ten thousand *ri* away!

Sugano, p. 38; Andō, p. 38. From *Teizan kō shishō* (A Book of Poems by Lord Teizan)

Title: "Southern Barbarians" refers to Christian missionaries from Spain, who were active in the Philippines and already proselytizing in Japan. Masamune wanted to eradicate the missionaries in order to prevent them from spreading their "evil doctrines" in Japan.
Line two: "Barbarian realm" could be a reference to the Philippines, where Christian missionary activities flourished in the sixteenth century (Sugano, p. 38). But it more likely refers to one or more of Japan's southern domains, which were by this time under the influence of Christianity.
Lines three and four: The first chapter of the Taoist classic *Chuang Tzu* (ca. third century B.C.), by the Chinese philosopher of the same name, is titled "Hsiao-yao Yu" (Free and Easy Wandering). It mentions a mythical roc being carried away on a whirlwind to the great southern ocean. Like the roc, Masamune is waiting for the chance to go south and root out his Christian foes, an objective he never achieved. A *ri* was, in Tokugawa times, a distance of about a third of a mile.

---

[5]Ibid.

☻ 7 A Poem to Commemorate My Planting a Plum Tree in the Back Garden after Returning from Service in Korea

Today our army which crossed the vast seas has come back to our land.
We fill the sleeves of our coats of mail with the buds of fragrant plants;
Elegant for a thousand ages, noble and so pure.
Once it was the flowers of a different realm that I viewed while at my leisure.

Inoguchi, p. 117

☻ 8 Recited in a Drunken State

My youth has passed me by in a flash.
The world is at peace, but my hair has gone grey.
Heaven has granted me this old shell of a body;
Why go on living if I can't enjoy myself?

Hirano, p. 162

Title: Inoguchi, p. 117 has a slightly different version of this poem with the title "Enjoying Myself."

Fujiwara Tamekage, fl. ca. 1600

Little biographical information about Fujiwara Tamekage is available beyond that
he was one of *Fujiwara Seika's sons and a native of Kyoto. We also know that
he was a minor kanshi poet who flourished around 1600 and made his career as
a Neo-Confucian scholar.[1] In Tamekage's first poem, the limpid tones of a flute
rise through the foggy moonlit air at dawn, breaking the silence and mesmerizing
even the clouds, painting an arrestingly atmospheric portrait of daybreak in
spring. The second verse, a nocturnal poem, is striking for its somewhat unusual
image of dewy flowers glistening in the light of the full moon.

◐ 9 A Poem Using the Rhymes Found in "Listening to the Rain on a Spring Night"

The willows have yet to wake from their slumber; dense and dark the fog.
The hazy light of the moon so round shines into my window.
Who can it be, playing the flute, making it seem like spring?
The clouds are stilled by the lingering sound as it flows through cerulean skies.

Iwanami, p. 172. From *Hakuō shū* (The White Sea Gull Collection)

Title: The poem referred to here has not been identified.

---

[1] Iwanami, p. 498.

52

☾ 10 Plants in the Moonlight

The wind and dew so bracingly fresh, now in the middle of autumn.

Beside the stone steps flourishing shrubs, with flowers that glisten like crystal.

How I dread the coming of dawn, for when the plants on Yao's steps

Start shedding their leaves, the moon will sink as well.

Iwanami, p. 172. From *Hakuō shū*

Line one: "The middle of autumn" here refers to the period around the fifteenth day of the Eighth Month.

Lines three and four: The plant alluded to here is the mythical *ming-chieh*, which supposedly grew in the palace of the legendary Emperor Yao (putative reign ca. twenty-fourth century B.C). It produced a leaf on the first day of the lunar month and one each day till the full moon. From then on it began to lose its leaves. The point of Tamekage's poem is to express regret over the waning of the moon which accompanied this loss of leaves.

Hayashi Razan [Dōshun], 1583-1657

The leading disciple of *Fujiwara Seika and perhaps the most important Confucian scholar of the early Edo period, Hayashi Razan was born in the Shinmachi area of Kyoto. An outgoing and precocious child with a love of learning, Razan began to immerse himself in Confucian doctrine in his mid-teens. Before long, he was lecturing on the Chu Hsi commentaries to the classics. Razan became a principal advisor to Shogun Tokugawa Ieyasu in 1605, contributing to the establishment of the shogunate and its Neo-Confucian-based hierarchical class system, as well as to the development of its Confucianist system of education. As a staunch promoter of Neo-Confucianism, he was a formidable critic of Christian doctrine, attacking Buddhism and the Wang Yang-ming school of Confucianism as well.

In 1606 Razan was given the title of *hakase* (doctor) by Ieyasu and became First Secretary of the shogunate, responsible for drafting documents and laws and recording the official acts of the government. He went on to serve the next three shoguns as well. In 1630 Razan established the Hayashi School for Confucian studies, known also as the Kōbunkan academy, on a piece of land in Shinobugaoka (modern Ueno in Tokyo) donated by the shogun Tsunayoshi. This was to serve as an important center for the dissemination of the official Neo-Confucian orthodoxy for virtually the entire Edo period. The academy was the precursor of Shōheikō (Shōheizaka Gakumonjo), the official shogunate-sponsored school of Confucianism later established in the Yushima area of Edo in 1690. Generations of Hayashi scholars served as its head, although other outside scholars sometimes held this position during the nineteenth century, Asaka Gonsai (1790-1860) being a case in point. Following a reorganization in 1790, the school became the official Confucian training academy not only for scholars from the various domains but for shogunal retainers (*hatamono* and *gokenin*) as well. It was officially closed in 1871.

Razan was a prolific scholar whose works in the fields of philosophy and religion number several hundred volumes. Sir George Sansom colorfully describes him as "a man of demonic energy, a voracious reader, and an indefatigable writer...who was distinguished by the breadth rather than the depth of his learning...[and who] could overcome most of adversaries by sheer weight of knowledge."[1] In seeming disregard of the Chu Hsi orthodoxy—and even his own writings in which he relegated the production of belles-lettres to a secondary position behind the all-important mastery of Confucian texts—Razan kept up a lively interest in Chinese ghost and supernatural stories, many of which he translated. Tragically, the Great Edo Fire of 1657 destroyed his personal library, which held many of his own manuscripts. Razan was reportedly so distraught over the loss that he died four or five days later.[2]

Razan's poetry is appealing, if conventional, tending toward natural description with little personal revelation. The second poem below, on the death of his brother, is an exception, displaying an emotional intensity that is relatively uncharacteristic of early Edo kanshi.

---

[1]Sansom, *A History of Japan, 1615-1867*, p. 73.

[2]*NKD*, p. 552.

◍ 11   The Clear Moon over Musashi

Musashi province, autumn scene, the moon enchantingly fair.

Above vast moors and level plains, the sky so beauteous and clear.

Flattening the greenery, we drive on through, but leave no tracks behind.

The full moon shines for a thousand *ri*, the grasslands stretch to the horizon.

Iwanami, p. 173. From *Razan shishū* (The Collected Poems of Razan), 1662

Line one: Old Musashi province corresponds to modern Saitama prefecture and the eastern part
of Kanagawa prefecture near modern Tokyo.
Line four: A *ri* (Ch. *li*) was about a third of a mile.

◍ 12   Going to the Grave of my Younger Brother Choton and Seeing the Withered Plants of the Previous Year Half-Buried in the Snow; Written on the Fourth Day of the First Month of 1639

For more than fifty years we were one flesh and blood.

Now I weep and wail as the wind blows across your fresh grave.

The warbling oriole has become your friend,

Remaining with you among the plants and patches of snow.

Iwanami, p. 174. From *Razan shishū*, 1662

Line one: The poet's brother had died the previous year, on the fifteenth day of the Eighth
Month, at the age of fourteen (Iwanami, p. 424). Thus, "fifty" years in the first line (*gojū*) must
be an error for "fifteen" (*jūgo*), which could have been the boy's age by the traditional *kazoe-
doshi* method of reckoning.
Line three: Known for its beautiful call, the oriole is considered the bird of joy and music. It
also represents the five human relationships and symbolizes friendship.

◉ 13   Viewing Cherry Blossoms in the Moonlight

Pale moonlight shines on the railing, heady the scent of blossoms.
The lovely atmosphere of a night in spring surpasses a mid-autumn evening.
Hazily shines the light of the moon—neither bright nor dim.
A brisk breeze is wafting its way through all the scent and color.

Iwanami, p. 174. From *Razan shishū*, 1662

Ishikawa Jōzan, 1583-1672

Among the most accomplished of the early Edo poets, Ishikawa Jōzan was a native of Mikawa (in modern Aiji prefecture), the home of Shogun Tokugawa Ieyasu, whose clan his family had long served. Jōzan is considered the first Edo kanshi poet to devote himself primarily to the pursuit of poetry.[1] As a youth Jōzan underwent military training and later distinguished himself in Ieyasu's service during the Siege of Osaka (1615), in which the rival Toyotomi forces were defeated. But because he had disobeyed orders, killing an enemy soldier without authorization, he was dismissed, and his outstanding service went unrewarded. Thereafter, at the age of thirty-two, he went to live as a monk at Myōshinji, a Zen temple in western Kyoto.

In 1617 Jōzan began to pursue an academic livelihood under the guidance of *Fujiwara Seika, becoming friendly with *Hayashi Razan and *Hori Kyōan who were also Seika's students. Between 1623 and 1635, he tutored the Asano family of Hiroshima, in order to support his mother. After her death, Jōzan went into retirement at Ichijōji in northeastern Kyoto. He continued to receive a stipend from the Asano family and, being extremely frugal, was able to save enough money to build a hermit's retreat, which was known as Shisendō.[2] He was to live out his days there in isolation, allowing himself only the occasional company of his friend Katakura Chōshū and a few young men who acted as his assistants. Jōzan lived to ninety and never married.

In his retirement, he devoted himself exclusively to the writing of kanshi. As Burton Watson points out, Jōzan worked in the Chinese eremitic tradition of such great poets as T'ao Yuan-ming, Wang Wei (701-761), and Liu Tsung-yuan

---

[1] Matsushita Tadashi, *Edo jidai no shifū shiron* (Tokyo: Meiji Shoin, 1957), pp. 261-267.

[2] Watson 1990, pp. 5-6.

(773-819).[3] He greatly admired the poetry of the mid-T'ang dynasty, especially that of Tu Fu (712-770), yet had a keen appreciation for the Sung poets as well. Watson further observes that in form, at least, Jōzan's kanshi, mostly *zekku* and *risshi*, follow High-T'ang models, but his critical concepts are more in line with the Spiritualist style of the late-Edo poets, who looked to the Sung for their inspiration.[4]

We have selected some of what we consider Jōzan's most successful poems. Perhaps the most charming and typical of his works are those which describe the tranquility and pleasures of Shisendō, his retreat. These provide a vivid portrait of a proud, self-reliant man who is fully satisfied with his solitary life in retirement, growing flowers and sweet potatoes, and oblivious to the goings-on in the nearby village. "Dwelling in tranquility," he writes in one of the poems below, "I've no taste for society:/The world and I have forgotten each other."

⊙ 14   A Sudden Rain Shower

Shades of darkness enshroud half the sky,
Rumbling thunder passes over distant mountains.
Cool the evening; the drizzle has ended.
The moon shines clearly through broken clouds.

Iwanami, p. 177. From *Shinpen fushō shū* (A Collection of Worthless Works [New Edition]), 1704

---

[3]Ibid., pp. 7-8.

[4]Ibid., p. 7. See the section on the poet Priest Gensei, below, for further discussion of this style.

◙ 15 Falling Leaves Mingling with the Rain

Frosty leaves are blowing about, scattered by the wind;
A sudden shower and they mingle with the raindrops, whirling here and there.
Parted from their branches the leaves are driven against the windows and doors.
Their sound blends with the patter of raindrops falling from the eaves
    of my study.

Iwanami, p. 178. From *Shinpen fushō shū*, 1704

◙ 16 An Impromptu Poem Written on an Autumn Night

The wind dies down, brightly glow the fireflies.
The moon descends, mournful cries of wild geese.
On the dewy steps the scent of garden plants.
The times move me to sing the "Fragrant Orchid Song."

Iwanami, pp. 178-179. From *Shinpen fushō shū*, 1704

Line four: The "Fragrant Orchid Song" was supposedly written by Confucius upon seeing some orchids growing alone in a valley among common weeds. Their situation reminded him of his own: like the orchids, he was elegant and refined, yet was unappreciated and forced to keep company with the base and unworthy (Iwanami, p. 179).

◙ 17 A Poem Written while Ill on a Summer Night

My body is frail and my days are nearly done.
My heart's at ease, but tonight I cannot sleep.
The croaking of frogs and the song of the cuckoo
Mingle with the rain, breaking my sickbed sleep.

Iwanami, p. 178. From *Shinpen fushō shū*, 1704

◎ 18 Mount Fuji

Celestial visitors come to play from the peaks beyond the clouds.

Ancient sacred dragons dwell deep within her cavernous depths.

A pure white fan turned upside down in the sky above the eastern sea:

With snow so like the finest silk and a plume of smoke for a handle.

Sugano, p. 39. From *Shinpen fushō shū*, 1704

Line four: The smoke rising from this volcano reminds the poet of the handle of a fan. Line four and line three in the original are reversed in the translation for clarity.

◎ 19 Waking from a Dream

I awake from a dream in the fifth watch,

The village drum heralding the dawn.

Shadows from the dying lamp play upon my wall,

As I lie alone in bed, listening to the leaves fall.

Emaciated with age, I find my pillow too hard;

The night is cold, my bedclothes feel too thin.

Lazy and idle, I dwell in poverty and seclusion,

Doing just as I please when the spirit moves me.

Hirano, p. 165

Line one: The fifth watch was the two-hour interval between 3:00 A.M. and 5:00 A.M..

◎ 20 A Country Temple

An isolated village by flowing waters,

A winding path to the cottage of a monk.

In the deep shade, a stand of tall bamboo:

The evening sun has reached this pure, secluded place.

Hirano, p. 165

◑ 21 A Temple in nearby Woods

How old is this temple I do not know,
But solemn offerings are made here even today.
An ancient gate from a bygone age;
A thatched hall deep among cypresses and pines.
As the night nears its end the lamp burns faintly.
Birds cry out in the deserted forest.
Spring, and we offer toasts with wine for our deafness,
Drinking our fill as we pray for a good harvest.

Hirano, p. 165

◑ 22 Passing Thoughts

Retiring from the world was once far from my mind;
Now my last years I spend in constant tranquility.
I pick flowers along the woodcutter's path
And plant sweet potatoes here at my retreat.
This robe of coarse cloth displeases me not;
My sash of light gauze has length to spare.
The spring days are a perennial source of joy,
As I open and close my scattered books.

Hirano, p. 166

Line six: The poet's sash has "length to spare" because he has grown thin on his spartan diet.

This verse brings to mind a pair of poems titled "On Returning to My Garden and Field," written by T'ao Ch'ien (365-427). See Wu-chi Liu, trans., in *Sunflower Splendor: Three Thousand Years of Chinese Poetry*, ed. by Wu-chi Liu and Irving Yucheng Lo (Bloomington and Indianapolis: Indiana University Press, 1975), p. 52.

◙ 23   Living at Ichihara

1   In dark and distant mountains I dwell.

What part does the village play in my life?

The sound of the stream washes away dreams of visitors.

The lamplight dampens my will to write verse.

5   A tea-stand rests atop the brazier's flame,

Here in my thatched hut in the midnight frost.

The two of us talk of the present and past,

Tallying the dead and the living among our friends.

Poor and lowly, I am content to follow the elders of Shang,

10   Wandering hither and yon like the madman of Ch'u.

Dwelling in tranquility, I've no taste for society:

The world and I have forgotten each other.

Hirano, p. 166

Line nine: The Shang dynasty lasted ca. 1600 B.C. to ca. 1028 B.C. Which elders are being designated here is not clear, but the poet probably intended this to mean simply the Shang forefathers or ancestors in general.

Line ten: "The madman of Ch'u," a reference to Lu Chieh-yü, also known as Lu T'ung, who lived during China's Spring and Autumn period (722-468 B.C.) in the state of Ch'u. During the reign of King Shao, he refused to serve as an official because he felt the times were irredeemably corrupt. He withdrew from society, feigning madness.

This poem, its ending in particular, seems to echo an eight-line verse by the High T'ang poet Meng Hao-jan (689-740), the last couplet of which reads: "I will lodge on this mountain forever,/I and the world are done with each other." Trans. by Stephen Owen, *The Great Age of Chinese Poetry: The High T'ang* (New Haven: Yale University Press, 1981), p. 73.

Hori Kyōan [Kyōin], 1585-1642

Hori Kyōan was a native of Ōmi province in what is today Shiga prefecture. He had originally wanted to be a doctor but turned instead to Confucian learning, becoming a well-known scholar of the Shushi (Ch. Chu Hsi) or Teishu persuasion.[1] Much of the political appeal of Teishu doctrine lay in the standards of moral behavior it prescribed. Confucianism demanded the complete obedience of sons to their fathers and subjects to their rulers. In broader terms, it emphasized the centrality of loyalty to one's superiors at every level, viewing this as essential to maintaining the social and political status quo. The doctrines of Teishugaku were eventually adopted as the official orthodoxy of the Tokugawa shogunate, largely because of their manifest utility as a philosophical tool for buttressing the authority of the shogun.

A brilliant and erudite young man, Hori Kyōan received instruction from *Fujiwara Seika and was grouped with *Matsunaga Sekigo, *Hayashi Razan, and *Naba Kassho as one of the "Four Kings" of Seika's school.[2] From age twenty-seven he served the daimyo Asano Yoshinaga (d. 1613) of the Kii domain and then later went off to serve the Owari domain. Among his various official achievements was the compilation of genealogies for the Tokugawa shogunate. He was also an accomplished waka poet and classical scholar. As in many of the early Edo kanshi, moonlight is a conspicuous image in Kyōan's verse, providing a romantic backdrop against which nocturnal beauty is set, this fashion deriving from T'ang poetic traditions.

---

[1]Teishu or Teishugaku (Teishu Learning) refers to a set of Neo-Confucian doctrines which came into prominence during the early Edo period. The word Teishu is derived from the surnames of the three leading Chinese figures in Sung dynasty Neo-Confucianism: *Tei* is the Japanese reading of the surname Cheng, referring to Ch'eng Hao (1032-1085) and Ch'eng I (1033-1107); *shu* is the Japanese reading of the surname Chu, referring to Chu Hsi (1130-1200), the father of Neo-Confucianism.

[2]*NKD*, p. 607.

☾ 24   Pounding Cloth by the Light of the Moon

In the chilly evening sky tonight the moon is shining brightly.
They're pounding cloth in all the houses, cutting and stitching it, too.
The dawn moonlight pierces the blinds, depriving me of my sleep,
As the din of mallets continues on till the bell of the fifth watch tolls.

Iwanami, p. 181. From *Kyōin shū* (The Kyōin Collection)

☾ 25   Casting Off My Melancholy

Tonight, as the moon shines full and round,
A friend comes to meet me in his tiny boat.
The bright moon knows no worldly cares.
Raising our cups we toast it drunkenly, celebrating life.

Iwanami, p. 180. From *Kyōin shū*

☾ 26   Looking at the Mountains and Waiting for the Moon

In an upstairs room I sit erect, waiting for the moon.
The distant mountains already dark, yellow the nearer hills.
The autumn wind seems to know what I want,
Scattering the drifting clouds, revealing half a moon.

Iwanami, p. 180. From *Kyōin shū*

Matsunaga Sekigo, 1592-1657

Matsunaga Sekigo, a native of Kyoto, was the son of the famous literary figure Matsunaga Teitoku (1571-1653), who was an early Edo poet and the founder of the Teimon school of comic linked verse. Sekigo began writing poetry at a very young age and by fourteen was proficient in *The Four Books*. He was tutored by his uncle *Fujiwara Seika and went on to become a leading Teishu scholar. Sekigo opened his own school in 1648 and trained thousands of students during his career, among them the major scholars Kinoshita Jun'an (1621-1698) and Utsunomiya Ton'an (1633-1709). He served as an official in the Kanazawa domain and was once invited to lecture in the Osaka Castle by Toyotomi Hideyori (1593-1615). Sekigo enjoyed the patronage of the emperors Go-Yōzei and Go-Mizunoo and was given his own academy, named Sekigodō, in recognition of his scholarly achievements.[1]

The first of the poems below is distinguished for its fresh, painterly quality, and Sekigo's image of the carpetlike patchwork of rice fields is particularly striking. As he gazes at the picturesque scenery dotted with the same "bean-sized people and inch-long horses" typical of Japanese painting, art and nature seem to become one. The second verse is the earliest in this collection on the subject of nocturnal travel. Though brief and written in the plainest language, the poem succeeds in capturing the atmosphere of an awakening countryside, with the silence of night giving way to the first sounds of animals heralding the dawn in the roadside villages. In the early Edo period, few poets seem to have considered the lives of the common folk a worthy subject, and poems touching on such themes did not appear in any quantity until the eighteenth century.

---

[1]*NKD*, p. 625.

⏏ 27 On the Road

Rice paddies, thousands of acres, spread out like carpets on the ground;
A pair of white egrets wing their way across the setting sun.
The dark trees in a distant village are enshrouded by evening mist.
Bean-sized people and inch-long horses inhabit this painted screen.

Iwanami, p. 182. From *Sekigo shū* (The Sekigo Collection)

Line one: "Thousands of acres" is literally "a thousand *kei*," one *kei* being a unit of about fifteen acres.

⏏ 28 Travelling Early in the Morning

Rushing through the stars in the predawn light, the carriage bears us away.
Crowing roosters and barking dogs in every village we pass.
Nothing to see but trailing clouds above the eastern peaks,
As up and down for miles we go until the break of day.

Iwanami, p. 183. From *Sekigo shū*

⏏ 29 Mount Suribari

By a winding stream, surrounded by mountains, I walk an endless path.
After the rain, the waterside village seems greener than before.
Gazing up at the narrow road, I stand at the foot of Mount Suribari.
No one in sight, all is silent; autumn grasses growing lush and dense.

Iwanami, p. 182. From *Sekigo shū*

Title: Located southwest of Maibara (west of modern Gifu) in Shiga prefecture. This verse was one of a series of fifty-one poems written between the second and the eighth day of the Ninth Month of 1600 while Sekigo was on the road to Kanatsu from Fukui in modern Ishikawa prefecture (Iwanami, p. 428). He was about eight at the time.

Naba Kassho, 1595-1648

The son of a prosperous farmer, Naba Kassho was born in Himeji, a town in old Harima province, part of modern Hyōgo prefecture. Kassho displayed great precocity from an early age and as a young man was recognized as one of *Fujiwara Seika's four most promising students.[1] He began serving the Kumamoto domain at age twenty-nine, remaining there for seven years before returning to Kyoto in 1630. He lived there for four years before taking a post in the Kii domain in what is today Wakayama prefecture. Kassho was respected as an upright man of firm principles who always spoke his mind. A distinguished Po Chü-i (772-846) scholar, he produced an annotated woodblock edition of Po's poetic works which preserves an early Northern Sung text thereof. Kassho's edition was considered sufficiently valuable to be included in the Chinese *Ssu-pu ts'ung-k'an* collectanea.[2]

The first poem below reflects the oft-encountered poetic theme of nostalgia for the lost glory of epochs past. It also serves to remind us of the ephemerality of human life, expressed here by the images of water flowing past never to return, and drifting clouds which similarly disappear. The awareness of the transience of all living things (*mujōkan*) derives from basic Buddhist teachings and is one of the main thematic undercurrents in traditional Japanese literature, whether written in the vernacular or in Chinese.

At first glance, the second poem appears to be about a nameless rustic fisherman, a stock image in kanshi where such figures are always romanticized. Upon closer examination, the subject turns out to be the poet himself, lamenting his own miserable condition and contrasting it with the carefree life of the birds overhead. The same mildly pessimistic note is sounded in the third verse, where

---

[1]See *NKB*, p. 496.

[2]Ibid.

the poet again articulates certain basic Buddhist concepts: that our temporal world remains in flux and that happiness and good fortune are always short-lived.

☾ 30   Visiting Ginkakuji Temple

Desolate and lonely the temple of the shogun,
Lush and verdant the myriad plants and trees.
The moss grows thickly, for visitors are few;
The Ancient One who reposed among the pines is no more.
When will these waters cease to flow?
Whither will the drifting clouds return?
I sigh aloud on the mountain path at dusk
While birds from the dark forest go flying past.

Hirano, p. 168. Probably from *Naba ikō* (A Posthumous Text of Naba's Works), 1666

Line four: The "Ancient One" refers to the eighth Muromachi shogun, Ashikaga Yoshimasa (1436-1490), who built this retreat.

☾ 31   Encountering Rain while Travelling by Boat to Imagire

Short straw cloak and tattered straw hat; soaked to the skin by rain!
I look like an angler homeward bound, my fishing done for the day.
In life there never is any rest from hardship and from sorrow.
A pair of birds from the bay fly past, without a care in the world.

Iwanami, p. 184. From *Naba ikō*, 1666

Title: Imagire, a locality on the shores of Lake Hamana in modern Shizuoka prefecture.

◉ 32 Gazing Afar after Snow Has Fallen

A thousand trees have come into bloom—suddenly spring is here!
The myriad paths are spread with jewels; immaculate, no dust.
The sky is blue, the bright sun shines, but then it rains for a spell.
How much like the human realm—those folk who are down on their luck.

Iwanami, p. 185. From *Naba ikō*, 1666

◉ 33 Su Wu's "Felt and Snow"

A frozen pit and the violent Ch'in realm were where the two were held.
Heaven awoke and was moved by their plight; both of the captives were freed.
For a ram to give birth to a sheep was akin to a horse growing horns on its head;
The letter attached to a goose's foot worked as well as the white-headed bird.

Iwanami, p. 184. From *Naba ikō*, 1666

Title: Su Wu was an envoy of the Former Han dynasty (206 B.C.-A.D. 8) who was sent on a mission to the Hsiung-nu, a nomadic people living on the northern periphery of China. He was held captive by them for nineteen years. Su Wu refused to shed his allegiance to the Han court and spent many days in a dungeon, the frozen pit in line one, without food. He is said to have survived by eating snow and chewing on a felt rug, hence this title.

Emperor Chao Ti, having made peace with the Hsiung-nu in 86 B.C., sent an envoy to ask that Su be released. The Hsiung-nu lied to the envoy, telling him that Su was dead. The envoy then tricked the Hsiung-nu, saying that the Emperor had shot a goose which had a letter tied to its leg, the letter revealing that Su was in fact still alive. This anecdote is alluded to in the last line of the poem.

Su was duly released, returning to China in 81 B.C. According to the historical accounts, he had been told by the enemy while in captivity that he would be released "when a ram gave birth to a kid," in other words, never. This story is alluded to in the third line, although the "kid" is a "sheep" in the poem.

Line one: The two men referred to here are Su Wu (see preceding note) and Prince Tan, the son of Wang Hsi, who was a ruler of the state of Yen during the Warring States period (403-221 B.C.). Prince Tan was held hostage in the state of Ch'in, whose ruler, Wang Cheng (r. 246-209 B.C.), told Tan that he could go free if horns could be found on a horse's head, or if a bird with a white head were to appear. This anecdote is alluded to in lines three and four of the poem. Although neither of these miraculous events seemed possible, the bird with the white head was eventually seen, and Tan was thus released.

Emperor Go-Mizunoo, 1596-1680

Emperor Go-Mizunoo, known also as Prince Kotohito, reigned between 1611-1629. He was the son of Emperor Go-Yōzei, whom he succeeded to become Japan's 108th emperor. Go-Mizunoo was compelled in 1620 to marry the daughter of Shogun Tokugawa Hidetada, a girl named Tokugawa Kazuko, who became his official consort four years later. Displeased with his forced marriage to Kazuko, he also chafed at other kinds of shogunal meddling in court affairs. He was particularly aggrieved by new regulations passed in 1613 and 1627 which severely undercut his authority, putting him firmly under the thumb of the shogun by defining his role as that of scholar and poet, while at the same time denying him his traditional power to select priests for the highest ecclesiastical rank, *shie* (the Purple Robe). Consequently, when his daughter Okiko was seven, Go-Mizunoo yielded the throne to her, and she became the Empress Meishō (r. 1629-1643). He had originally planned to pass the throne to his son, but the latter's untimely death caused him to select Okiko, who became the first empress to rule since the eighth century.[1] Over the next half century, Go-Mizunoo ruled from behind the scenes as a retired sovereign, remaining active from the cloister throughout the next four imperial reigns. He was a devout Buddhist, scholar, and poet, perhaps better known for his waka than for his kanshi, and he left us a waka collection titled *Ōsō shū* (The Sea Gull's Nest). He was a cultivated and refined person whose sensitivity toward nature is apparent in the poems below. In both, he expresses apprehension at the prospect of anything hindering his ability to appreciate the natural beauty around him. Today, the gardens of the Shūgakuin Detached Palace, built by Go-Mizunoo in northern Kyoto, stand as an enduring memorial to his aesthetic sensibilities and love of nature.

---

[1]On the emperor's turbulent reign, see Sansom, pp. 27-28.

◘ 34 On the Bamboo Planted in Front of the Window

On the new bamboo, so dignified and tall, a chill has now descended,
Gratifying the poet in me as I stand before my window.
In summer, we must expect sudden showers; in winter, the snow must fall.
But I fear the bamboo with its cool shade will obscure the light of the moon.

Hirano, p. 160

◘ 35 In Appreciation of Flowers

What need is there for me to seek a further source of delight?
A moment's glance is worth a thousand in gold, for my cares all disappear.
Yet when the flowers are in bloom I regret the auspicious omens:
Rain after ten days, wind after five—both my enemies!

Hirano, p. 159

Line four: Rain that fell once every ten days and wind that blew once every five days were considered desirable for creating a peaceful and prosperous world, according to *Lun-heng* (Critical Essays), written by Wang Ch'ung (27-97?).

Nakae Tōju, 1608-1648

One of the leading intellectuals of the seventeenth century, Nakae Tōju came from a samurai family living in the province of Ōmi, modern Shiga prefecture. He was renowned for his efforts to establish a more action-centered and intuitive Confucianism based on the teachings of the Chinese scholar Wang Yang-ming (J. Ō Yōmei, 1472-1529), who emphasized the cultivation of the inner self. Following the death of his father in 1616, Tōju was raised by his grandfather, who served Katō Sadayasu, the daimyo of Yonago domain in the province of Hōki, located in modern Tottori prefecture. When Sadayasu was transferred to Ōsu in Iyo in 1617, Tōju and his grandfather moved there as well. Upon his grandfather's death in 1625, Tōju became family head and began to serve Sadayasu, following in his grandfather's footsteps. But he retired nine years later without official permission, offended, George Sansom tells us, by the unfriendliness of his colleagues.[1] He thereupon returned to his home to teach and to be near his widowed mother. His school was small, with fewer than sixty students, and he never earned much from this endeavor, depending upon gifts from his students to make ends meet.[2] Tōju became known for his attachment to the ideal of filial devotion and was called the Sage of Ōmi. He was also known as Tōju Sensei (Wisteria Tree Master), a name derived from the fact that an old wisteria tree grew near the room where he taught in his village.[3]

---

[1]Sansom, p. 74. Another source cites "political and academic rivalries within the domain" as contributing to his decision to leave. See Seiichi Iwao, ed. [trans. by Burton Watson], *Biographical Dictionary of Japanese History* (Kodansha: Tokyo and New York, 1978), p. 221.

[2]Peter Nosco, *Remembering Paradise: Nativism and Nostalgia in Eighteenth-Century Japan* [*Harvard-Yenching Monograph Series*, no. 31] (Cambridge: Harvard University Press, 1990), p. 35.

[3]Iwao, p. 221.

At thirty-seven, Tōju read the complete works of Wang Yang-ming and, through this new-found knowledge, came to reject the teachings of Chu Hsi. Tōju is considered the founder of the Japanese Yōmeigaku school of Neo-Confucianism, which was based upon Wang Yang-ming's doctrines. Sometimes referred to as the Idealist or Mind school, Yōmeigaku was one of the principal branches of Ming Neo-Confucianism in Japan. Instead of the mere acquisition of knowledge, it emphasized meditation, self-discipline, and ethical activism in order to develop the intuitive faculties of the individual. In place of "the extension of knowledge through the investigation of things" seen in *The Great Learning*, Wang advocated "the extension of intuitive knowledge" through investigation of one's inner self, this accomplished through meditation that would supposedly lead to intuitive development and enlightenment.[4] Wang Yang-ming thus brought Neo-Confucian teachings philosophically closer to the ideals of Buddhism, those of the Zen sect in particular. Wang also rejected the dualism of Chu Hsi Confucianism, which drew a clear distinction between Heaven and man and between "heavenly principle" and "human desire." The Idealists regarded Heaven and Man instead as part of one realm. People within this vast realm were seen as sharing a fundamental equality transcending all class and social differences, a view which further illustrates the determination of the Idealists to close the gap between Neo-Confucian teachings and the essential beliefs of Buddhism.

In the first poem below, Tōju uses the image of the moon to signify the inner intuitive soul lying at the core of Wang Yang-ming thought: "The mind should make tranquility its goal/For then the bright moon will not sink beneath the waves." In the second verse, the poet farewells his disciple Kumazawa Banzan (1619-1691), reflecting the intimacy which traditionally bound teacher and student in China and Japan, in what was virtually a father-son relationship. The theme of parting, with its attendant sense of loss and uncertainty about the possibility of reunion, is commonly seen in kanshi and was inspired principally by the T'ang

---

[4]John K. Fairbank, Edwin O. Reischauer, and Albert O. Craig, *East Asia: Tradition and Transformation* (Boston: Houghton-Mifflin Company, 1973), pp. 192-193, 419.

74

poetic tradition.   Most typically it is encountered in the context of male friendships.

◐ 36   Thoughts as I Look at the Moon from a Boat;
Written in the Winter of 1634

If a man's judgment is the least bit flawed,

For the next thousand miles he will be off-course.

The mind should make tranquility its goal,

For then the bright moon will not sink beneath the waves.

Iwanami, p. 187. From *Tōju sensei ikō* (A Posthumous Text of Master Tōju's Works), 1795

Line four: Here the moon signifies one's inner intuitive soul, harking back to the philosophy of Wang Yang-ming (1472-1529).

◐ 37   Farewelling Kumazawa on His Departure to Bizen

Barely a few days left in the year;

Who'd have thought we'd be here at this kiosk?

Bidding farewell to someone so talented,

I heave a sigh at my wretched old age.

Although my sideburns are as white as the plum blossoms

These eyes of mine are as green as the willows.

Here above the blue waters we are overwhelmed by sadness,

As the west wind brings us to our senses.

Inoguchi, p. 118

Title: Kumazawa Banzan (1619-1691) was an important Yōmeigaku scholar and one of Nakae Tōju's most prominent students. Banzan was twenty-nine and Tōju forty at the time. Bizen was part of modern Okayama prefecture.
Line two: The kiosk is a simple restaurant with pennant decorations outside.
Line six: "Green eyes" is meant as an expression of intimacy with and sympathy for someone.

Yamazaki Ansai [Suika], 1618-1682

Yamazaki Ansai, known also as Suika after the syncretic Shinto Suika sect which he founded, was a native of the Ikadachi district of Ōmi province in what is today Shiga prefecture. An austere boy, he had read *The Lotus Sutra* and *The Four Books* by age eight. Ansai's relations with his family were strained at best; apparently they found him haughty and lacking in frivolity, and to make matters worse he had a rebellious, impertinent streak, which led his parents to conclude that the priesthood would be the best way to straighten him out. So at twelve, Ansai started his Buddhist training at Enryakuji on Mt. Hiei.[1] However, the monastic life did not agree with him, and three years later his father moved him to the Zen temple Myōshinji in western Kyoto. Ansai remained at Myōshinji for four years but reportedly was disliked by everyone there.[2] When he was nineteen, he went to Tosa in distant Shikoku to serve as priest of Kyūkōji temple, where he stayed for six years. During this time, he read Neo-Confucian texts with Nonaka Kenzan (1615-1663) and Ogura Sansei (1604-1654), both students of the Confucian Nangaku (Southern Learning) scholar Tani Jichū (1598-1649).

Ansai reveals in his biography that the turning point in his career occurred one day when he was twenty-three, while he was listening to a lecture presented by Tani on the Confucian classic *Doctrine of the Mean*.[3] He decided then and there to leave the world of Buddhism and instead seek an education in Teishugaku, as if to follow in the footsteps of Tani, who had himself left the Buddhist priesthood to devote himself to Confucian learning. Inoguchi Atsushi relates that this marked change of course, made without the required permission, angered the daimyo of Tosa. Ansai's mentor Kenzan tried to apologize on

---

[1]Inoguchi, p. 122.

[2]Ibid.

[3]As related by Hiroshi Miyaji in the entry "Yamazaki Ansai," *KEJ*, vol. 8, p. 312.

Ansai's behalf, but the daimyo remained unmollified. Using money obtained from Kenzan, Ansai escaped to Kyoto, where he taught Neo-Confucianism and pursued a new-found interest in traditional mythology and Shinto. In 1665, Ansai's situation improved, as he came under the protection and patronage of the well-placed daimyo of Aizu, Hoshina Masayuki, who was the son of Shogun Hidetada.[4] Ansai played a major role in the reform of education in the domain, then returned to Kyoto after his patron died. It is not clear whether Ansai ever actually resided in the Aizu domain for any length of time; most likely, he merely made periodic visits from Edo to implement his educational reforms.

Ansai's interest in Shinto deepened as he grew older, and he was initiated into the esoteric Ise (Watarai) Shinto sect in 1669. Shortly thereafter, he embarked upon the study of Yoshida Shinto, also known as Yuiitsu (Primal) Shinto, a sect which Koschmann identifies as being one that "considers Shinto to be the origin of Confucianism, Taoism, and Buddhism as well."[5] His published works challenged Buddhism from a Shinto-Confucian standpoint, although as George Sansom points out, Ansai was not the first to use Shinto ideas "as an ally of Confucianism against Buddhism." *Hayashi Razan had previously done much the same thing, and even earlier *Fujiwara Seika had conceived a unity between Shinto and Confucian doctrine, establishing an intellectual tradition that was to flourish throughout the Edo period.[6] Ansai founded the Suika (or Suiga) Shinto sect and continued to work toward a complex reinterpretation of Shintoism from a Neo-Confucian viewpoint. His idealized conception of the imperial institution and emphasis upon the veneration of the imperial house were highly influential

---

[4]Inoguchi, p. 122.

[5]J. Victor Koschmann, *The Mito Ideology: 1790-1864* (Berkeley, Los Angeles, and London: University of California Press, 1987), p. 8.

[6]Sansom, p. 86.

in later Edo times, especially during the anti-shogunate movement of the nineteenth century.[7]

Ansai was reputedly a strict but effective teacher, emphasizing the practical application of the doctrines he studied. Not one to mince words, he voiced sharp criticism of the Hayashi family, whose members, in his view, failed to practice what they preached, and according to Sansom, Ansai considered *Hayashi Razan "a common Confucianist drudge."[8] Despite his fearsome, uncompromising manner with students, he reportedly attracted more than six thousand of them over the years—about a third of the total number of students undergoing training in Neo-Confucianism in his day.[9]

Ansai left an extremely large collection of writings on a range of subjects. So diverse were his philosophical interests over his lifetime that *Itō Jinsai is said to have remarked in jest that "Ansai's enthusiasms went from one subject to another so frequently that if he had lived longer he would no doubt have become a Christian missionary."[10] His kanshi poetry, on the other hand, is not well known, and relatively few verses of interest by him exist. Inoguchi characterizes his poems as direct expressions of personal feelings, relatively free of literary embellishment.[11] The examples below, however, show him as a fairly typical early Edo poet in his use of poetic language and no more inclined toward direct expression of private feelings than any of his contemporaries.

---

[7]Iwao, p. 277. For a cogent summary of what J. Victor Koschmann calls Ansai's "Confucianized Shinto" synthesis, which draws upon the earlier seminal research of Herman Ooms, see Koschmann, pp. 9-10.

[8]Sansom, p. 75.

[9]Inoguchi, p. 122. Although Peter Nosco has identified *Itō Jinsai's Kogidō academy as the most successful privately-funded academy in Japan prior to the eighteenth century, one wonders if Ansai's was not more successful still, as he had several times more students than Jinsai over his lifetime. See the Jinsai biography, below, for details.

[10]As paraphrased in Sansom, p. 86.

[11]Inoguchi, p. 124.

◐ 38 My Feelings

I sit and muse on how the Heavenly Lord has washed away the dust of the world.

The rain has passed, and as I gaze around me everything seems refreshed.

The light breeze and the clear moon are just as in ancient times;

But a companion possessing a calm, pure mind is the one thing that I lack.

Sugano, pp. 40-41; Hirano, p. 169; Andō, p. 48. From *Suika bunshū* (The Collected Works of Suika), 1714-1724

Lines three and four: Sugano, p. 41, observes that the language of these lines contains phrases almost identical to lines in the biography of the Neo-Confucianist Chou Tun-i (1017-1073) contained in *Sung shih* (The History of the Sung Dynasty). He suggests that the poet is alluding to Chou Tun-i as the ideal companion.

◐ 39 Orioles in Autumn

The sun and moon give way to each other throughout the seasons of the year.

Flowers scatter, leaves turn dark, then take on reddish hues.

All of a sudden, before our eyes, gold-clad lads a-warbling.

And in the autumn wind and light I hear the winds of spring.

Hirano, p. 170

Line three: "Gold-clad lads" (*chin-i kung-tzu*) is a Chinese nickname for the oriole first used by Emperor Ming Huang (685-762), sixth emperor of the T'ang dynasty.
Line four: The oriole is associated with early spring; the poet is taken by surprise since it is autumn.

Priest Gensei, 1623-1668

Gensei is considered one of the foremost poets of the early Edo period. He was often called Fukakusa no Gensei (Gensei from Fukakusa), in reference to a hilly area in modern Fushimi ward in Kyoto, his place of origin. Gensei's mother was forty-one years old when he was born, and once when Gensei was very young, she took him to Kenninji temple, where the head monk reportedly exclaimed, "How amazing for an old woman to have given birth to such a splendid young boy!"[1] At around the age of six, Gensei began his formal literary and military education, studying waka with Matsunaga Teitoku (d. 1653). When he was thirteen, he was taken to Edo, where he served Ii Naotaka (1590-1659), the daimyo of Hikone, to whom he was distantly related. Six years later, Gensei went with his mother to Izumi, in the area of modern Osaka, where he saw a statue of Nichiren (1222-1282). This experience apparently made such a deep impression on him that he decided then and there to become a Nichiren priest.[2] Gensei took his vows at twenty-six and went on to establish the Zuikōji temple of the Nichiren sect in Fukakusa, Kyoto. He retired six years later to lead the life of a poet-recluse, continuing to write poetry in Japanese and Chinese even when he was extremely ill.

Gensei was reputedly a man of boundless energy, well-read and endowed with a remarkable memory. A prolific writer, he loved all poetry, both Chinese and Japanese, and was also an expert in the tea ceremony. His special gift, however, was for kanshi, and he is ranked with *Ishikawa Jōzan as one of the two greatest poets of the Kanbun period (1661-1673).[3] Gensei was happy to

---

[1]Inoguchi, p. 120.

[2]Ibid. Nichiren, who was trained in the Tendai tradition, founded the Buddhist sect which bears his name. Its teachings stressed the primacy of *The Lotus Sutra* and the formulaic utterance of its title: "Praise to the Sutra of the Lotus Blossom of the Fine Dharma." See Miner, p. 209.

[3]*NKD*, p. 216.

give instruction to anyone, whether lay person or priest, friend or stranger. He adhered strictly to Buddhist law, including its prohibitions, always wearing the simplest clothing. Serious and upright, Gensei had great compassion for his fellow man, which won him the sobriquet Nyorai Incarnate (*nyorai no keshin*).[4] Gensei was devoted to his parents and cared for them with great attentiveness, lodging them in Chikuyōan, his cottage in Fukakusa. Both parents lived to the age of eighty-seven, and the filial Gensei only outlived his mother by twenty-seven days.[5]

Gensei is considered a forerunner of the Japanese Spiritualist style of kanshi, which was inspired by the *hsing-ling* (J. *seirei*) style later associated with Yuan Mei (1716-1798) and others. *Hsing-ling* poetry rejected conventionalism and the imitation of earlier masters, advocating instead the cultivation of "native sensibility" and spiritual depth.[6] It placed particular emphasis upon the free expression of the poet's own personal feelings. "The poet," wrote Yuan, "is one who has not lost the heart of a child."[7] In Japan, *seirei* did not fully come into its own until the latter half of the eighteenth century when it was practiced by such masters as Rikunyo (1734-1801) and Yamamoto Hokuzan (1752-1812).

The poetry of Gensei is striking for the freshness of its imagery and its inventive treatment of even the most common subjects, such as the "smiling" chestnuts in the first selection. This poem's charm lies both in the novel personification of the humble chestnut and in the poet's tender description of the seasonal changes it experiences. In the fourth verse below, the image of the poet's imprint in the moss is particularly appealing, reminding us how long he has sat absorbed in the beauty of the scenery, totally at one with his surroundings as he watches the transformation of day into night.

---

[4]*Nyorai* (Skt. *tathāgata*) means "one who has attained buddhahood."

[5]Inoguchi, p. 120.

[6]"Native sensibility" is James J.Y. Liu's term—see Liu, pp. 73-74 for an informative discussion of *hsing-ling*.

[7]As quoted in ibid., p. 74.

☪ 40   Chestnuts

Chestnuts in bunches, surrounded by leaves;
greenish prickles like a hedgehog's spines.
Buffeted fiercely by the wind from the west but not yet willing to fall.
After the frost they open their mouths coquettishly and smile.
Then I look out and see the apes filling my mountain garden.

Iwanami, p. 341. From *Sōzan shū* (The Grass Mountain Collection), 1674

☪ 41   Nighttime Conversations in Mountain Homes

A dog is barking in the woods, the night is wearing on.
East and west all talk has ceased; nothing more to discuss.
Vulgar stories, petty gossip—who would choose to listen?
Clouds block my brushwood gate, cold the mountain moonlight.

Iwanami, p. 342. From *Sōzan shū*, 1674

☪ 42   On the Road to Takatsuki

Green fields stretching endlessly, as far as the verdant hills.
Villages and monasteries away in the hazy mist.
Autumn sunlight, infinitely radiant, autumn all around.
Chilly cerulean skies; white clouds, calm and still.

Iwanami, pp. 343-344. From *Sōzan shū*, 1674

Title: Takatsuki, a castle town in the old province of Settsu, part of modern Osaka-fu.

82

☾ 43 Viewing the Grass Hills in the Evening

Loving the mountains, I often go outdoors
And repose upon pine roots, my stick set aside.
The autumn river divides the plain below;
The evening mist obscures the faraway village.
Dew appears and turns the forest white,
Stars come out as the branch tips darken.
Then I realize how long I've been sitting:
In the late autumn moss, the imprint of my body!

Inoguchi, p. 121. From *Sōzan shū*, 1674

Title: "Grass Hills" is a reference to Gensei's native Fukakusa.

☾ 44 On the Road to Fushimi

As I trudge along with my bramble staff, my mind is miles away.
I gaze afar at the mountains blue, a river flowing nearby.
Many indeed are the visitors who come from the world of dust.
Yet they notice not the peach-tree blossoms growing beside the road.

Hirano, p. 172. Probably from *Sōzan shū*, 1674

Line three: In Buddhist thought, dust is synonymous with worldly cares, the mundane world of men.

Itō Jinsai, 1627-1705

Itō Jinsai, posthumously known as Kogaku Sensei (The Master of Ancient Learning), was a native of Kyoto. The son of a lumber seller, he is perhaps the first major kanshi poet to have come from a merchant-class background. Jinsai started reading *The Great Learning* at eleven, and although he was encouraged to train as a medical doctor like many other promising young men of his day, he devoted himself instead to mastering Neo-Confucian doctrine. By his late twenties he had progressed sufficiently to write several seminal treatises, including *Taikyokuron* (A Treatise on the Ultimate) and *Seizenron* (A Commentary on the Goodness of Human Nature). He rose to become the most influential Confucian scholar and commentator of the seventeenth century.

In his late thirties, influenced by Zen ideals and the doctrines of Wang Yang-ming, he began to question Neo-Confucian teachings, which he had come to see as mere interpretations of the classics. In his view, these teachings ran counter to the original doctrines of Confucius and Mencius, and he maintained that it was necessary to concentrate upon studying the ancient classics themselves in order to understand the essence of Confucianism. "The *Six Classics* have always been our stock-in-trade," he writes in the first poem below, asking, "Why labor in pursuit of anything else?" Rejecting Teishugaku, Jinsai went on to establish a major school called Kogigaku (The School for [the Study of] Ancient Meaning), also known variously in Japan as Kogaku (Ancient Learning) and Fukkogaku (Antiquarian Studies). Western scholars sometimes refer to this as the school of Pristine Confucianism. Jinsai's new school was one of the three principle Antiquarian schools in existence by the end of the seventeenth century.

As David Pollack points out, a chief characteristic of Jinsai's literary thought is its emphasis upon the complementary nature of literature and the ancient Way, with literature serving as a device for illustrating the Way. Poetry is a means of expressing human emotions and human nature, observed Jinsai, and is not meant to be a vehicle for explaining morality. It must depict all authentic emotions, even those pertaining to that which is "low and near-to-hand," the humble rather than the lofty.[1] Jinsai also rejected what Pollack calls "the clever depiction of 'scene' in poetry for its own sake," for as Pollack explains, in Jinsai's view "it served no purpose other than to create the illusion of a world, uninformed by the reality of emotion."[2]

Jinsai endeavored to abide by the values of humanity and righteousness (*jingi*) in his own daily life, becoming a living example. He taught his students that it was not sufficient to merely understand these principles; one had to put them into practice. His school emphasized the importance of loyalty, compassion, and faithfulness, believing that an ethical society free of deception and treachery could someday be realized. Unlike many prominent scholars of his day, Jinsai refused to accept a government post and instead devoted himself exclusively to scholarship. Among his five sons, Tōgai, the eldest, and Rangū, were the most distinguished, carrying on the noble-minded traditions of Kogaku.

During his lifetime, Jinsai taught more than one thousand students (some accounts say three thousand) from all across the country at his private school, the Kogidō academy, located in Horikawa, Kyoto. As many as half of those enrolled over the years were from merchant, peasant, or medical backgrounds, with only thirty-nine percent being samurai or *rōnin*.[3] Peter Nosco notes that this school was the most successful self-funded private academy in Japan prior to the eighteenth century, even though it was not the first such academy to appear. He links the rise of the private school in Tokugawa Japan to the "civilization" or "vocational rehabilitation" of the samurai, whose martial abilities had little value in a nation at peace and who had no choice but to learn new Confucianist

---

[1]David Pollack, *The Fracture of Meaning: Japan's Synthesis of China from the Eighth through the Eighteenth Centuries* (Princeton: Princeton University Press, 1986), pp. 198-199.

[2]Ibid., p. 201.

[3]Richard Rubinger, *Private Academies in Tokugawa Japan* (Princeton: Princeton University Press, 1982), p. 55.

leadership skills.[4] Jinsai's academy, Nosco points out, followed a pattern of development that became typical among subsequent private institutions of this sort, beginning informally as a reading and study group and only later becoming a formal academy.[5] Inspired by Jinsai's success, many other scholars opened similar private ventures, catering to the growing numbers of literate townsmen and to the increased demands placed upon samurai to acquire a high level of moral education which would serve them in their professions.[6]

Although preoccupied much of the time with teaching, Jinsai also enjoyed his peace and quiet, as we see in the second poem below, where he writes about his cozy, secluded study. The dearth of visitors to this private refuge brings him satisfaction rather than loneliness. Genial, and gentle in temperament, Jinsai is said to have never in his life had an altercation with anyone.[7] Once, after another scholar attacked him in a published work, he was urged by a student to defend himself, but he reportedly just smiled and said nothing. When pressed to explain, he stated that according to *Lun yü* (The Analects of Confucius), a gentleman never enters into disputes with others. He added, moreover, that if the man who had criticized him were correct in his views, then he was a valuable friend, and if he were wrong, he would eventually wake up to his error.[8]

Jinsai left behind a large corpus of commentaries on the Confucian classics, among them *Rongo kogi* (Old Interpretations of the Analects of Confucius, ca. 1712). Although he worked hard all his life, he never realized his dream of retirement. The third poem below describes with evocative imagery a place he had in mind: an idyllic, secluded woodland retreat in the hills of Ichijōji, northeast of Kyoto, where persimmons and wild meadow mushrooms grew in profusion. In the last of our selections, there seems to be an element of wistful

---

[4]Peter Nosco, *Remembering Paradise*, p. 33.

[5]Ibid., p. 35.

[6]Ibid., pp. 36-37.

[7]Andō, p. 53.

[8]Inoguchi, p. 125.

longing in Jinsai's sentimental description of the humble fisherman, whose relaxed and carefree lifestyle doubtless seemed enviable to this busy city-dwelling scholar.

◐ 45   Your Education Must Begin Today

Your education must begin today.

Plan for the future, think of the past, tarry not a minute longer.

Tiny seedlings grow into great, green trees;

Spring waters wind on and form a raging flow.

When your knowledge grows, your horizons expand.

Things once mastered become no effort at all.

The Six Classics have always been our stock-in-trade.

Why labor in pursuit of anything else?

Iwanami, p. 192. From *Kogaku sensei shishū* (A Collection of Poetry by the Master of Ancient Learning), ca. 1717 (following date in postscript)

Lines seven and eight: *The Six Classics* constitute the basic canonical texts of Confucianism. The sentiments expressed here represent a rejection of Neo-Confucianism with its emphasis upon commentaries, which Jinsai implies are not worth reading. Jinsai adhered to the Kogigaku school of Confucianism, which advocated returning to the original texts and disregarding most of the commentaries. The latter were seen as having departed from the true, original meaning of the classics.

1. An original document, dated 1852, written by
Takahashi Yoshizumi (?-?), quoting Kogaku scholar
Itō Jinsai (1627-1705). (Translated in the List of Illustrations.)

88

◎ 46 An Impromptu Poem

My study stands in the autumn cold among scattered pines and emerald bamboo.
Water bubbles on the brazier, the scent of tea is fragrant.
Forsaken the path before my door; people seldom come.
A few chapters from *The Great Learning* I read from time to time.

Iwanami, p. 193. From *Kogaku sensei shishū*, ca. 1717

Line four: *The Great Learning* (*Ta hsüeh*) was one of the Confucian classics.

◎ 47 Journeying to Ichijōji; Written on the Third Day of the Ninth Month of 1697

Green and vast the autumn scene, midway up the mountain.
Clouds mingled with ancient trees, the first geese flying by.
In mountain gardens the persimmons are ripe;
    crows carry them off in their beaks.
By valley streams mushrooms grow thickly;
    people take them home on their backs.
The city so distant I never see a dusty haze in the air.
The forest so dense that all I see is a light and cloudy mist.
If some day I should wish to find a place where I might dwell,
It would be right here, below Mount Hiei, by this country riverbed.

Iwanami, p. 193. From *Kogaku sensei shishū*, ca. 1717

Line one: Climbing high into the hills or mountains was not just a recreational pursuit but a perfect occasion for versification as well. As one scholar has observed, "[Chinese poets] felt a lofty vantage enabled one to see things in enlarged perspective, to surmount petty concerns, and to view matters in a grand manner." See David R. McCraw, *Du Fu's Laments from the South* (Honolulu: University of Hawaii Press, 1992), p. 101.
Line two: "First geese," a reference to the annual autumn migration of the geese to the south. This is a conventional reminder of the arrival of autumn.
Line four: Literally, meadow mushrooms (*shimeji* or *hon-shimejitake*, *Lyophyllum aggregatum*, sometimes translated as champignon), a highly prized mushroom in the *matsutake* family said to be even better tasting than the latter.

⊌ 48 A Poetic Inscription for a Picture of a Fisherman Painted on a Narrow Strip of Decorative Paper

High he stands upon a bank, always a rod in his hands.

Bushy eyebrows, snowy hair, in the twilight river chill.

Making fires, cooking fish, the only skills he knows.

But don't for a moment mistake him for that fellow from Ch'ichou!

Hirano, p. 177

Line four: The "fellow from Ch'ichou" was Lü Shang, a high official in China during the Chou dynasty (ca. 1027-256 B.C.) who went into exile to escape the despotic ruler Chou Hsin. Years later, when he was eighty years old, he was brought back into official service by King Wen who had come upon him fishing one day. The poet is suggesting that this humble fisherman is in no way comparable to the distinguished Lü Shang, even though both men enjoyed fishing.

Tokugawa Mitsukuni [Jōzan], 1628-1700

Tokugawa Mitsukuni was the grandson of Tokugawa Ieyasu, the unifier of feudal Japan. The second daimyo of Mito (now part of Ibaragi prefecture), Mitsukuni was also an outstanding Confucian scholar, historian, and man of letters and was renowned for his benevolent rule. Mitsukuni was rebellious and unruly during his adolescence, although he had overcome these problems by his late teens, apparently inspired by reading portions of *Shih chi* (The Records of the Grand Historian), from which he is said to have gained a deep appreciation of the Confucian ideals of moral uprightness and self-abnegation.[1]   In 1672 he established the Shōkōkan academy for historical research in Koishikawa, Edo, at the Mito domain residence, where he continued the compilation of his chef d'oeuvre, *Dai Nihon shi* (The Great History of Japan), a project which he had begun in 1657. A massive history of Japan from earliest times to the fourteenth century, this work, which was "intended as a moral exemplar on the pattern of Chinese histories,"[2] did not reach its final completed form until 1906. Sansom praises the compilation as "the only Japanese work which resembles in form and quality the great Chinese histories, since it includes their standard features and is extremely accurate."[3] Evidently, Mitsukuni had been concerned that his work would not be properly finished in the event he died during its compilation, a sentiment revealed in the final verse below, written upon the death of his sister. The tortoise poem, the first of the following selections, suggests that Mitsukuni often wished he could have lived a quiet life in obscurity, instead of allowing his sense of duty to take precedence over his love of solitude and leisure. Obsessed

---

[1]For further details concerning how *Shih chi* shaped his outlook, see Kate Wildman Nakai, "Tokugawa Confucian Historiography," in Nosco, pp. 73-75.

[2]Koschmann, p. 34.

[3]Sansom, p. 94.

with completing *Dai Nihon shi*, Mitsukuni immersed himself in historical scholarship, which may help to account for the prevalence of Chinese historical allusions in his poetry.

Mitsukuni's philosophy became the foundation for Mitogaku (Mito Studies) which emphasized the following three unities: Shinto and Confucian thought, literary and military training, and loyalty to parents and the emperor.[4] Mitogaku scholars also advocated uniting all forces within the country against the threat from foreign powers, giving rise to the imperial loyalists' slogan of *sonnō jōi*, "revere the emperor and repel the barbarians." Mitsukuni and later generations of Mito scholars gave precedence to things Japanese, promoting Shinto over Buddhism, for example, while also working to protect the imperial house from encroachment by the shogunate. During the 1660s, Mitsukuni destroyed more than half of all the temples in Mito and replaced them with Shinto shrines, one in every village.[5]

By promoting paper production, shipbuilding, horse-breeding, and gold mining, Mitsukuni also brought increased economic prosperity to his domain. He reduced the tax burden upon the peasantry, implemented a program of famine relief, and tried to raise the moral tone of his samurai, whose values he felt had been corrupted by the times.[6] Years later, the Mito scholar Fujita Yūtoku (1774-1826) identified various long-standing "evils" in Mito, these including dissipation (*shida*), forced labor (*kenpei*), and extortion (*rikieki*). In using the term *shida*, he meant that the people were "extravagant and deceitful," adding that they "spurn simple manners and crave elegance, hate hard work and delight in relaxation."[7] "Such tendencies," observes Koschmann, "marked a process of degeneration from the system established by Tokugawa Ieyasu" whereby,

---

[4]*Sources of Japanese Tradition*, vol. 2, ed. by Ryusaku Tsunoda, William Theodore de Bary, and Donald Keene (New York and London: Columbia University Press, 1958), p. 85.

[5]Koschmann, p. 146.

[6]*KEJ*, vol. 8, p. 51.

[7]Quoted in Koschmann, p. 89, based on the scholarship of Takasu Yoshijirō presented in *Mitōgaku taikei* (Tokyo: Mitōgaku Taikei Kankōkai, 1941), vol. 3, p. 23.

according to Fujita, peasants had experienced neither surplus nor insufficiency. The new, "degenerate" society, on the other hand, was one where money ruled and where decadence and conspicuous consumption had begun to trickle down from the comparatively rich merchant class to the peasantry itself.[8] It was this type of socio-economic revolution and its attendant rising expectations which Mitsukuni was attempting to check in the domain and which helped shape kanshi during the latter half of the Tokugawa period.

☽ 49   Snow: A Poem Using the Character *Ki* (Tortoise)

Last night the snowflakes shone in the moonlight—a wonder to behold!
The wind of dawn is bitterly cold, goose-flesh covers my body.
I lie upon pillows in the window's bright light,
  as Yuan An would rather have done,
Just like the tortoise that dragged its tail
  through the mud and the snow.

Iwanami, p. 188. From *Jōzan bunshū* (Collected Writings of Jōzan), 1718

Line three: Yuan An (d. 92) was a high official in the Latter Han dynasty (25-220) renowned for his sincerity and rectitude. The emperor he served was a minor whose power was often usurped by imperial relatives. Mitsukuni is saying that Yuan would rather have stayed in bed until late (as the poet himself was now doing) instead of rising early to serve the young sovereign, but his sense of duty did not allow it.
Line four: The tortoise reference is from *Chuang Tzu*. The king of the state of Ch'u sought out Chuang Tzu, hoping to offer him high office. Chuang Tzu replied that he would prefer to remain in obscurity, like a tortoise that "drags its tail through the mud."

[8]Ibid.

🌙 50 Rain at the Beginning of Autumn (*Risshū*)

The Great Fire has vanished to the west,
And cool air wafts through the hills beyond the city.
The summer heat lingers, but the rain on the dryandra leaves
Freshens the air, bringing autumn skies.

Iwanami, p. 188. From *Jōzan bunshū*, 1718

Title: *Risshū* is one of twenty-four seasonal divisions of the lunar calendar, the fifteen-day period immediately before the autumnal equinox. Its onset, around the eighth of August by our Western calendar, traditionally marks the first day of autumn.
Line one: "The Great Fire" is another of the aforementioned twenty-four seasonal divisions, signifying the height of summer and coming immediately before *risshū*. Each season had a corresponding compass direction, the west being associated with autumn.
Line three: For notes on the dryandra tree, see poem 2, above.

🌙 51 The Reed Plumes

Wet reeds laden heavily with fresh, pure dew,
White plumes shining brightly in the moonlight.
The wind blows through the yellow leaves, playing Heaven's pipes,
Sounding like the soughing music of Hsinyang.

Iwanami, p. 189. From *Jōzan bunshū*, 1718

Line three: "Heaven's pipes" refers to the sounds of nature, especially the wind. This comes from the "Ch'i Wu Lun" (Discussion on Making All Things Equal) chapter in *Chuang Tzu*. See Burton Watson, trans., *Chuang Tzu: Basic Writings* (New York and London: Columbia University Press, 1964), pp. 31-32.
Line four: Hsinyang was a river near Kiukiang, in China's Chiangsu province. It is mentioned in the poem "P'i-p'a hsing" (Song of the P'i-p'a) by Po Chü-i, where he describes seeing guests off at this river by night in autumn and hearing the mournful rustling sound of the wind blowing through the maples and reeds.

◉ 52   Encountering Signs of Spring while Feeling Melancholy; Written in 1690

My feelings are entangled with the willow branches; I cannot set myself free.

The orioles heralding the arrival of spring only bring me grief.

Alas, the lady has passed away! Whatever shall I do?

What I fear now is that I have no one who can finish my *Han shu* for me.

Iwanami, p. 190. From *Jōzan bunshū*, 1718

Line four: *Han shu* (The History of the Han Dynasty) was written by the Chinese historian Pan Ku (32-92). It was not completed by Pan himself, but posthumously by his sister. "My *Han shu*" is an allusion to the work which Mitsukuni was compiling at the time, titled *Dai Nihon shi* (The Great History of Japan). Although he had begun this project in 1657, he had not yet finished it when this poem was written. Here he is expressing the fear that, like Pan Ku, he might not live to see the work brought to completion, and that, since his sister had died, there would be no one to finish the compilation for him.

    Dai Nihon shi was a great historical chronicle inspired by Chinese models and covering Japanese history from the time of the putative first emperor Jinmu down to Emperor Go-Komatsu (the one hundredth emperor, d. 1433). It comprised 397 volumes and was written in Chinese. The work was presented to the shogunate in 1720, with 250 volumes then complete, but was expanded over the years, reaching its final form in 1906.

◉ 53   An Account of My Thoughts as I Listen to the Rain One Night at the Beginning of Winter

Clear and cold the water flows in the stream beside the path.

Late autumn, and the yellow chrysanthemums lie scattered by the eastern hedge.

On the hills all around the leaves have fallen, mournfully blows the wind.

I sit by my lamp as the rain drips down, my heart overflowing with emotion.

Iwanami 190. From *Jōzan bunshū*, 1718

☺ 54   Fallen Leaves after Rain

Endless rain and heavy fog; wet weather day after day.

Evening comes, and a gentle wind blows, chasing the dense clouds away.

Night falls, and I am startled by a sound—is it water dripping from the eaves?

At dawn I see the fallen leaves lying deep before my window.

Iwanami, p. 191. From *Jōzan bunshū*, 1718

Lines three and four: The sound the poet had heard was leaves falling against his window rather than water dripping. Poetic misapprehension, particularly regarding natural phenomena, is common in the Japanese poetic tradition. See Brower and Miner, pp. 169, 187-188, 191-192.

Hayashi Baidō, 1643-1666

A shogunal Confucian scholar and prolific kanshi poet from Edo, Hayashi Baidō was the eldest son of the Confucian scholar and historian Hayashi Gahō (1618-1680). He studied the Teishu orthodoxy in Kyoto under Hayashi Dokkōsai (1624-1661). Although his untimely death at the age of twenty-four cut short a promising career, he left behind a number of scholarly works and anthologies, including an annotated ten-*maki* collection of poems by contemporary writers and an impressive collection of his own verse in forty-one *maki*. Two verses from the latter work follow. In the first poem below, we see the moon used symbolically, this time as an image of the eternal and unchanging nature of the universe, as contrasted with the transient world of men. The deserted, weed-infested military camp serves as a chilling reminder of the impermanence of life, evoking feelings of grief and desolation in the poet. This poignant moment of recognition is one that is captured time and again in Japanese literature.

◉ 55   A Deserted Military Camp in the Moonlight

A deserted camp in a meadow of weeds; I gaze up at the moon.
Coming to this spot has stirred my emotions, my hood is wet with tears.
The moon comes and goes as in ancient times, following its natural course.
Nothing to see but cawing crows, nary a soul in sight.

Iwanami, p. 176. From *Jisen Baidō shishū* (Baidō's Collection of Selected Poems), 1668. This collection is part of the *Baidō Hayashi sensei zenshū*, published the same year.

☾ 56 Hearing Wild Geese while on My Travels

Time passed slowly this autumn night at the quiet and lonely inn.

Behind me by the wall stands a single lamp, its scented oil gone cold.

The wind at dawn interrupted a dream where I was back at home.

Then I heard the cries of the first wild geese, the waning moon high in the sky.

Iwanami, p. 176. From *Jisen Baidō shishū*, 1668

Toriyama Shiken, 1655-1715

Little is known about the life of Toriyama Shiken, a native of Fushimi district in Kyoto who in his later years lived in Osaka. He was considered an expert in literary criticism and taught Chinese poetry throughout his life, encouraging his students to follow High T'ang models. He had a poor opinion of *Ogyū Sorai's verse, considering it little more than "fourth-rate late T'ang-style poetry."[1] Shiken never held an official post. Indeed, the first of the poems below indicates a preference for a leisurely life, one free of the entanglements of the "red dust." The second and the fourth verses celebrate natural beauty, with the introduction of humble folk—a priest and a woodcutter—serving to reveal what this poet and so many others saw as an ideal: life in obscurity in quiet harmony with nature. Among Shiken's literary contributions are an annotated edition of poems by the T'ang dynasty poet Han-shan and two collections of his own verse.

◙ 57 Gazing Afar from a Tower

High in a tower a hundred feet up, I sit in the setting sun.
The hazy trees on the hills where I live are distant and dimly seen.
The white clouds in the sky above do not serve the red dust;
Free and easy they drift along, straight toward the horizon.

Iwanami, p. 197. From *Shiken ginkō* (A Book of Poems by Shiken), 1719

Lines three and four: "Red dust" is a Buddhist term connoting the mundane world with its cares and commitments. The poet seems to lament being tied to this world, unlike the clouds whose freedom he envies.

---

[1]*Kokushi daijiten* Iinkai, ed., *Kokushi daijiten*, vol. 10 of 15 vols. (Tokyo: Yoshikawa Kōbunkan, 1989), p. 480.

☾ 58   Crossing a Ford in the Countryside

A path through water-oats and cattails leads to a remote riverbed.
At the water's edge floats a solitary boat in the slanting rays of the sun.
Who can it be, calling over and over, his voice coming through the clouds?
I can tell it's a priest from the mountain temple, returning after begging for alms.

Iwanami, p. 197. From *Shiken ginkō*, 1719

We may imagine that the priest is calling across the river to summon the ferryman.

☾ 59   Travelling Early in the Morning

The shadows upon the river grow faint, the lingering moon hangs low.
Everywhere throughout the forest the crows still roost in the trees.
Astride my horse, I gradually awaken, the day is just growing light.
A cock is crowing by a village store beyond the apricot trees.

Iwanami, p. 198. From *Shiken ginkō*, 1719

☾ 60   Thoughts while Walking beyond the City on a Spring Day and Passing the Ruins of an Old Castle

Out walking in the outskirts I passed through an old fortress.
I rambled around, going just where I pleased.
In the ruined garden, peach blossoms were bursting into bloom.
In the empty moat, the water was half dried up.
Flowers and spring will always be with us,
But people and their times are another matter.
I tried to leave but couldn't tell north from south,
Until a wood-cutter heading home called across from a hillock.

Iwanami, p. 198. From *Shiken ginkō*, 1719

Arai Hakuseki, 1657-1725

Arai Hakuseki, a native of Edo, was a Teishugaku scholar, man of letters, statesman, and historian. The son of a retainer who served the lord of the Tsuchiya clan—which was enfiefed in Kururi, Kazusa province—Hakuseki was born in the Tsuchiya's temporary Edo residence in the Second Month of 1657. His birth came a mere three weeks after the great Edo fire which burned for two days, destroying much of that city. The circumstances of his entry into the world seem to have presaged a brilliant life, for Hakuseki was a stunningly precocious child. A pet of the Tsuchiya retainers, he was called the "fire boy," because he was born with a deep wrinkle above the bridge of his nose which was seen as resembling the character for fire.[1] By the age of three he could copy lengthy texts, and at four he was already known for his remarkable memory.

Hakuseki possessed enormous self-discipline and a love of learning. We know much about his early years owing to the existence of a fine autobiography titled *Oritaku shiba no ki* (Told around a Brushwood Fire, ca. 1716-1717). Earl Miner characterizes this work as "the sole prose biography in classical Japanese literature worthy of being set beside Rousseau's *Confessions*."[2] According to this work, at the age of nine Hakuseki set himself the goal of reading three thousand characters each day and another thousand in the evening. Hakuseki tells us that he threw ice water over himself to fight off sleep at night, and that by eleven he had sufficient skill as a writer to take over the task of handling his father's correspondence.[3] Once when Hakuseki was a struggling student, a wealthy farmer named Kawamura Zuigen, said to have been the richest man in Japan at the time, offered Hakuseki, whom he recognized as an enormous talent,

---

[1]Inoguchi, p. 127.

[2]Miner, p. 142.

[3]Inoguchi, p. 127.

his granddaughter (some accounts say his niece) as a bride. At the same time, he also offered Hakuseki the gift of a house with land, worth three thousand *ryō*, which the latter could use to fund his education. A bold and free-spirited man who lived on his own terms, Hakuseki bluntly refused to accept Kawamura's generosity, evidently reluctant to incur a debt which he felt would become an encumbrance in future years. Hakuseki is said to have cavalierly told Zuigen, "I'm all right as I am," adding that if he never became a daimyo in his lifetime, then in death, at least, he would become the King of Hades, alluding to a similar statement often made by Han Ch'in-hu (527-581), advisor to the future first emperor of the Sui dynasty.[4]

In his late twenties Hakuseki studied Neo-Confucianism under Kinoshita Jun'an (1621-1698). He was also well-read in the Yōmeigaku philosophy introduced into Japan by *Nakae Tōju. Earlier, in 1677, Hakuseki's father had been dismissed from his post for complicity in a local political dispute, and Hakuseki became a *rōnin*, or a masterless (in effect unemployed) samurai. But his obscurity was not to last for long, and he eventually rose to become one of the most important political figures of his age. Hakuseki enjoyed the patronage of Shogun Ienobu, whom he served from 1709 as a trusted counsellor. Some believe that many of the most important decisions of Ienobu's administration were actually made by Hakuseki himself and that he may have even been the most politically influential scholar in Japanese history.[5] During his career, Hakuseki fostered currency, legal, and judiciary reform and made important contributions to political life in his efforts to strengthen the authority of the shogunate. He was fortunate enough to enjoy the favor of the next shogun, Ietsugu, as well, but retired to devote himself to scholarship after Yoshimune became shogun in 1716.

One of Hakuseki's most famous works was *Seiyō kibun* (Hearing about the West), which deals with such subjects as astronomy and the geography of Europe. The sources of this information were the writings of Matteo Ricci and

---

[4]Ibid.

[5]Miner, p. 142; *KEJ*, vol. 1, p. 72.

conversations Hakuseki had with an Italian Jesuit named Giovanni Battista Sidotti.[6] Hakuseki was one of the most respected poets of his day, his reputation extending as far as China and Korea. He particularly admired the work of Tu Fu, although his own poems lack Tu Fu's emotional power. The verses translated below are perhaps most notable for their crisp, masculine vigor and their striking use of color and olfactory imagery. The first poem depicts Hakuseki as a blunt, martial-seeming man, full of pride verging on vanity about his personal appearance. The amour-propre displayed here harks back to his behavior when he haughtily declined Zuigen's offer, as related above. The other verses, however, show a quieter, more sensitive and contemplative side, that of a man enjoying the peace and solitude of retirement in a rural setting. This balance between the martial and the aesthetic within Hakuseki's character represents an ideal that the more well-bred men of the samurai class sought to cultivate.

◉ 61   Inscription for My Portrait

A countenance dark, the color of iron, with silvery temple hair.
Eyes that flash like purple gems, a lightning gaze that can kill.
My body small, a mere five feet, yet every inch unflinching!
But in these peaceful times, there's no reason to place my portrait
    in the Ch'ilin Pavilion.

Sugano, pp. 41-42; Andō, p. 56. From *Hakuseki shisō* (A Draft of Hakuseki Poems), 1712

Line four: The Ch'ilin Pavilion was built by Emperor Wu (r. 140-86 B.C.) of the Former Han dynasty after a *ch'ilin*, a mythical beast resembling a unicorn, was reportedly captured. In 51 B.C., Emperor Hsuan had the portraits of eleven meritorious officials painted and displayed in this pavilion. Hakuseki lived in a time of relative peace, and there were few opportunities for him to distinguish himself militarily, despite his martial appearance. Here, he implies that only those with military merit ought to have their portrait preserved for posterity.

---

[6]Miner, p. 142.

☺ 62 Busy Swallows near Motionless Blinds: An Ode Using the Word *Bō* ("Busily") for Its Rhyme

Red-cheeked "black-coats" fly among the carved beams,
Flitting here, flitting there, busily back and forth.
All day long nary a soul has come to this hall so vast.
In the pearl-studded blinds the wind is still; sweet the scent of flowers.

Iwanami, p. 199. From *Hakuseki shisō*, 1712

☺ 63 An Impromptu Poem

Dawn breaks above the blue mountains.
Sparrows leave the forest, chirping as they fly.
Young bamboos rise out of the haze,
A solitary flower glistens with dew.
I brew some tea, steam clouds swirling around my bed.
I brush my snowy hair, which droops like the ties on a cap.
I find myself sitting with no duties to perform,
Waiting for sunrise by the eastern window.

Iwanami, p. 200. From *Hakuseki shisō*, 1712

Line six: The ties are those on an official's cap, the recollection of which seems to lead the poet to the observation about his idleness in the next line.

☺ 64 Written on a Spring Day

Willow down floating through the air, borne away by the river's flow.
Paris grass growing everywhere throughout the fragrant islet.
Fine wine, the color of blue grapes, in the ornate golden jar.
If we don't get drunk this clear spring day, we'll never dispel our cares!

Iwanami, p. 199. From *Hakuseki shisō*, 1712

Line two: Paris grass is *Paris tetraphylla* (J. *tsukubane*), a herb.

Muro Kyūsō [Shundai], 1658-1734

Muro Kyūsō was a native of Bitchū in modern Okayama prefecture. The son of a doctor, he showed exceptional promise as a child. His gifts were noted early on by Maeda Tsunanori (1643-1724), the lord of the Kaga domain, who employed him as a retainer when Kyūsō was only fourteen and had him lecture on *The Great Learning*. Tsunanori was deeply impressed with Kyūsō's intellect and saw him as a rising star who would enrich the academic and political life of his domain. Thus he sent the boy to study under Kinoshita Jun'an in Kyoto. Kyūsō followed Jun'an to Edo in 1682 when the latter became a Confucian official in the shogunate. The following year, upon the death of his father, Kyūsō went with his mother to Kanazawa, remaining there for the next twenty-five years.[1]

Kyūsō followed pure Neo-Confucian interpretations of the classics, rejecting the various heterodoxies (*isetsu*) current in his day. In 1701 he compiled the *Akō gishiroku*, chronicling the famous vendetta of the forty-seven loyal retainers.[2] In 1711, Arai Hakuseki recommended him to the shogunate, and he became a tutor and political advisor to Shogun Yoshimune in Edo. Shortly thereafter, he accepted an appointment as a professor at the Takakura Yashiki academy, moving to Surugadai. Kyūsō distinguished himself in the areas of political and economic theory as well as in Chinese literature. Even when he was in his seventies and in poor health he battled on, producing impressive works of scholarship and gaining a reputation for being one of the finest Chinese prose stylists of his day.

Kyūsō was an outspoken critic of what he considered the depraved morality of his time. In his view, the samurai class had become excessively materialistic, and this had fostered rising expectations and greed. He also felt that samurai had lost their sense of duty, a value which he believed should come even before life

---

[1]Inoguchi, p. 140.

[2]See notes to poem 107 for details.

itself. In his collection titled *Shundai zatsuwa* (Small Talk from Shundai), Kyūsō wrote, "As I remember my youth, young men of that time never mentioned prices, and there were some who blushed when they heard lewd stories. Thus have social standards changed in fifty years or so."[3]

The first of the two poems below describes an attitude typical among scholar-officials who, having chosen a career in officialdom, discover that their hearts still lie in the countryside of their childhood. After the hurly-burly of their official careers has passed, their greatest concern is for safeguarding their solitude and rediscovering this peaceful life of inaction and simple pleasures. The poem conveys the Taoist notion that simplicity is Nature's ideal and that people must avoid becoming enmeshed in the ties and complexities of public service. Many kanshi similarly celebrate the joys of solitary communion with nature, which is seen as the source of the greatest human contentment.

The second verse possesses an appealing wistfulness and demonstrates the facility of kanshi poets to focus upon individual phenomena within nature and somehow tie these to the human world. By subjectively endowing the willow tree with human emotion—seeing it "farewell" the spring season prematurely—he makes it a participant in human affairs, thus heightening the bonds between himself and nature. Moreover, the "error" of the willow trees in shedding their down too early and the futility of this seemingly noble gesture of farewell creates a sense of bittersweet pathos (*mono no aware*), a quality that Japanese writers have traditionally seen as inherent in all living things.

---

[3]As quoted in Sansom, pp. 84-85.

☉ 65   Returning to My Fields

1   After my official career began
     I never for a day forgot the hills and the mountains,
     Much less the landscapes of mulberries and elms.
     Now I find I am growing old.
5   Fish leap up but never jump the banks;
     Animals dart out but prefer their dark lairs.
     It's seldom right to rebel against one's nature,
     So I've returned to plow my fields in the southern plains.
     Eight or nine houses stand near mine,
10   But I keep my distance, here among the clouds.
     In the morning I go out once the others have left;
     In the evening I come back before they return.
     Thick trees surround a distant village;
     Thin, dark smoke rises from a nearby town.
15   The cows and sheep return at dusk
     When the mountain peaks are bathed in evening light.
     Drunk, I lie beneath the eastern eaves;
     Happiness is found in being true to one's nature.

Inoguchi, p. 142

☉ 66   Willow-Down

Suddenly rising from my neighbors' homes on the northern and southern sides:
Floating willow-down, high and low, blown in endless drifts.
Here in the capital it flies about, looking like flakes of snow.
But it bids farewell to no traveller; it farewells the spring in vain.

Inoguchi, p. 141

Line four: "In vain" because there is no one to be farewelled and the departure of spring is not yet imminent. Willow branches were traditionally given to people about to embark on a journey; here the willow seems to be shedding its down in a similar gesture of farewell to spring.

Ogyū Sorai [Ken'en], 1666-1728

A native of Edo, Ogyū Sorai was one of the most prolific and influential intellectuals of the Edo period, a philosopher who, in the words of the Japanese historian Bitō Masahide, "worked to refashion Confucian thought to conform to Japanese society."[1] Besides being the preeminent Neo-Confucian scholar of his age, he was a distinguished kanshi poet and philologist as well. Sorai was already a fluent reader by the age of five. He could write entries in Chinese from dictation for his father's diary by about seven and began composing Chinese poetry at nine, around which time his family arranged for him to receive formal instruction from Hayashi Hōkō (1644-1732). Sorai's father Hōan was a shogunal physician, but through some misdeed on his part he was exiled to Kazusa in 1679, taking the young Sorai with him.

The years spent in adverse circumstances in the provinces appear to have had a considerable effect upon Sorai's intellectual development. He was able to witness the living conditions of the peasantry firsthand and would later expound his views in such works as *Taihei saku* (Policy for Peace, ca. 1719-1723) and *Seidan* (Political Discussions, ca. 1727),[2] where he advanced the theory that the concentration of population in the cities was the source of all social ills and that people should return to live in their villages of origin.[3]

After years of exile in Kazusa, Sorai's father was finally pardoned, returning to Edo with Sorai in 1690 and becoming the personal physician of Shogun Tsunayoshi. Following Hōan's death, Sorai, already well used to poverty, eked out a meager living for several years by teaching Confucianism in an outdoor

---

[1]Bitō Masahide, "Ogyū Sorai and Japanese Confucianism," trans. by Samuel Yamashita, in Najita and Scheiner, eds., *Japanese Thought in the Tokugawa Period, 1600-1868*, p. 159.

[2]Kato, pp. 61, 63.

[3]Ibid., p. 69.

classroom setting. At one time he was reduced to accepting leftovers from a tofu shop next to Zōjōji temple in Edo,[4] later repaying the kindness by sending two helpers to work at the shop after he became an official.[5] When Sorai was thirty-one, Tsunayoshi appointed him chief secretary to Yanagisawa Yoshiyasu (1658-1714), Tsunayoshi's senior councillor. Sorai gave lectures and advised Yoshiyasu's circle and had fifteen assistants at his command. His stipend increased, and by age thirty-five he was receiving the handsome annual salary of two hundred *koku*. Although now extremely wealthy, Sorai was such a bibliophile that he continually sold off family property to purchase whole libraries, one after another, as if trying to compensate for those years of deprivation in Kazusa where there were "no teachers, no friends…and no books," as he later lamented in his treatise *Sorai sensei gakusoku* (Master Sorai's Academic Principles, 1711-1717).[6]

When Yoshiyasu was enfiefed as daimyo of Kōfu in 1704, Sorai accompanied him there. Following the death of Tsunayoshi in 1709, Yoshiyasu lost his power base and went into retirement, instructing Sorai to teach full-time in Edo and bring glory to the domain by striving to become the foremost scholar in the land. Taking this injunction to heart, Sorai turned to private teaching full-time while continuing to devote himself to scholarship. He attracted many of the most promising students in Japan, including *Hattori Nankaku, *Dazai Shundai, Yamagata Shūnan (1687-1752), and *Takano Rantei, who all went on to become outstanding poets and scholars.

At thirty-eight, Sorai made an attempt to become one of *Itō Jinsai's students, submitting a letter requesting admission to his school. The fact that such an already distinguished scholar would, in mid-career, seek to study with another teacher is testimony both to Sorai's intellectual appetite and to Jinsai's enormous reputation. However, Jinsai was recuperating from an illness at the

---

[4]*NKD*, p. 92.

[5]Inoguchi, p. 131.

[6]Trans. as "Instructions for Students" (1976). See Richard Minear, "Ogyū Sorai," in *KEJ*, vol. 6, p. 72.

time and neglected to respond to the letter. Sorai misinterpreted Jinsai's dilatoriness and for the rest of his life felt enmity toward him, attacking Jinsai's scholarship at every turn, even though both men had much in common as advocates of a return to the original Confucian texts.[7]

Around the year 1717, Sorai established the Ken'engaku school, which stood in opposition to the Teishugaku orthodoxy. Known also as Kobunjigaku (The School of Classical Philology), this school based itself upon mid-Ming intellectual traditions, attempting to revise the line of inquiry represented by Itō Jinsai's Kogigaku school by going back even further textually, beyond Confucius and Mencius, to *The Five Classics*. Although he had received instruction in Teishugaku in his earlier years, Sorai later came to believe that pre-Han texts were where the real heart of Confucianism lay, and that to get at these truths it was essential to emphasize close analysis of these texts and the language used therein. This, then, was Kobunjigaku, which literally means "the study of old phrases and syntax."[8] So that the texts might be read in what he considered an uncorrupted form, Sorai advocated abandoning the traditional *kundoku* reading and translation method whereby the Japanese decoded Chinese text, translating it into a special style of literary Japanese. Sorai believed that *kundoku* stood in the way of determining the original and proper meaning of the Chinese classics.

Sorai viewed man as essentially a social animal, whose nature, to cite Bitō Masahide, "require[d] that he be part of a group." As Bitō further explains, Sorai felt that the individual, lacking innate goodness, needed both instruction and "correctional" social interaction with his peers for his moral improvement, an attitude which well reflected the Japanese social consciousness of the times.[9] Sorai's fundamental thesis that man could be educated and molded by models of virtue, making him able to bring order to his own society, had a major impact on

---

[7]For details, see Inoguchi, p. 132.

[8]Maruyama, pp. 76-77.

[9]Bitō, pp. 158-159.

the development of political thought in the latter half of the Edo period.[10] But, as Samuel Yamashita points out, Sorai also had a well-developed understanding of the uniqueness of the individual. Just as carpenters and swordsmiths had to take into account the natural properties of the woods and metals they fashioned into objects, so too were people obliged to consider their own gifts and predispositions as they went about refining their own unique natures.[11] His appreciation for human diversity and individuality appears unprecedented in the Japanese Confucian tradition.[12]

Sorai's seminal scholarship drew the attention of Shogun Yoshimune, who desired to appoint him to a post. However, Sorai declined to serve, preferring at this stage to avoid the risk of political entanglements. Nonetheless, several years later, in 1721, he did undertake an annotation assignment at Yoshimune's request. Yoshimune continued to pursue him to the day Sorai passed away, still intent upon appointing him to a position in the shogunate. According to *Dazai Shundai, one of Sorai's disciples, Sorai worked himself to death. His teachings lived on, however, as the preeminent philosophy of the times for some three decades thereafter, gradually losing ground in the 1770s and 1780s, by which time the school had fallen into a state of internal decay and factionalization.[13]

Sorai was well-versed in economics, politics, music, linguistics, and the military arts, as well as in all aspects of Chinese civilization. But he was not a modest man and had a rather high opinion of his own scholarly worth, once commenting, "If you could add my learning to Itō Jinsai's virtue and Kumazawa Banzan's talent, you'd have the greatest sage in the East."[14] Although

---

[10]Ibid.

[11]Yamashita, "Nature and Artifice in the Writings of Ogyū Sorai," in Nosco, p. 155.

[12]Nosco, "Introduction," in Nosco, p. 15.

[13]On the decline of the Sorai school, see Maruyama, pp. 135-141.

[14]Inoguchi, p. 133.

notoriously critical of other scholars, he was lax with his own students, which Inoguchi suggests was one reason why so many flocked to his academy.[15]

The best of Sorai's poems possess vigor and vitality. He took T'ang verse as his models and rejected Sung styles, yet he also admired the Ming poets, whose verse he helped popularize. Significantly, Sorai advocated the liberation of poetry and prose from the constraints of Confucian morality, a viewpoint opposed to the basic Chu Hsi notion that only literature which embodied Confucian principles was worthwhile. The selections below display nostalgia for the past as well as a poignant sentimentality about friendship, parting, and the impermanence of life, all common themes in Edo kanshi. The close kinship Sorai felt with his like-minded friends comes through with an unusual degree of intensity. He also takes particular pleasure in observing the quiet rhythm of life in the countryside, demonstrating a remarkable ability to encapsulate in a few vivid images the humble, bucolic charm of the rural environment.

◙ 67   Seeing a Friend Off at Dusk in the Rain

On the path by the river where willow branches trail,
We said our farewells in the rain as night fell.
I feel so forlorn, for he's now far away.
The sky is dark and cloudy, my horse so slow.
The river's roar muffles the temple bell's toll.
The plants on the bank are now sure to flourish.
Who can doubt that when morning comes
My heart will be in disarray with sorrow?

Iwanami, pp. 202-203. From *Sorai shū* (The Sorai Collection), 1736

---

[15]Ibid.

☾ 68   Something on Their Minds

1   The pale sun is sinking slowly,
     As I sit and gaze at the lush courtyard plants.
     The north wind plucks at my robes,
     And I heave a sigh, for the year is now ending.
5   Each of us is destined to grow old,
     So why lament when old age arrives?
     Wealth and honor come but rarely;
     Glory and fame cannot be guaranteed.
     In the main hall I set forth wine,
10   The better to enjoy the season's finest days.
     The zither and whistle converse with each other.
     Drunk, we grow noisy, then our tears fall like sleet.
     These gentlemen have something on their minds:
     Four good friends, seated around the table,
15   Sharing a sadness that few can understand.

Inoguchi, p. 136

☾ 69   Farmhouses on the River

The lane follows the river's twisting course.
Between the farmhouses fences are few.
By the low riverbank people wash their plowshares;
After the rain they dry their fishing clothes.
Calves bearing firewood drink from the river;
Farmers on skiffs return from harvesting wheat.
Children are playing upon the sand,
As sea gulls wheel about overhead.

Inoguchi, p. 136; Iwanami, p. 202. From *Sorai shū*, 1736

☻ 70 A Poem about the Former House of Lord Hideyoshi

His galleons which crossed the vast ocean shook the great Ming realm.
Who would believe that at this spot brambles and weeds now grow?
The wind and rain on the thousand mountains pound fiercely time and again—
A noise akin to the sound of his voice when he roared at his troops long ago!

Sugano, p. 43. From *Sorai shū*, 1736

Line one: The galleons belonged to Toyotomi Hideyoshi (1536-1598), the co-unifier of feudal Japan. During the 1590s, he came into conflict with the Ming dynasty when his army invaded the Korean peninsula, seeking to conquer China. He withdrew in 1598, his military expedition having failed in its objective. Hideyoshi's base was in Hizen (in Kyushu), the formerly prosperous place where, according to the poet, "brambles and weeds now grow."

☻ 71 Hearing a Flute

Who was it, playing that lovely flute,
Its music drifting into the traveller's room?
An urgent-sounding tune brought fleeting sadness,
A languid song evoked lasting sorrow.
"Fallen Plum Blossoms," a piece so forlorn;
"Broken Willow Branches," a most melancholy tune.
Here in my room the music lingers on,
As the hills before me capture the evening sun.

Iwanami, p. 204. From *Sorai shū*, 1736

Line six: "Broken willow branches" refers to the Chinese practice of presenting a willow branch to a friend who is leaving. The words for willow and "stay" sounded similar in Chinese; hence, giving this token signified that one wanted the departing friend to stay.

Itō Tōgai, 1670-1736

The eldest son of the illustrious scholar Itō Jinsai, Tōgai followed in his father's footsteps, becoming a prolific Kogaku scholar, philologist, and leading poet in his own right. A native of the Horikawa district in Kyoto, Tōgai seemed destined for the life of a scholar even at the age of three, by which time he could already read many characters. Although he lost his mother when he was young, he became deeply devoted to his step-mother, and his family life was apparently marked by few upsets thereafter.

Tōgai led a placid life of teaching and scholarship, remaining always at his family's residence in Horikawa. He was the first teacher of Confucian studies to take over the operation of a private academy from his father, and the school continued to prosper under his leadership.[1] He had many outstanding and devoted disciples, who are said to have loved and respected him like a father. Following the precedent set by Jinsai, Tōgai never accepted an official post, although he was offered one by the lord of Kishū, who was prepared to give him the princely salary of five hundred *koku*. This reluctance to accept an official post is alluded to below in the poem titled "Quietly Gazing at the Autumn Scenery at the Edge of Town." His contemporary *Ogyū Sorai apparently regarded Tōgai as a rival, and whenever Sorai had a visitor from Kyoto he would ask him about Tōgai's latest scholarship.[2]

Tōgai's impressive corpus of 242 volumes surpasses in bulk, if not in originality, even that of his renowned father. Although he broke little new ground, he was a more versatile scholar than Jinsai. He wrote on every imaginable subject, from the Chinese classics to Japanese institutional history and philology, and compiled numerous anthologies of his own verse and that of his

---

[1]Nosco, *Remembering Paradise*, p. 36.

[2]Inoguchi, p. 143.

father. Tōgai's posthumous name, Shōjutsu Sensei, means "The Master Who Carried on his Forebear's [i.e., his Father's] Work" and was given in recognition of the fact that he had labored at compiling Jinsai's entire scholarly corpus. Yet in spite of his obvious intellectual prowess, there is evidence that Tōgai entertained doubts about the intrinsic worth of the scholar's life. This sentiment appears in his poem titled "Self-Ridicule," below, where he says it is "...worthless just to sit around, wasting grain and silk:/Talking idly, reading books, and studying the ways of the sages."

Poetry was Tōgai's greatest love, and he especially admired the verse of Tu Fu, whose works he took as his model. The first poem below is undoubtedly one of his best, the image of the blue waters flowing through the red sunlight amidst ripe harvest grain and shady mountain-mulberry trees leaving an unforgettable impression of bucolic beauty and tranquility. The poet ruefully observes that as a human being he can never fully enter the natural world and become one with the trees and animals, interpreting the bird's flight from him as a desire to remain apart.

◙ 72   Quietly Gazing at the Autumn Scenery at the Edge of Town

Shady the mountain-mulberry trees in the village.
Ripe the rice and millet growing in the fields.
Blue waters flow through the red sun in the river,
White clouds linger midway up the mountain.
Weak is my will to advance in the world.
Now, as in the past, few appreciate the finer things of life.
To my shame I have a calculating mind,
Which makes the mountain birds fly away from me in fear.

Inoguchi, p. 144

Lines seven and eight: These lines contain an allusion to a Taoist story of a boy who was able to make friends with sea gulls because he had "forgotten all schemes." See McCraw, p. 25.

◙ 73 Enjoying the Cool Breezes

Bamboo and cedars, tall and bushy, fill my garden,
Blocking out the sunset as evening shadows deepen.
I raise the blinds and sit outside by the railing.
On a fragrant wind comes a lone cricket's chirp.

Inoguchi, p. 145

◙ 74 Nighttime Rain Outside My Window in the Mountains; Written on the Second Day of the Ninth Month at Mr Asai's House

My vine-covered window really keeps out the rain.
Book in hand, I sit here all night long.
Gradually I notice the spring waters flowing more loudly;
Now and then I hear the rustling of leaves.
Sleeping birds roost far from the wind,
Hungry flying squirrels dart about in the night.
I think back to the pleasures of Lushan long ago,
A single lamp casting its light upon my solitude.

Iwanami, p. 195. From *Shōjutsu sensei shishū* (Master Shōjutsu's Collection of Poetry), 1758-1761

Title: Mr. Asai has not been identified.
Line six: Flying squirrels make a mournful, screeching cry, adding to the melancholy atmosphere of the scene.
Line seven: Lushan (Mt. Lu), in China's Chiangsu province, a place of scenic beauty. "The pleasures of Lushan" alludes to a line by Po Chü-i where he describes the aesthetic enjoyment of sitting in a rough dwelling on a rainy night at Lushan (Iwanami, p. 195).

75 Wind in the Mountain Dwellings

A few thatched huts nestling by a mountain;
No checkpoint here, just a pair of pines.
Gusts of fresh wind sweep through with a rustle.
Now and then cassia pods are blown down into the garden.

Iwanami, p. 196. From *Shōjutsu sensei shishū*, 1758-1761

Line two: Checkpoints were established in early times by the government to monitor the movement of people, thus providing added security. This secluded hamlet was too small and remote to warrant such measures.

76 Self-Ridicule

The sun rises and climbs to its zenith, then goes to sleep again.
Remarkable how rapidly the months and years pass by!
How worthless just to sit around, wasting grain and silk:
Talking idly, reading books, and studying the ways of the sages.

Inoguchi, p. 146

⏺ 77 Hakuunji Temple

Hidden deep within the clouds, Hakuunji temple.

A mountain path winds its way far into azure skies.

I gaze up at the pagoda that reaches high into another world.

Dogs and roosters are heard from afar, way off in the clouds.

In a stream ahead, the waters have risen; clearly it has rained.

Ancient trees, cool and shady; I await no breeze.

Before my eyes the Sixteen Realms lie within my view:

Could it be that I am sitting in the Palace of the Immortals?

Inoguchi, p. 146

Title: Hakuunji means "Temple of the White Clouds." Its location is uncertain. Perhaps it was the same temple as Hakuunkyōji, located on Mt. Atago to the west of Kyoto.
Line seven: "Sixteen realms" probably just means a vast region. It could instead denote the sixteen great kingdoms of India at the time of the Buddha or hark back to the sixteen states of ancient China established between 304 and 439.

⏺ 78 A Poetic Inscription for a Painting of a Falcon

No rings or halters bind this bird, it sits upon no glove.

A striking sight, that craggy head, pecking all day long.

Golden pupils shine like stars, an iron bill so sharp.

It slowly glides from place to place, husbands its strength and seizes each chance.

The falcon spots its prey and strikes, descending from the sky.

Once those claws ensnare their quarry, how the blood does flow!

In forests deep the wily hare has nowhere to escape;

Its burrow may have three ways in, but all were dug in vain.

Inoguchi, p. 146

Yanada Zeigan, 1672-1757

Yanada Zeigan was a native of Edo and a Teishugaku scholar of some repute. At the age of eleven he began his formal education under the guidance of Hitomi Kakuzan (1620-1688) of Kyoto, showing a particular aptitude for poetry and early on becoming a devoted reader of *Yamazaki Ansai's Confucian scholarship. A man of diverse intellectual interests, Zeigan was also a student of both Zen and Shintoism and pursued an interest in the military arts as well. Apparently he believed that Confucianism, Shinto, and Buddhism were fully compatible philosophical systems.[1] But as the first poem below suggests, he was at the same time critical of the intellectual blindness and spiritual imperfections he saw among the most devout adherents of these religions.

In his mature years Zeigan taught in Edo, where he became acquainted with the illustrious scholar and statesman *Arai Hakuseki. Arai considered him a phenomenal talent and even showed him his own work in progress, regarding him, it seems, not merely as a follower but as an intellectual equal.[2] Hakuseki's teachings, and those of *Muro Kyūsō, were to have had an important influence upon Zeigan. At forty-eight, Zeigan agreed to accept an appointment in the Akashi fief, this after previously declining to serve the lords of Kii and Kanō. He was given a stipend far smaller than what had been offered by the other two domains, and some people criticized him for accepting such a relatively poor salary. It seems, however, that Zeigan had his reasons for preferring the Akashi post: the natural beauty of the area and its relative closeness to Kyoto may have been considerations.[3] Zeigan apparently spent the rest of his days there, living to the age of eighty-six.

---

[1] Inoguchi, p. 157.

[2] Ibid.

[3] Ibid., p. 158.

120

☾ 79   A Miscellaneous Poem

The orthodox Confucianists are besotted with their doctrines.
Refined men of talent are intoxicated by their own refinement.
The temples bells will awaken them from their dreams,
And when the valley clouds have all dispersed,
    their towers will be flooded with moonlight.
The foolish ape grabs in vain at the moon in the water;
The blind horse, trusting its hooves,
    walks among flowers at the edge of the cliff.
Here is a message for all wise priests:
Don't be like the ape and the horse and go astray in life!

Inoguchi, p. 162

Title: "Miscellaneous poem" (*zatsuei*) denotes informal verse written on a variety of themes. The terms *zatsudai*, *zasshi*, and *zattai* are also seen in the poetic titles of compositions in this anthology to designate informal, non-occasional poetry.
Line four: Clouds suggests ignorance; moonlight, Buddhist enlightenment.

☾ 80   On a Winter's Day in a Village by the River

Yellow clouds enshroud the trees, the evening sun hangs low.
Familiar with this riverside village, I do not lose my way.
A white-haired fisherman comes along, bringing me the news:
"West of the jetty where people are fishing the plum trees are in bloom!"

Inoguchi, p. 162

◘ 81 Drifting on Lake Biwa at Dusk in Autumn

North of the lake, south of the lake, the shades of night are deepening.
I cease my poling, turn my head, and look for the lone pine tree.
From both shores where the waves are crashing, autumn winds arise,
Bringing the sound of evening bells from Mt. Hiei off in the clouds.

Sugano, p. 48. From *Zeigan sensei bunshū* (The Collected Works of Master Zeigan), 1742-1746

Line two: The tree in question was the famous Karasaki pine, a well-known landmark on the western shores of Lake Biwa near the modern city of Ōtsu in Shiga prefecture.

◘ 82 Evening Rain at Hine

Night falls in the empty forest, mournful the cries of birds.
In the misty rain, a brambly dais; weeds in profusion all around.
No one knows of this ancient road where carriage bells once rang out.
Unbearable now to see cobwebs hanging from the eaves of that hut of thatch.

Iwanami, p. 205. From *Zeigan sensei bunshū*, 1742-1746

Title: Hine corresponds with the modern area of Ōazana-Hineno in Izumisano city in Osaka-fu.
Line three: The location of this road, which presumably led to Hine, is unknown today. Hine was a favorite stopping place for the ancient nobility. The ninth-century emperor Kanmu is known to have visited Hine in 804, sojourning there on his way to Izumi during an imperial tour. See Iwanami, p. 434. Kanmu's carriage bells are perhaps what is alluded to here.
Line four: The hut in question may have been the shrine Hine Jinja, which is located in Hineno (Iwanami, p. 434). In Zeigan's day there was another small shrine not far from Hine at the site of Chinu no Rikyū (The Chinu Detached Palace). The thatched hut may instead have been this old shrine, which apparently disappeared in the 1730s. The Chinu Detached Palace was said to have been frequented by Emperor Genmei (r. 708-714) and Princess Sotoori-hime. Local legend has it that Sotoori-hime liked to practice her calligraphy here (Iwanami, p. 434).

◙ 83 A Poem on Globe Amaranths

Red globes, red for a thousand days—

I wonder how they do it!

As red as folks drunk on Nakayama wine,

Whom even the autumn wind can't awaken!

Hirano, p. 194

Title: The word for globe amaranths is literally "red for a thousand days."
Line three: Wine from the town of Nakayama was said to cause a drunkenness that lasted a thousand days. Nakayama should probably be identified with the modern locale by that name in the town of Kawaichi, Chiba prefecture.

◙ 84 Bush Warbler in a Bamboo Cage

One day you left the mist and haze.

A painted cage is now your home.

Your lovely voice sounds just as it did when you were living in the wilds;

But don't you yearn for the flowers of the forest where you used to dwell?

Inoguchi, p. 162

Miyake Kanran, 1674-1718

Miyake Kanran was born in Kyoto, and in his early years he studied with Asami Keisai (1652-1711), a scholar in the tradition of *Yamazaki Ansai, before entering the school of Kinoshita Jun'an. In 1697, Kanran took a post in the Mito domain at the invitation of *Tokugawa Mitsukuni, his assignment being to assist with the compilation of the massive history *Dai Nihon shi*. In 1710, he became an administrator of the domain school, Shōkōkan, where the *Dai Nihon shi* project was based. The following year he left Mito to serve the shogun in Edo, joining *Muro Kyūsō as a shogunal retainer on the recommendation of *Arai Hakuseki.

The poem below, with its conventionally somber images of twilight crows, falling rain, and mist, creates a melancholy yet romantic atmosphere, here intensified by the presence of the haunting music of the biwa. The instrument is being used to accompany a chanted recitation from the classic war tale *Heike monogatari* (The Tale of the Heike), which in medieval Japan constituted the ultimate literary embodiment of the sadness of human transience and lost glory.

◔ 85   A Small Gathering at a House in the Pines

Peach trees bloom in silence by the bamboo hedge.
Twilight crows gather west of the misty wall.
Deep in the house, an unflickering silver candle; rain is falling outside.
Someone is reciting a tale from *Heike* to the strains of music from a lute.

Hirano, p. 198

Line four: *Heike monogatari* is the most celebrated narrative in the war-tale genre and is best known to us today through the Kakuichi version, completed in the fourteenth century. This work, which for centuries was recited by blind jongleurs, tells the sorrowful tale of the Heike clan's fall at the hands of the Minamoto clan in the lengthy Genpei Wars of the late-twelfth century, a major watershed in Japanese history.

Priest Daichō, 1676-1768

Priest Daichō was a native of Matsura (some accounts say Imari) in Hizen, part
of modern Saga prefecture in northwest Kyushu. He took his Buddhist vows at
fifteen and became priest of Ryūtsuji temple in Hizen. Daichō was educated in
Kyoto and Edo, studying both Buddhist and Confucian texts. He also received
training in Zen at Dairyūji temple in Shikagawa, Edo, where he became chief
priest in 1723. In Edo, he was an associate of *Ogyū Sorai and *Hattori
Nankaku. He spent a period learning Chinese in Nagasaki and also taught in Edo
and Saga at different times in his career. Daichō lived to the advanced age of
ninety-three. His poem titled "At a Mountain Temple" is a mere four lines in
length but conveys with remarkable effectiveness a sense of isolation, suddenly
broken by the unexpected appearance of the mysterious stranger. The temple
mentioned here was perhaps the Manpukuji (est. 1661), located in Kyoto not far
from Uji, where Daichō practiced Zen for a period in his youth and resided again
in his later years. The second verse assembles an evocative series of tranquil
autumnal images, blending solitude with impoverished rusticity (*wabi*), the latter
quality suggested by the references to the barking village dog and the weed-like
mugwort.

◑ 86   At a Mountain Temple

Cold pine temple, doors unlocked.
Autumn rain, shining in the lamplight.
A slender form comes into view—
I know not where this priest is from.

Iwanami, pp. 347-348. From *Matsura shishū* (The Matsura Poetry Collection)

◔ 87 Composed on a Boat on the Yodo River

Autumn gradually deepens on the Yodo River,
But little boats can still float on its waters.
The red glow of sunset has only just faded,
Yet the blue of the hills has not yet vanished.
In a lonely village a dog barks at the moon.
Lamps are burning on both sides of the river.
I thought I heard rain through my mugwort-covered window;
It was nothing more than the blustery wind.

Iwanami, p. 347. From *Matsura shishū*

Line two: Presumably because the river had not yet frozen over.

Gion Nankai, 1677-1751

Gion Nankai, an eminent scholar, poet, and painter, was born in the domain of Kii, part of modern Wakayama prefecture. When he was still a boy, his father took him to Edo, where at the age of sixteen he studied under Kinoshita Jun'an. Early on, he showed great promise both in Chinese poetic composition and in calligraphy, eventually becoming a master of both. In 1697, when he was twenty, he returned to Kii to take up a post as domain scholar. But in 1700 he was dismissed and placed in confinement in a small village for some minor offense, the nature of which is unknown. Nankai is said to have been profligate and shiftless as a young man, so his personal habits, which included a fondness for liquor, may have been what led to his dismissal.[1]

After Nankai was pardoned a decade later, he was invited to assist with the reception of a delegation from Korea, reportedly composing poetry with one of its members. In 1713 he received an appointment as professor and head of the new domain school. Largely self-taught as an artist, Nankai is viewed as a first-rank Nanga master in the *bunjinga* (literati painting) tradition, which he helped to found. Many of his art works were accompanied by poems, the two elements forming an organic artistic whole.

Nankai preferred T'ang poetic styles over Sung. With *Yanagawa Seigan and *Arai Hakuseki (whose poetry is generally ranked below Nankai's), he is traditionally considered one of the three greats of Japanese poetry.[2] As Donald Keene points out, Nankai believed that poetry "must be the vehicle for elegant language and thoughts," a "voice" to reflect human emotions, rather than a tool for disseminating moral principles.[3] However, he also observes that, while

---

[1]*WWW*, p. 541.

[2]*NKD*, p. 162.

[3]*WWW*, p. 542.

Nankai's poetry has a lovely but remote quality, it seems to lack an individual voice.[4]

In his language and vocabulary, Nankai is generally more challenging and esoteric than many other kanshi poets, his verses possessing a special elegance of their own. Some scholars have compared him to Li Po, and the third poem below would seem to support this comparison. This verse offers a romanticized portrait of the life of the fisherman, who is always surrounded by nature and passes his days in relative ease and tranquility compared to people in other callings. Although the fisherman's life was a humble one, his lot seemed enviable to Nankai and other poets, in part because his life was free of political risks. Envy of the freedom of others is also a theme in the untitled verse about the parrot, below.

The final selection, "In Mourning for My Cat," is unusual in its choice of subject, bringing to mind an ancient passage in *Uda tennō gyoki* (The Memoirs of Emperor Uda), dated the sixth day of the Second Month of 899, in which the emperor lovingly describes his attachment to his cat. He writes,

> I once said to the cat, "You possess the forces of *yin* and *yang* and have a body that is the way it should be. I suspect that in your heart you may even know all about me!" The cat heaved a sigh, raised his head, and stared fixedly at my face, seeming so choked with emotion, his heart so full of feeling, that he could not say a thing in reply.[5]

---

[4]Ibid., pp. 543-544.

[5]Trans. in Judith N. Rabinovitch with Akira Minegishi, "Some Literary Aspects of Four *Kambun* Diaries of the Japanese Court: Translation with Commentaries on Excerpts from *Uda Tennō Gyoki*, *Murakami Tennō Gyoki*, *Gonki*, and *Gyokuyō*," in *The Humanities* [*Journal of the Yokohama National University*], Section II (Language and Literature) 39 [Oct. 1992]: 8.

◉ 88   Lament for My Younger Brother Shigetomo

How sad it is that in this world life should be so hard!

I cannot bear being near your coffin, tears soak my robes.

It should be you who is burying me, yet I am burying you;

You never once offended Heaven, but Heaven has done you wrong.

Your orphaned children gathered here—worry not for them.

Which of your friends in the world beyond will divine your dwelling place?

I feel ashamed for in the end there was nothing I could do.

But they'll envy you in the Jewelled Tower, for the brushes you bear are new.

Hirano, p. 203

Title: The brother's actual name is debatable, as other readings of the characters are also possible.
Line two: The phrase "I cannot bear being near your coffin" is an emendation of the original wording which reads, "[I] can bear being near your coffin," an apparent error.
Line eight: Since the deceased was a scholar, he was buried with his writing brushes so that he could use them in the next world.

This verse brings to mind lines in T'ao Yuan-ming's forlorn "A Lament for My Cousin Zhongde," wherein he asks, "How could I have thought you would die first?/Fate had marked you, in the end there was no escape[.]" Trans. by Helen Craig McCullough in *Brocade by Night: 'Kokin Wakashū' and the Court Style in Japanese Classical Poetry* (Stanford: Stanford University Press, 1985), pp. 38-39.

◉ 89   A Poem about Cranes on an Islet; Composed Mid-Autumn 1726, Following the Rhymes of Another Poem

Autumn winds blow as moonlight shines upon this seaside realm.

A beautiful lady mournfully gazes, leaning on a post.

Still raised, the speckled-bamboo blinds; the sky looks like the sea.

Jewels of dew, the cry of a crane, the third watch of the night.

Hirano, pp. 203-204

Title: There were probably several poets writing verses in groups or in pairs at this gathering, one writing a companion poem for his partner's verse, using the same rhymes.
Line four: The third watch was between 11:00 P.M. and 1:00 A.M.

🔘 90   The Fisherman

A straw hat, cloak, and fishing pole are the only things he owns.

He travels not by horse or cart, no headdress adorns his head.

All his life he spends each day upon the misty waves,

And in his cups he never feels the chill of wind and snow.

Roosting egrets, sleeping sea gulls: these are his companions.

White duckweed, red smartweed—where might rapids lie?

You mustn't talk about the risks of boating on rivers and lakes.

Can't you see that the journey through life has perils of its own?

Iwanami, p. 210. From *Nankai sensei kōshū* (The Later Collected Works of Master Nankai)

Line six: Smartweed is also known as water-pepper or knotweed (*Polygonum hydropiper*, J. *tade no hana*). It grows in damp places and produces a pale pink spiked flower in the autumn.

🔘 91

Upon the boat in a gilded cage a parrot, feathers white.

It enviously watches while I dance and listens as I sing.

But now I am no different from that bird inside the cage.

I cannot fly away with my man—what ever can I do?

Nakamura, p. 202. From *Enan chikushi* (Bamboo Branch Songs from South of the River)

The genre of poetry this verse represents is known as *chikushi*, "bamboo branches," or *chikushi shi*, "bamboo branch songs," deriving its name and inspiration from the Chinese *chu-chih tz'u* genre. In China, and later in Japan, it was a form of popular poetry which dealt with romantic love, popular customs and habits, and daily personal life. These poems were originally written in imitation of rural folk poetry (William H. Nienhauser, Jr., ed. and comp., *The Indiana Companion to Traditional Chinese Literature* [Bloomington: Indiana University Press, 1986], p. 373). The genre is said to have been inaugurated by the T'ang poet Liu Yü-hsi (772-842), reaching its peak with the Yuan poet Yang T'ieh-ya (1296-1370). In Japan, these poems became popular in the eighteenth century, especially in *Ichikawa Kansai's circle.

☾ 92   In Mourning for My Cat

1   Soft fur the color of tortoise-shell, a mind that was always quick.
The nights were quiet and peaceful, for all the mice had fled.
He belonged to us for less than a year—why did he suddenly die?
Maybe in taking care of him I didn't do my best.
5   In vain I recall how he sat on my lap, showing his master such love.
I hear him still at the foot of the stairs, meowing up at the children.
Camphor I placed inside his cage—alas, to no avail.
In the peonies' shade he's resting yet, in those hopeless dreams of mine.
If I'd wrapped his body in drapes and covers, what would've been
the point?
10   I sit here now beside the lamp, my old eyes blurred with tears.

Iriya, p. 20

Line seven: Camphor, uyaku, refers to a special variety of this plant, dendai-uyaku, used to treat the ailments of dogs and cats.
Line nine: An allusion to a section in Li chi (The Book of Rites) entitled "T'an Kung" (Sandlewood Bow), which states that old drapes should be saved for wrapping a dead horse for burial and old covers should similarly be used for dead dogs, to show one's affection for these animals.

Dazai Shundai, 1680-1747

A native of Shinshū in modern Nagano prefecture, Dazai Shundai was a distinguished and prolific scholar and man of letters. As a youth, he went to Edo with his father, who served the daimyo of Iida. In Edo, Shundai studied the Confucian classics with Nakano Iken, then entered the service of Matsudaira Tadanori, the daimyo of Izushi in what is now Hyōgo prefecture. Although he repeatedly asked to be allowed to withdraw from official service on grounds of illness, his request was never granted. At the age of twenty-one, Shundai finally left his post without authorization, apparently on account of his mother's ill health. For this action, considered a criminal offense, he was sentenced to ten years' incarceration with labor.

Following his release from prison, Shundai took instruction in Kobunjigaku from *Ogyū Sorai in Kyoto, thus ending his engagement with the Neo-Confucian orthodoxy. However, in time he came to find the school too liberal and rejected some of its concerns, in particular its emphasis upon philology. After Sorai's death, the school split into two factions, with *Hattori Nankaku heading the group interested in poetry and letters and Shundai taking command in classics as well as the more pragmatic disciplines of economics and politics.

A well-rounded scholar, Shundai was knowledgeable, not only about poetry and letters, but also about astronomy, calendrical studies, linguistics, and a variety of other subjects, including music. Among other things, he produced an annotated edition of the old-script text of *Hsiao ching* (The Classic of Filial Piety) which was circulated even in China, attracting much scholarly attention.[1] He is perhaps most famous for his seminal works that questioned the value of traditional agriculture as compared to commercial mercantile activity in the feudal economy, urging daimyo to "abandon the traditional piety that a rice economy was the only

---

[1]Inoguchi, p. 147.

legitimate basis for wealth...."[2] Tetsuo Najita relates that, while not going so far as to abandon the concept of the four-level class system, Shundai provocatively proposed that daimyo promote commercial mercantilism, arguing that the very survival of the status quo depended "less on ethical exhortations and more decisively on effective, empirical political action."[3] In Dazai's progressive treatises, writes Tetsuo Najita, we see "an insistence that history be viewed empirically...an emphasis on the ineffectualness of past guidelines drawn from the world of the ancient sages for action in the present...and an acute awareness of the possibility of political failure as a problem of structure and not of morality."[4]

Shundai had a large following of students throughout his life. He is described as being blunt, bold, and severe in manner, but above all, a man of high principles, impeccably decorous in his treatment of others and never compromising his standards for the sake of self-advancement. Consistent with his own behavior, he maintained that human relationships should always be governed by the principles and practice of *rei*—propriety and decorum—and that personal impulses should be restrained. On one occasion, Shundai reportedly gave the heir of a certain domain a stern dressing down for failing to come to greet him on his first visit, accusing the young man of unrighteous conduct. The heir evidently accepted the criticism with good grace and acknowledged that he had committed a breach of etiquette.[5] In his later years, Shundai declined all invitations to serve in feudal domains. Growing increasingly stubborn and set in his ways, he retired to a quiet life in Shishien (The Garden of the Purple Mushroom of the Immortals), his retreat, content to spend his final years in humble circumstances.

The first selection describes the remains of the old imperial capital of Nara and is filled with nostalgia for the former glory of this city. Old capitals and

---

[2]Koschmann, p. 83.

[3]Tetsuo Najita, "Method and Analysis in the Conceptual Portrayal of Tokugawa Intellectual History" in Najita and Scheiner, eds., *Japanese Thought in the Tokugawa Period*, p. 21.

[4]Ibid., p. 22.

[5]Inoguchi, p. 147.

abandoned castles in Japanese poetry generally serve as a reminder of the impermanence of all things, particularly man's own creations. Though natural phenomena—the willows, cherry blossoms, and deer that we see in this poem—may be transient, Nature has the capacity to rejuvenate itself endlessly, still flourishing amidst the ruins of our past. The same theme is evident in the third poem, where the tides and mountains alone remain, seemingly impervious to change.

◙ 93   Recalling the Past while at Nara

In the boundless lands south of Kyoto the ancient capital lies:
Third Avenue, Ninth Avenue—these roads still cross the city.
Wheat ripens in the old royal paddies as peasants wander by.
Mugwort grows on the imperial road as peddlers travel past.
Slender willows droop down low, ever evoking sadness.
Tranquil blossoms lie scattered about, showing no emotion.
The temples now are all that remain from a thousand years ago,
And the belling of wild deer is heard in the light of the setting sun.

Sugano, p. 45; Iwanami, p. 211. From *Shundai sensei bunshū* (The Collected Works of Master Shundai), 1752

Line six: This suggests that the flowers cannot share the poet's feelings of nostalgia for the old city.

☉ 94　Climbing Up Hakuunzan

On White Cloud Mountain clouds of white are flying through the sky.

Halfway up the emerald slopes several houses stand.

I walk as far as I can go on a white cloud-covered road,

White clouds enshrouding me head to foot as homeward bound I go.

Inoguchi, p. 147

Title:　Hakuunzan (White Cloud Mountain) cannot be identified.
Line one:　The phrase "white clouds" appears four times in the poem, breaking the rules of versification and thus making this a most unconventional—and consequently well-known—composition (Inoguchi, p. 147).

☉ 95　Recalling the Past while at Inamura

From the beach look south at the vast misty waves;

Through here, they say, the great army passed.

The ocean tides may have since returned,

　　but human history was forever changed.

The deserted mountains stretch far into the distance,

　　in the abundant rays of the setting sun.

Sugano, p. 44; Iwanami, p. 212; Andō, p. 64.　From *Shundai sensei bunshū*, 1752

Title:　This poem indirectly alludes to the story of Niita Yoshisada's attack upon Kamakura at Inamuragasaki (Cape Inamura) during the Genkō Rebellion, which began in 1331. According to legend, Niita at one point tossed his sword into the waters and prayed for divine assistance, whereupon the seas miraculously withdrew, allowing him to attack and destroy Hōjō Takatoki (1303-1333), the ninth and last regent of the Kamakura shogunate.

Hattori Nankaku, 1683-1759

A distinguished Confucian scholar, competent kanshi poet, and Nanga painter, Hattori Nankaku was born in Kyoto, the second son of a prosperous merchant. At fourteen, he was sent away to Edo to be taught by *Ogyū Sorai, and in time Nankaku became one of his leading disciples, being ranked with *Dazai Shundai as one of the "Two Jewels" of the Sorai school. From age sixteen, he served Yanagisawa Yoshiyasu, Shogun Tsunayoshi's senior councillor who was later enfiefed as lord of Kōfu. In 1716 (some accounts say 1718) Nankaku left Yoshiyasu's household to open an academy. Students came from as far away as Kyushu, attracted by his reputation as an affable and humble scholar. Nankaku had three sons and five daughters. The three daughters who reached adulthood were married off to disciples of his, who carried on the family's academic traditions. In his later years, Nankaku came under the protection of Lord Hosokawa of Higo. In frail health as he grew older, Nankaku visited few people other than Hosokawa, advising him on administrative policy and giving instruction in Kobunjigaku.[1]

Nankaku has been described as a magnanimous, refined, and graceful person. He also believed in following his own heart. As Kato Shuichi observes, "Rather than expound the virtues of righteousness and benevolence (as a Confucianist) or play a role in society (as a retainer or adviser) he preferred to follow his own tastes and seek pleasure."[2] Nankaku also believed that literature fell outside the boundaries of moral didacticism and that a person's literary worth as a writer had nothing to do with his moral conduct. *Emura Hokkai once compared him to three other leading post-Genna poets,[3] namely *Arai Hakuseki, *Yanagawa

---

[1]Inoguchi, p. 163.

[2]Kato, p. 124.

[3]Genna was the period from 1615-1624.

Seigan, and *Gion Nankai, asserting that "his natural endowment was not as great as Hakuseki's, in his craftsmanship he was no match for Yanada Zeigan, and in the richness of his poetic language he was not the equal of Gion Nankai."[4] But he went on to affirm the basic merit of Nankaku's verse nonetheless, adding that "one could not really place him below any of these three [in total effect]."[5] Hokkai was somewhat extravagant in his praise here, for Nankaku seems at best an average poet who wrote fairly conventional verse, much of it devoid of personal sentiment and originality. Nankaku's other works include *Daitō seigo* (An Account of the Great Eastern World, 1750), an anecdotal history of Japan, and *Tōshisen kokujikai* (A Japanese Glossary of Selected T'ang Poems, 1792). He also left us his *Nankaku sensei bunshū* (Master Nankaku's Literary Collection), the publication of which was completed the year before he died. The following poems are among his best.

◎ 96   Journeying by Night Down the Sumida River

The moon is floating on the river that flows past Golden Dragon Hill.
The waters toss, the moon bobs about, the golden dragon drifts along.
My little boat travels, never stopping; the sky the color of the water.
Autumn winds blow across from both shores as I float between the two realms.

Sugano, p. 49; Iwanami, p. 214; Andō, p. 66. From *Nankaku sensei bunshū* (The Collected Works of Master Nankaku), 1727-1758

Title: The poet is travelling down the Sumida River (Sumidagawa), eventually reaching the Edo River (Edogawa).
Line one: Golden Dragon Hill (Kinryūzan) is today known as Mt. Matsuchi (Matsuchiyama). This is a knoll near the Sumida River in the Asakusa area in Tokyo.
Line two: "Golden dragon" again refers to the hill whose reflection is seen in the river, appearing to move with the boat.
Line four: The poet is now on the Edo River, which formed the boundary between the provinces of Shimōsa and Musashi, north of modern Tokyo.

---

[4]Inoguchi, p. 163.

[5]Ibid.

◎ 97   Early Coolness

After rain the setting sun shines faintly in the western hills.
Who'd imagine that the autumn chill would return so soon this night.
The white clouds never waited for the autumn winds to blow.
They've fled already, hither and yon, for the sake of this melancholy one!

Iwanami, p. 216. From *Nankaku sensei bunshū*, 1727-1758

Line four: The clouds may have helped the poet to relieve his melancholia by scattering, leaving
a clear sky.

◎ 98   Walking in the Mountains in Late Spring

Peach and pear blossoms, one on the other, float past upon the water.
I've walked all over these deserted hills, and along the river I return.
I was unaware that the beauty of spring had left the human realm,
But some of the flowers still remain and are blooming on the trees.

Hirano, p. 207; Iwanami, p. 215. From *Nankaku sensei bunshū*, 1727-1758

Tasaka Hazan, fl. ca. 1750

Tasaka Hazan, whose dates are unknown, flourished in the mid-eighteenth century. A native of Nagato province in what is today Yamaguchi prefecture, he entered the academy of Yamagata Shūnan (1687-1752) and became a Kobunjigaku scholar, later serving the Hagi domain as a Confucian official. Six volumes of his poetry survive, and as the following two verses show, he was a moderately competent poet.

◙ 99   Returning Home in the Evening

On my staff I rest by the springtime river at dusk.
East and west no shadows can be seen.
Enshrouded by patchy haze, the willows are dark;
The setting sun gives the flowers a ruddy glow.
Outside the pine gate waits my little boy.
My thatched study stands among bamboo and trees.
Here I rest my legs after coming back,
As the light of the new moon shines through the latticed window.

Iwanami, p. 220. From *Hazan shishū* (The Collected Poems of Hazan), 1765

☻ 100 Song of the Reed Whistle

The north wind blows on the wild geese that fly through distant clouds.
The snow has stopped and above my village, the chilly evening moon.
High in the watch-tower a hundred feet up the beacon fires are burning.
I hear the reed whistle as I gaze toward Ch'ang-an, ten thousand *ri* away.

Iwanami, p. 221. From *Hazan shishū*, 1765

Line four: Ch'ang-an, in Shensi province in north-central China, was the western capital of China
during the T'ang dynasty. Today it is called Hsi-an (Sian).

Oka Chōshū [Raiseiken], ?-1766

A Teishugaku scholar, Oka Chōshū was a native of Sanuki, part of modern
Kagawa prefecture. He went to Edo to continue his training at the school of
Hayashi Hōkō, excelling in the composition of poetry. His family had long been
in the service of the Takamatsu domain, and Chōshū likewise served there as a
Confucian scholar and official, from 1740.

The poet's identification of the sound of rain on plantains with the rustling
of leaves is a common motif in kanshi, where poets often "mistake" one sound
for the other. This contrived poetic bewilderment[1] is reminiscent of that seen
in traditional Japanese court poetry, where falling cherry petals are conventionally
mistaken for snow. This technique, which, as Brower and Miner put it, involved
"a barrier of rhetoric between the perceiving sensibility and the poetic materials,"
is ultimately traceable to the Six Dynasties tradition in China, where the use of
elaborate figurative language to create a sense of puzzlement over the exact nature
or source of a particular phenomenon was a common poetic feature.[2]

---

[1] Here we use Brower and Miner's term—see Brower and Miner, p. 187.

[2] Ibid., p. 169.

◑ 101 A Sudden Shower

Night falls at the mountain inn with its speckled bamboo blinds.

A sudden shower brings an early coolness.

What makes this seem like an autumn evening?

The pattering of rain on the plantain leaves.

Iwanami, p. 186. From *Raiseiken shikō* (A Book of Poems by Raiseiken), 1778

<u>Line four</u>: The rain on the plantains imitates the sound made by falling leaves being blown about, reminding the poet of autumn. The anticipation of this season implicit in the third line suggests that the poem was written in late summer.

◑ 102 Returning by Night along the River

Fireflies flit about beside the river.

Few the travellers on the road tonight.

Along the way, the night cool as water.

Singing loudly, I walk home in the moonlight.

Iwanami, p. 186. From *Raiseiken shikō*, 1778

Tani Bizan, 1701-1773

Tani Bizan was a native of Awa province, part of modern Tokushima prefecture. Facts about his career are scarce, although it is known that he studied with *Itō Tōgai and was himself a Kogaku scholar and kanshi poet of some renown.[1] The charm of the first poem derives from the novel image of the firefly, suddenly emerging from the gloom as if to keep the poet company only to disappear an instant later, creating an atmosphere of utter loneliness and isolation seldom surpassed even this tradition renowned for its love of *sabi*. The second selection is written in the persona of a woman, something rather uncommon in the poetry of male kanshi poets although quite common in the waka tradition. We are reminded how vulnerable Edo women were to abandonment by their husbands.

◙ 103 Evening Rain Seen through the Mountain Window

The wind in the pines is blowing rain into the solitary shelter.
My lamp has gone out; the light of evening is now a dusky blue.
Deep as the ocean the traveller's desolation, here at the ends of the earth.
A firefly illuminates my loneliness, then vanishes through the latticed window.

Iwanami, p. 231. From *Fuyō shishū*, 1755

---

[1]Iwanami, p. 493.

☽ 104 A Woman's Misfortune

1 When I was thirteen years of age my family suffered misfortune.
When I was fifteen I left my village and journeyed far away.
Falling on hard times I married a dissolute man,
Who wandered away to some distant place and seemed to forget about me.
5 I used to have a perfect face, a beauty second to none.
But now my countenance, rosy once, shows the sadness of a broken heart.
Spring finds me lamenting beside my window, each night like a year.
My brocade blanket glitters brightly, but the mandarin ducks have
    gone cold.
Don't you see that the drake may have left, but the duck remains on
    the nest?
10 The orchid that withered away in the autumn bears a thin layer of frost.

Iwanami, p. 230. From *Fuyō shishū* (The Lotus Poetry Collection), 1755

Line eight: The brocade blanket is a wedding blanket, the mandarin ducks being a symbol of conjugal love and fidelity.
Line nine: The text appears to have a scribal error here, in that the words for duck and drake have been inadvertently transposed. We have emended the text and translated accordingly.

Akiyama Gyokuzan, 1702-1763

Akiyama Gyokuzan was a native of Higo, part of modern Kumamoto prefecture. He studied Sorai-style Neo-Confucianism with a local domain scholar and at twenty-three followed the Higo daimyo to Edo, where he attended the Hayashi academy. Gyokuzan next embarked upon a decade of research at Shōheikō and then studied further under *Hattori Nankaku. When Gyokuzan returned to Higo, he served as a tutor and chief advisor to the daimyo. In 1754, he was appointed as professor in the recently-opened domain school, Jishūkan (est. 1752). In what was to be the last year of his life, Gyokuzan was allowed to stay behind in the domain while the daimyo proceeded to Edo to take up his mandatory period of residence there. He continued to write verse until his death at age sixty-two.

Gyokuzan's own eight-character Chinese epitaph written moments before his death reads: "The clear mirror [i.e., the water] is bottomless; the moon reflected in the water is just like me."[1] The moon in Japanese literature is typically a symbol of religious awakening, inspiration, or knowledge. It also has connotations of spiritual purity and a clear conscience. Here, Gyokuzan was perhaps implying that he had in his lifetime attained a state of spiritual perfection.

The first of the three verses below is unusual among kanshi in that it shows the poet making fun of himself in a somewhat iconoclastic way. In this refreshingly honest verse, Gyokuzan indirectly calls into question the efficacy of paying homage to the gods, suggesting that they are amused by people's folly in imagining that going to such lengths to show their devotion will benefit them. The second poem paints a delightful portrait of the peaceful, otherworldly beauty of a remote temple. This is one of many Edo poems about a visit to a secluded temple or shrine, a transcendental experience typically likened to discovering heaven. Such poems seldom describe the temple itself or its religious activities,

---

[1]Inoguchi, p. 165. It would of course have been more natural for Gyokuzan to say that he was like the moon, rather than the other way around.

focussing instead on the aesthetics of the natural setting, as if visiting the temple environs were an end in itself. The scattering of the cherry blossoms is conventionally an occasion for lamentation in Japanese poetry. Here, however, the poet views their demise in a more sanguine light, pointing out that the flying petals blown about by the wind create an effect as lovely as the flowers in full bloom.

The third verse belongs to a thematic genre we may refer to as tomb poems. These express the nostalgic and melancholy feelings experienced upon visiting the grave of a well-known historical or literary personage. With most such poems, the poet's sadness is largely occasioned by the perception that no one else shares his memory of the deceased and the times in which that person lived.

☺ 105 On the Hakoyama Road

White clouds, new leaves on the trees—beautiful Mount Hako!
Scholars and writers year after year visit this spot then go home.
Today the spirits that inhabit the mountain must surely be laughing at me
For foolishly dragging my proud bones here along with those other old folk!

Hirano, p. 211. From *Gyokuzan shū* (The Gyokuzan Collection), 1754

<u>Title</u>: This mountain has not been unidentified.

◙ 106 Written while Spring Rain Fell during a Visit to Myōkai Temple; I Was Assigned the Rhyme-Word "Mist"

Bamboo monastery, lonely and secluded,
Faraway place in the springtime shade.
Visitors get lost on the winding paths.
Birds scatter, dispersing the light mist—
A scene so mystical one forgets the world.
Gazing at the clouds I shake off all ties.
What does it matter if the flowers fall,
For the sky will be filled with a shower of petals.

Hirano, p. 209. From *Gyokuzan shū*, 1754

◙ 107 Sengakuji Temple

The autumn wind blows the trees by the sea,
Soughing mournfully as it whips up the waves.
Above the shore lies T'ien Heng's tomb,
Making the moonlight seem all the more cold.

Hirano, p. 210. From *Gyokuzan shū*, 1754

Title: This temple belongs to the Sōtō Zen sect and is the burial place of Akō (Asano) Naganori (1665-1701) and his forty-seven loyal followers, who committed suicide after avenging the death of their lord, who was the daimyo of Akō (Harima). While receiving an imperial messenger at Edo castle in 1701, Naganori was humiliated in some way (the details are unclear) by the shogun's master of ceremonies, a samurai named Kira Yoshinaka (1641-1702), whom Naganori then struck with his dagger. Although Yoshinaka suffered only minor cuts, Naganori was forced to commit suicide for his actions, which were considered a capital offense, whereupon his followers, the "forty-seven loyal retainers," now masterless *rōnin*, launched their famous vendetta against Yoshinaka to avenge the death of their lord. In the Twelfth Month of 1702, Yoshinaka was beheaded in an attack led by Ōishi Yoshio (1659-1703), one of Naganori's samurai, after which those involved in the vendetta turned themselves in to the authorities. Fourteen months later, they were all ordered to commit ritual disembowelment (*seppuku*). The Japanese ever since have felt deeply moved by the loyalty of these retainers, and their story has been much celebrated both in the traditional theater and in other literature.
Line three: T'ien Heng, who lived at the end of the Warring States period (403-221 B.C.), was a Chinese rebel who committed suicide after the establishment of the Han dynasty and like Naganori was later followed in death by his retainers.

Takano Rantei, 1704-1757

A native of Edo, Takano Rantei was the much-loved only child of a comic linked-verse master named Katsuharu and the grandson of a prosperous merchant. Katsuharu was fifty when Rantei was born. As a child, Rantei showed enormous promise, so he was sent to receive instruction from *Ogyū Sorai, who was reportedly amazed by his stellar talent, once exclaiming, "I've come up against the walled fortress of Chao Pi," an allusion to a Chinese military hero of the Ming dynasty.[1]

Because Katsuharu was not particularly interested in making money, the family fortunes steadily declined. To make matters worse, at seventeen Rantei lost his sight. Thereafter, following Sorai's advice, he devoted himself to writing poetry, especially the "modern" regulated forms in which he excelled, while also pursuing an interest in collecting antiques and old paintings. An admirer of the Ming poet Li P'an-lung (1514-1570), Rantei has been described as comparable to *Hattori Nankaku in his poetic style,[2] but he is undoubtedly the better poet. Nothing in the verses below reflects Rantei's disability, and it is remarkable that he was able to describe in such realistic detail scenes that he might never have actually seen. We may imagine that, having memorized so many poems, he was capable of manipulating vocabulary and natural images to produce convincing descriptions of the world around him. Rantei loved Kamakura and built a retreat there, near Engakuji temple, enjoying visits from priests of local temples. Only about one thousand of his approximately ten thousand poems survive, perhaps in part because of his reluctance to allow his disciples to publish his works, on the grounds that he was not yet satisfied with them.[3]

---

[1]Inoguchi, p. 154.

[2]*NKD*, p. 387.

[3]Inoguchi, p. 155.

◎ 108 Passing through Shichirigahama Beach

The great Sea of Tōnan stretches out, extending to the clouds.

Floating foam encroaches on the sand, retreating night and day.

Crashing waves pound the heavens, like horses leaping skyward.

The roar of the surf shakes the earth, causing a thunderous rumble.

A black dragon emerges from its lair, the full moon in its grasp,

As the fairy immortal appears on her dais, festooned with purple clouds.

Many old men have fished the seas at the mouth of the Shichiri shallows,

But has any of them, in a thousand autumns, ever asked about Tzu Ling's jetty?

Inoguchi, p. 156. From *Rantei sensei shishū* (A Collection of Poetry by Master Rantei), 1757

Title: Shichirigahama is a beach near the city of Kamakura extending from Inemuragasaki to Koyurugigasaki. From here one can see Mt. Fuji, Mt. Hakone, Ōshima Island, and the Miura Peninsula.
Line five: *Chuang Tzu* contains references to a dragon which had a pearl under its chin. It was believed that thunder and rain were caused by dragons playing with pearls or balls in the heavens.
Line six: "Fairy immortal" refers to Ho Hsien-ku, the only female among the eight immortals of Taoism. Symbolized by the lotus and sometimes by the peach, legend has it that she was attacked by a demon, only to be rescued by one of the immortals who brought her into their group.
Line eight: Tzu Ling was Yen Kuang, a close friend of Kuang Wu, the first emperor of the Eastern Han dynasty. He was a reclusive fellow who loved fishing, and there was a spot known to later generations as the Tzu Ling Shallows, presumably the same place alluded to here. Perhaps the intent of the poet here is to suggest that the fishermen, unlettered rustics that they are, have no knowledge of famous anglers who preceded them.

◎ 109 Floating in a Boat on a Moonlit Night where the River Forks

The waters fork and the river splits apart—autumn on the great river Sumida.

A bright new moon hangs overhead; the river flows for ten thousand leagues.

Gazing up at the azure heavens, I was about to play my jewelled flute

When a tiny wisp of floating cloud drifted down onto my boat.

Sugano, p. 47; Andō, p. 70. From *Rantei sensei shishū*, 1757

Line one: The Sumida River (Sumidagawa) merges with the Imado River (Imadokawa) here, the latter seeming to cut off the former where they fork.

☾ 110   Written in Fondness for the Flowers

Flowers bloom, but no one comes to see them.
Flowers fall, but no one notices.
If the spring breeze has any compassion,
It will blow them to where my master dwells.

Inoguchi, p. 156. From *Rantei sensei shishū*, 1757

☾ 111   One of the Eight Famous Sites of Ōmi Province: Onjōji Temple (Miidera)

Dense white clouds above the mountain temple,
No human footprints in the surrounding woods.
An aged priest is ringing the bell.
Its echo resounds through the empty valley.

Iwanami, pp. 237-238. From *Rantei sensei shishū*, 1757

Title: The evening bell at Miidera was the fourth of the so-called Eight Famous Sights of Ōmi, which were identified as such in the late-fifteenth century. The others were as follows: (1) the autumn moon at Ishiyama; (2) the evening snow at Mt. Hira (Hirayama); (3) the setting sun at Seta; (5) boats leaving the port of Yabase; (6) the sky and wind at Awazu; (7) the night rain at Karasaki on Lake Biwa; and (8) the wild geese alighting at Katata. Miidera is near Ōtsu in Shiga prefecture east of Kyoto.

Ishijima Tsukuba, 1708-1758

Ishijima Tsukuba was a native of Hamamatsu in Tōtōmi, part of modern Shizuoka prefecture. A Kobunjigaku scholar, he began reading the Chinese classics with his father at the age of six and later studied with *Ogyū Sorai and *Hattori Nankaku. Tsukuba served the Hamamatsu domain, finally retiring to Yamashita in Tsukuba. He is said to have loved drinking and never had a family of his own. In his later years, Tsukuba opened a school near Kichijōji temple, Edo, where he mainly taught Kobunjigaku, acquiring a reputation for his scholarly acumen and punctiliousness. He was always poor and never owned many books, borrowing from his friends when he needed to prepare a lecture.

The first selection below begins in a conventional fashion, praising the neighbor's plum flowers, but ends with a novel twist: the introduction of the notion of borrowed scent, an image reminiscent of the *shakkei* (borrowed scenery) concept in Japanese landscaping.[1]

112 The Neighbor's Flowers

I sit and gaze at my neighbor's garden—the peach and plum blossoms of spring:
Beyond the fence on every branch, blooming freshly in wild profusion.
All day long the wind from the east has brought their scent my way.
What need is there at this time of year to importune their owner?

Iwanami, p. 236. From *Kikaen bunshū* (Collected Writings from the Garden of Water Chestnuts and Lotuses), 1758

Line four: Literally, "What need is there...to make inquiries of their owner?" The poet does not have to ask permission to go over and smell the flowers since the wind is bringing their scent to him.

---

[1]In landscape gardening, the term *shakkei* refers to the incorporation of external landscape beauty beyond the garden proper as a means of enhancing the manmade beauty of the setting.

☺ 113   Kaigakurō on Mount Takao: A Miscellaneous Poem

A mountain lodge, tranquil in the midday sun.

I watch the clouds float past in the sky.

No one journeys across the river.

The chirping of cicadas mingles with the woodcutter's song.

Iwanami, p. 236.   From *Kikaen bunshū*, 1758

Title: This verse is the fourth in a series of twelve poems.   Mt. Takao (Takao-san) is to the west of Kyoto.   Kaigakurō is most likely an inn, although it has not been positively identified.

Yuasa Jōzan, 1708-1781

Yuasa Jōzan was a native of Bizen in what is today Okayama prefecture. A precocious child, he is said to have memorized most of the major war tales by about the age of ten. As a youth, he avidly read the works of *Itō Jinsai and *Ogyū Sorai with a Confucian teacher in Bizen. As a result of this exposure to Kogaku, Jōzan came to reject orthodox Neo-Confucian doctrine. In his late teens he went to Edo to study with *Hattori Nankaku, working also for a period with *Dazai Shundai. Jōzan's father and grandfather had served the Okayama domain, and after becoming head of the family at twenty-four, Jōzan was appointed to various Okayama administrative posts, receiving a large salary of around four hundred *koku*. He did much to expose venality and administrative abuses in the domain and improve the economic situation of the impoverished Okayama peasants. In his brave, forthright remonstrations with his superiors he courted disaster, eventually being placed under house arrest in 1769.[1]

Known for his dedication and gallantry, Jōzan was sought out by other Kobunjigaku scholars, most notably Matsuzaki Kankai (1725-1775), and the syncretic scholar Inoue Randai (1705-1761), who became one of his closest friends. Throughout his life he remained committed to the reinvigoration of Sorai's Kobunjigaku, even though it was at odds with the official Teishu creed of the domain school. Jōzan was knowledgeable in history and excelled in Chinese poetry and prose as well. He was also skillful in the martial arts, which he practiced every day, even as an old man. His lively and well-known collection of anecdotes, *Jōzan kidan* (Anecdotes about Jōzan), brings to life the stories of remarkable samurai of the Sengoku period (1467-1568) of civil war. He was

---

[1]Inoguchi, pp. 170-171.

apparently fond of telling his disciples, "A samurai may give up letters, but he must never give up the martial arts."[2]

Jōzan's martial proclivities show through in the first poem, a verse possessing remarkable robustness and vitality, both in its powerful description of stormy seas and in the poet's boisterous defiance of the "beasts" (literally, "sea turtles and crocodiles") lurking beneath the waters. Turbulent ocean imagery occurs again in the second poem, only this time the poet's mood turns to one of awe and fear, caused by his sudden apocalyptic vision.

⬤ **114 A Poem Inspired by the Experience of Returning by Boat on the Sanuki Sea and Encountering Fierce Winds and Waves**

Given orders, I set my sail and headed across the Southern Sea,
Running straight into mighty winds and waves that towered high.
Like bolting horses those furious billows that suddenly besieged us.
Rising, I brandished my trusty sword and roared at the beasts of the deep!

Hirano, p. 212; Inoguchi, p. 170.

Title: This poem was written when the poet was forty-three years old. Jōzan was en route to the castle town of Marugame in Sanuki, modern Kagawa prefecture (Inoguchi, p. 171).
Line one: The Sanuki Sea is off northern Shikoku island.

---

[2]Ibid., p. 171.

■ 115 A Poem Sent to Toshinari

The wind was whipping up billowing waves as I leaned against the rails.
I was singing aloud a mournful song, when suddenly my hair stood on end.
Look over there, away on the horizon, at the color of the floating clouds.
One among them is cold and purple—a cloud that's come for me!

Hirano, pp. 212-213

Title: Toshinari is a tentative reading; this individual has not been identified.
Line four: Purple clouds have a special significance in Pure Land Buddhism. In deathbed scenes depicted in art and literature, when the moment of death approaches, the dying person sees a purple cloud trailing in the west. On this cloud rides the Amitābha Buddha, who descends to earth to meet the dying one and lead him to the Pure Land. Jōzan may have viewed the cloud as a sign of the coming of Amida Buddha, even though he was obviously not on his deathbed and was merely musing fancifully.

Emura Hokkai, 1713-1788

A renowned poet and scholar, Emura Hokkai was born in the Akashi domain of Harima, part of modern Hyōgo prefecture. His father Itō Ryūshū (1683-1755) was also a Confucian scholar of some distinction, and Hokkai was the second of three brilliant brothers, who were all gifted in Chinese studies. As a youth he received instruction for three years from the prominent scholar-poet *Yanada Zeigan. Soon his love of Chinese poetry eclipsed his original interest in haikai, and at twenty-two he began teaching the classics, taking over the students of his father. In 1734, upon the death of the Confucian scholar Emura Kian (1666-1734) of the Miyazu domain in Tango north of Kyoto, Hokkai adopted the Emura name to satisfy a request that Kian had made to his father to provide an heir to carry on the Emura family line.[1]

Hokkai's chief love remained Chinese poetry, and after some thirty years of service to the Miyazu domain at the domainal residence in Kyoto, he decided at the age of fifty-one (fifty-four by some accounts) to retire and thereafter taught kanshi poetry at a school he had founded in Kyoto. He also established a poetry society called Shijōdō Shisha,[2] whose purpose was to teach kanshi writing and disseminate the members' views on poetic theory. Together with Irie Hokkai (1714-1789) of Edo and Katayama Hokkai (1723-1790) of Osaka, he was known as one of the "Three Hokkais," a sign of his high status during his lifetime. Donald Keene, however, does not hold him in particularly high regard, noting that Hokkai denounced as "criminals" some of his more "adventurous" contemporaries who "addressed poems to prostitutes, wrote poetry while staying

---

[1]Ōsone, p. 95.

[2]This name means "[Poetic] Stick-Presentation Hall Poetry Society." "Stick" is a reference to the ceremonial walking sticks which poets supposedly carried while strolling and reciting verse. These are sometimes referred to in kanshi. See, for example, poems nos. 43, 17, 202, and 332 in this anthology.

156

in a brothel, or used phrases suggestive of immoral relations."[3] Keene writes,
"[S]uch 'criminal' poems are certainly more attractive than Hokkai's hackneyed
descriptions of dusk falling over the sea or of some lonesome crows in a withered
willow,"[4] the latter an apparent reference to the first of the two Hokkai verses
translated below. Hokkai is also noted for his five-volume history of Japanese
kanshi, titled *Nihonshi-shi* (A History of Japanese *Shih* Poetry, 5 volumes, 1771)
which critiques the work of kanshi poets from the late-seventh century to
Hokkai's day. Another major contribution was his *Nihon shisen* (An Anthology
of Chinese Poetry by Japanese Poets, ten volumes, 1774), which includes kanshi
written by some 520 poets from the early decades of the Edo period down to
about 1780.

◙ 116 Cold Crows on Withered Trees

A scattering of cottages with brushwood gates along a grassy path.
Snow in the air, a desolate scene; an old road leading uphill.
What person hired Kuo Hsi, that painter of mountains and rivers,
To draw cold crows on the withered willows growing on this steep slope?

Iwanami, pp. 246-247. From *Hokkai sensei shishō* (A Book of Poems by Master Hokkai, 1786)

Line four: Kuo Hsi was a famous Sung dynasty artist. The poet is imagining that he is walking
through a scene in a Kuo Hsi painting.

---

[3]*WWW*, p. 544.

[4]Ibid., p. 555.

☺ 117 The Egret

The egret makes no attempt to fly away.
Its crest is moist from the evening rain,
As if to vaunt its fine bright feathers,
It has chosen to stand beside the green grass.

Iwanami, p. 247. From *Hokkai sensei shishō*, 1786

Ryū [Tatsuno] Sōro, 1714-1792

The son of a tea-shop owner, Ryū Sōro was born in Fushimi in modern Kyoto. At age eleven, he lost his father, and the family lived thereafter in a state of penury, although Sōro still managed to continue his studies. The owner of a brush-shop in Kyoto offered to adopt him, so the young man came to Kyoto and began working there, sending money home to his mother every month. In the third verse below, we find him recalling his mother fondly and wishing he were back home.

Sōro read the classics and the works of T'ang and Ming writers in his spare time. He also familiarized himself with the teachings of *Ogyū Sorai and *Dazai Shundai and received instruction from Uno Meika (1698-1745). However, Meika came to form a low opinion of Sōro and eventually expelled him from his school. This upset Sōro deeply, and subsequently he never revealed to anyone that he had once been Meika's student.[1] In 1737 he opened a school of his own in Karasumakoji, Kyoto. Proficient at writing both kanshi and waka, Sōro in time acquired many followers. At age thirty-eight, he accepted an appointment as a Confucian scholar in the Hikone domain and remained there for eighteen years, returning to Kyoto in 1775 after he retired. Around this time, Sōro established Yūransha (The Secluded Lilies Poetry Society), which flourished in the 1770s. Together with Kontonsha (founded by Katayama Hokkai) it was one of the most important poetic groups at that time.

Sōro was reputedly an easy-going person who had rather low expectations of his students, allowing even those of low caliber to work with him, which tarnished the school's reputation. He was, however, meticulous about being paid for any professional writing tasks he was hired to perform and consequently had

---

[1]Inoguchi, p. 175.

many detractors in Kyoto.[2] A hint of this somewhat mercenary quality seems to come through in the last of the poems, where he admits, "...[T]o my shame a five-picul salary still seems sweet to me." In the first poem, however, he expresses a seemingly contradictory preference for a life in seclusion away from the secular world, speaking of "hankering for the pleasures of this world beyond the dust," in reference to the temple where he is sojourning at the time.

☪ 118 Staying at Byōdōin on the Usagi Road

Here to this temple I've come to stay;
The forest is deep and I relish the seclusion.
Monks chant on a dais in the moonlight,
As visitors moor their boats in front of the temple.
A bell tolling across the water sounds near;
The reflection of the pagoda floats upon the river.
I keep hankering for the pleasures of this world beyond the dust
And will spend another autumn here among the cassias.

Hirano, pp. 213-214. From *Sōro shū* (*Sōro bunshū*, The Sōro Collection), 1753 (following date in preface)

Title: Byōdōin, the Phoenix Temple, is a renowned Buddhist temple in Uji to the south of Kyoto established in 1052.

☪ 119 The Fisherman

Raincoat of straw and bamboo-leaf hat—he leads a meager life.
Upon the vast and misty waves is where he makes his home.
He drinks three cups of cloudy wine, then is drunk and dead to the world,
Asleep on his boat in the bright moonlight among the flowering reeds.

Inoguchi, p. 178

---

[2]Ibid., pp. 175-176.

◐ **120 My Thoughts in Autumn**

On the city wall the visitor's fur robes billow in the wind from the west.

When will I be able to return to the village that I call home?

I was roused from a dream in the fifth watch by rain falling on the plantains:

My mind had journeyed a thousand *ri* back to the fulling blocks of autumns past.

Ssu-ma, after wearying of travel, was moved to write *fu* verse;

Chung-hsüan, after roaming the land, ascended a tower where he recalled

     his past.

From afar, I can sense Mother leaning on the gate, expectantly gazing out,

At the white clouds off on the distant horizon, endlessly drifting by.

Hirano, p. 214. From *Sōro shū*, 1753

Line five: Ssu-ma is Ssu-ma Hsiang-ju (179-117 B.C.), the best known writer of *fu* (prose-poems) in the Chinese literary tradition. He was a scholar-official who served emperors Ching and Wu. His most famous piece is the "Shang-lin fu" (Prose-Poem on Shang-lin Park).

Line six: Chung-hsüan is Wang Ts'an (177-217), one of the leading scholars and *fu* poets of his age. At the time of the Tung Cho Rebellion he fled to Chingchou, where he wrote his best-known poem, titled "Teng-lou fu" (Prose-Poem on Climbing to the Loft). In this verse, which is alluded to in the poem, he describes his longing for his home. These allusions to Wang Ts'an and Ssu-ma Hsiang-ju serve to reinforce the theme of nostalgia for one's home district.

☾ 121 Written on a Wall

South of the painted bridge that stands near the Golden Tortoise Castle

Is a little cottage made of grass belonging to a penniless scholar.

The moon shines down on the rustic lane this lonely autumn night.

The willow catkins sway in the wind beside my rugged gate.

In my belly, the books I've consumed—a thousand works in all.

And at my waist, a roaring dragon—the single sword I bear.

The Pine and Chrysanthemum Lord of Ch'ai-sang I've admired all for nought,

For to my shame a five-picul salary still seems sweet to me.

Inoguchi, p. 178

Line one: The Golden Tortoise Castle, Kinkijō, has not been identified.
Line two: "Penniless scholar" refers to the poet himself.
Line seven: "The Pine and Chrysanthemum Lord of Ch'ai-sang" is a reference to the eminent Chinese poet T'ao Yuan-ming (365-427), a native of Ch'ai-sang.
Line eight: The poet feels embarrassed that, unlike T'ao Yuan-ming, who was content with poverty, he continues to long for an official post, preferably one with a salary of five *koku* (piculs) of grain per annum. A picul (about five bushels dry measure) was considered a volume sufficient to feed one man for a year.

Hara Sōkei, 1718-1767

Hara Sōkei, a native of Kyoto, studied Kogaku under *Itō Tōgai from the age of ten and later trained as a doctor. He opened a school in Kyoto and served the Karatsu domain in Hizen, Kyushu, first as a physician and then as a professor. A doctrinal purist, he accepted nothing less than the original Confucian texts themselves, in particular *The Analects of Confucius* and *Mencius*, rejecting post-Han dynasty Confucian scholarship and attacking the work of Sorai, Jinsai, and even Chu Hsi himself.[1] The gentler, wistful side of the man emerges in his poetry. The two somewhat melancholy verses translated below are permeated with *sabi*, an aesthetic quality identified with a stark, faded beauty and typically colored in the monochrome palette of late fall and winter—pale, muted colors and grayish tones.

◐ 122 A Grave by the Roadside

Forlorn the grave mound in the field,
Its headstone overgrown with moss.
The autumn grass has buried all footprints.
The mournful wind comes and goes at will.

Iwanami, p. 251. From *Sōkei shū* (The Sōkei Collection), 1810

---

[1]*NKD*, p. 555.

◐ 123 Hearing the Frosty Bell on a Cold Night

The light of the fading lamp is dim; gloomy this thatched abode.
I wake from a dream as the cold moonlight drifts in through the western window.
From afar the frosty tones of a bell—whence does its tolling descend?
Borne by the wind for half the night, piercing this homesick heart.

Iwanami, p. 252. From *Sōkei shū*, 1810

Ike Taiga, 1723-1776

Ike Taiga was an illustrious Nanga painter and man of letters. A native of Kyoto, where he spent his life, he lost his father at four. At fifteen, he and his mother opened a fan shop at Nijō Higuchi, where he carved seals in his spare time. This may explain why he used more than 113 seals and style names in his writings and artworks.[1] He took the name Taiga in 1742 and married the painter Gyokuran four years later. Taiga was particularly famous for his finger-painting, which he learned under Yanagisawa Kien (1704-1758), a well-known painter of bamboo. He was also an avid practitioner of Zen and Chinese calligraphy. At twenty-eight, Taiga visited *Gion Nankai, who was reportedly astounded by his artistic genius. Kato Shuichi observes, "[His paintings] are strikingly individualistic, in contrast to the essentially decorative work of the Kanō school, and indeed Taiga was probably the most individualistic painter of the eighteenth century."[2] The second of the two poems below shows the painter's eye for color and detail, capturing the ineffable beauty of the young girls.

---

[1]Roberts, p. 167.

[2]Kato, p. 124.

🌙 124-125   Two Poems Written Upstream

(No. 1)

Willows growing upstream, branches easy to break;

Orange trees by the fence, not yet in bloom.

Why should I buy land and grow millet?

My neighbor to the east is a maker of wine!

Iriya, p. 54

Line two: The trifoliate orange tree blooms late in spring.
Lines three and four: The poet seems to be alluding to T'ao Yuan-ming who grew his own millet for making wine.

(No. 2)

Golden orioles and butterflies, around me everywhere;

The greens of plants and the reds of flowers, here before my eyes.

Practicing the Way and discussing sutras are matters of the world of dust.

Delicate brows and beautiful hair—girls in the breezes of spring.

Iriya, p. 54

Lines three and four: For the poet, the beauty of his surroundings rather than philosophy and religious teachings constitutes the ultimate sublime reality.

Hosoi Heishū, 1728-1801

The son of a prosperous farmer, Hosoi Heishū was a native of Owari, part of modern Aichi prefecture. It is said that while his mother was pregnant with him, she often dreamed of the sun, the moon, and the stars. Her dreams were deemed prophetic when Heishū was born with moles between his eyebrows in what is described as an Ursa Major-like configuration.[1] A precocious child who read both day and night, he went to Kyoto at age sixteen to further his education but apparently returned a year later, unable to find a suitable teacher. His father had sent him off with the sum of fifty ryō, but Heishū, living frugally on rice husks and wearing only tattered clothing, managed to return with ten ryō to spare, having also managed to buy himself a pair of horses and a collection of books. His father, much impressed by his son's love of books and his frugality, offered to give him a house and some land. Heishū declined, asking instead for two hundred kin with which to buy more books. "These," he said, "will serve as my teacher."[2]

Around 1744, Heishū went to Nagoya and entered the school of Nakanishi Tan'en (1709-1752). With Tan'en's encouragement he went off to Nagasaki to learn Chinese the following year. Heishū often visited his home from Nagasaki, concerned about his mother's deteriorating health. This attentiveness manifested itself even in his dreams, as shown in the first poem below, but he was unable to be at his mother's side when she died.[3] Eventually Heishū followed Tan'en to Edo. There, he established a school and after Tan'en's death took over many of his students. Heishū was extremely poor at this time, but since his elder brother had meanwhile bankrupted the family, his father came to live with him.

---

[1]Inoguchi, p. 179.

[2]Ibid.

[3]Ibid.

To add to his burdens, two friends from Nagasaki with whom Heishū had earlier formed a blood-brother relationship joined the household as well.

Heishū was a leading exponent of Setchūgaku (Syncretic studies). As Maruyama notes, the views of the Syncretic scholars were too wide-ranging and diverse to be considered a school in the usual sense, but Setchūgaku can in general be characterized as a practical, moderate kind of eclecticism which drew from orthodox Teishugaku, Kogaku, and Wang Yang-ming Neo-Confucianism yet "reject[ed] factional extremes," to use Maruyama's words, adhering to no single Neo-Confucian school.[4] Accordingly, Heishū himself often said that what mattered in learning was the cultivation of virtue, not the creation of a variety of different philosophical schools.[5] Thus, he largely ignored the intellectual disputes going on amongst the different Confucian schools, concentrating instead upon producing students of high moral caliber.

Heishū was famous for his outstanding character and was reportedly an inspiring lecturer as well, moving people to mend their ways. Once, a local samurai was hiding in the school, lying in wait for Heishū and intending to kill him, for reasons that are unknown. The man heard Heishū lecture, and after listening to him for a while, was apparently so moved by his manifest virtue that he changed his mind, even throwing away his sword.[6]

In 1772, Heishū was invited by the daimyo Uesugi Harunori (Yōzan) of Yonezawa domain (part of modern Yamagata prefecture), to assist with educational reform and establish a domain school. In Yonezawa, he became a much-respected advisor, promoting benevolent rule, higher academic standards, and improved living conditions for the peasantry. Heishū won the acclaim of the local people, who called him a Nyorai Incarnate (a living Buddha) and bowed to him whenever he passed by.[7] He was to make several extended visits to

---

[4]Maruyama, p. 141.

[5]Inoguchi, p. 179.

[6]Ibid.

[7]Ibid.

Yonezawa from his home in Edo during the 1770s in his capacity as advisor. In 1780, Heishū was invited back to his native Owari to serve the daimyo as a lecturer, and in 1783 he became head of the domain academy, Meirinkan, reinvigorating the scholarly atmosphere there before finally retiring in 1792. Upon hearing of the death of his former lord, Uesugi Yōzan, in 1799, Heishū is said to have wept, exclaiming, "Now I am finished."[8] He died two years later.

◖ 126 Dreaming of My Parents

The fragrant grass grows lush and green, day by day renewed.
I'm moved to think of going home, for spring is hard to bear.
Three thousand *ri* away from here is the town that I call home.
The other night I had a dream—I saw my aged parents.

Sugano, p. 51; Inoguchi, p. 180; Andō, p. 80. From *Ōmeikan shi shū* (Collected Poems from the Ōmei Academy), 1764

The poet was in Nagasaki studying when this verse was written. He was in his early twenties.

◖ 127 Inscription for a Landscape Painting

I remember how when in my prime I travelled over rivers and through clouds,
East and west over ten thousand *ri*, back and forth I went.
Now as an old man recalling those times it all seems like a dream.
Yet I've managed somehow to paint those hills that have lingered in my mind.

Hirano, p. 217

---

[8]Ibid.

Priest Rikunyo [Rikunyoan, Rokunyo, Jishū], 1734?-1801

A distinguished scholar of Buddhism and Confucianism and one of the better-known Edo kanshi poets, Priest Rikunyo was a native of Ōmi Hachiman, located east of Kyoto on the shores of Lake Biwa. He was born either in 1734 or 1737.[1] After early schooling in Hikone, his home province, he was sent by his father, Naemura Kaidō, to Kawagoe, north of Edo, for further study in 1746. Rikunyo remained there for ten years, completing his education. Although Rikunyo's movements in these early years are difficult to trace, we know that he received the tonsure at eleven, under the mentoring of the Tendai high priest Kankoku of the Enryakuji temple on Mt. Hiei.[2] He returned to Kyoto from Kawagoe in 1757 to become a priest in Zenkōji temple on Mt Hiei. Some nine years later, he went to Edo to serve as priest in Kan'eiji temple in Ueno.[3] In 1767 Rikunyo left the priesthood, only to return some five years later to serve as a priest in the Shōgakuin temple and, somewhat later, the Myōshōin temple on the eastern slope of Mt. Hiei, in Kyoto.[4] For a period during his mid- to late thirties, he studied classical poetic rhetoric in Edo under Miyase Ryūmon (1719-1771), a former disciple of *Hattori Nankaku, but soon rejected his conservative Kobunjigaku-influenced teachings.[5] He was to travel back and forth between Edo and Kyoto many times in subsequent years, with stops in his native Hikone, before retiring to the western hills of Kyoto.

---

[1]We have followed Fujikawa, p. 3 in taking 1734 to be Rikunyo's birth year. Some other sources give his birth year as 1737.

[2]Fujikawa, p. 3.

[3]Watson 1990, p. 37; Fujikawa, pp. 3-4.

[4]*NKD*, p. 286; Inoguchi, p. 184.

[5]*NKD*, ibid.

Rikunyo was an innovative and influential poet. He came to dislike poetry imitative of T'ang models, and although he was trained in the formal *kakuchō* style, noted for its classical refinement, he much preferred the Sung-inspired *seirei* poetry. Rikunyo enjoyed the verse of the Southern Sung in particular, his favorite poets being Lu Yu and Yang Wan-li. A poem titled "The Cold Fly" by Yang Wan-li, which begins, "I see a fly/warming himself on the window sill,/rubbing his legs, enjoying the morning sun,"[6] may have been the inspiration for Rikunyo's verse titled "Frosty Dawn," below. Rikunyo found poetic material in his humble surroundings, incorporating subject matter which more conventionally-minded poets might have considered vulgar. His verse is fresh and plebeian, representing a more naturalized style of kanshi. Andō, however, is of the opinion that Rikunyo never fully assimilated the Sung style, noting a paucity of personal sentiment in his verse and characterizing his language as unrefined.[7]

◙ 128 Passing a Homestead on an Autumn Day

A brushwood gate facing a country stream,
A narrow road where people seldom pass.
Yellow butterflies seek out fragrant plants;
Red dragonflies alight on withered lotuses.
Aged eggplants have split down the middle.
On the cheeks of the cracked dates dimples have appeared.
Just chickens and dogs remain to guard the house:
The family has gone away to bring in the harvest.

Iwanami, pp. 349-350. From *Rikunyoan shishō* (A Book of Poems by Rikunyoan), 1778 (date of preface)

---

[6]Quoted from Jonathan Chaves' translation of the verse in *Sunflower Splendor: Three Thousand Years of Chinese Poetry*, p. 377.

[7]Andō, p. 247.

◔ 129 Morning Glories

The unruly tendrils of the morning glories transplanted beside the well
Have climbed their way along the railing, spreading everywhere.
Suddenly, unbeknownst to me, they've taken over the well rope,
And lately I've had to go next door to ask my neighbors for water.

Iwanami, p. 351. From *Rikunyoan shishō*, 1778

◔ 130 Returning from the Sumida River in the Evening

Evening at the weeping willow ford, I call to summon the boat.
The wild pheasant's cries linger in the mist that veils the riverbank trees.
At a wine stall where the customers tarry they've lit the lanterns early,
But paper kites still hang in the air, far off in the distant skies.

Iwanami, p. 352. From *Rikunyoan shishō*, 1778

<u>Line three</u>: "Wine stall" is more literally "pennant stall." Such shops were marked with pennants.

◔ 131 Frosty Dawn

At dawn when I woke up in my bed, the frost had half melted away.
The brilliant sunlight filling my window had already started to fade.
I lay there watching the cold flies gather on the other side of the screen,
Rubbing their front legs, falling down, then flying up again.

Fujikawa, p. 7

◙ **132**

Still too cold for signs of flowers, not a breath of wind.
Before the brazier, lost in the thoughts that come with growing old,
I suddenly recall my youth, as I sit with my chin in my hands—
Where did I once see a humming kite, aloft in the distant skies?

Fujikawa, pp. 7-8

Line four: It was the practice to attach a whistling device (*unari*) to the string of a kite.

Nishiyama Sessai, 1735-1798

Nishiyama Sessai, a native of Bitchū, part of modern Okayama prefecture, was the son of a doctor. He went to Osaka to study medicine at sixteen and also began reading the Confucian classics with Oka (Okada) Hakku (1692-1767). Hakku was apparently beginning to feel his age, for he soon found Sessai a new and younger teacher, Naba Rodō (1727-1789). Under Rodō's tutelage, Sessai concentrated on Kobunjigaku but later rejected this discipline in favor of orthodox Neo-Confucian thought. Together with *Shibano Ritsuzan, Sessai helped pave the way for Senior Councillor Matsudaira Sadanobu's anti-heterodoxy campaign of the Kansei Reforms (Kansei Igaku no Kin, 1790), which endeavored to weaken the influence of the Kobunjigaku and Kogaku schools, thereby bolstering the Chu Hsi orthodoxy which had been promoted as the ethical mainstay of the shogunate. Declining various appointments in provincial domains, Sessai eventually retired to his village where he taught and wrote Chinese verse.

Inoguchi writes that because Sessai as a young man often had severe fits of temper, he pasted on his wall the Ten Prohibitions of Buddhism so that he could contemplate them both day and night and thereby improve his behavior. By middle age, Sessai was apparently regarded as a model human being by his fellow villagers.[1] He may have improved his character, but a certain churlishness shows through nonetheless in the following single Sessai poem that we have managed to find.

---

[1]Inoguchi, p. 182.

◉ 133 Declining the Gift of a Brocaded Garment

All my life I've been used to cotton clothes;

In warm and cold weather they make me comfortable and free.

I've no love for the special warmth of a brocaded robe.

So don't make this gentleman compromise his good taste!

Inoguchi, p. 182

Title: Padded garments were used as coverlets at night. Sessai had apparently received it from a wealthy student (Inoguchi, p. 182).

Yabu Kozan, 1735-1802

Yabu Kozan was born in Higo province, modern Kumamoto prefecture. A
Teishugaku scholar by profession, he was educated as a young man in Kyoto and
Edo on a domain scholarship and became a professor at the Jishūkan, the
Kumamoto domain academy, in 1766. One of his goals was to bring the
teachings of the Jishūkan more squarely into line with Neo-Confucian doctrine,
but the academy was so firmly entrenched in Kogaku traditions that his attempt
was apparently unsuccessful.[1] During his lifetime, Kozan associated with such
prominent Confucian scholars as *Bitō Jishū, Rai Shunsui (1746-1816), and Nakai
Chikuzan (1730-1804). The first poem below is one of the longer selections in
the anthology that deals with with the peasant folk and their rural environment.
It focusses on the oft-romanticized figure of the carefree young cowherd,
describing the mundane details of his unhurried daily existence far removed from
the cares of city life. The understated simplicity and bucolic charm of this poem
give it a special appeal of its own. It is clearly reminiscent of a poem titled "The
Cowherd: A Song," by the eighth-century poet Ch'u Kuang-hsi.[2]

---

[1]Inoguchi, p. 673.

[2]For a translation of this verse, see Joseph J. Lee's rendition in *Sunflower Splendor: Three
Thousand Years of Chinese Poetry*, p. 99.

☺ 134 The Song of the Cowherd

1   Below the bank, fragrant plants in profusion;
    Upon the bank, weeping willows in abundance.
    They stand entwined, providing lovely shade,
    Their dark foliage shutting out the sunlight.
5   The cowherd is resting beneath the trees,
    A cool breeze blowing through his bamboo hat.
    An old cow has eaten her fill and stares vacantly;
    Her calf never strays from her side.
    Splashing water, the cowherd washes mud from his body,
10 Then breaks off a branch to swat at mosquitoes and gadflies.
    Lying on his back, with a river rock for a pillow,
    He and the cows forget each other.
    A distant temple bell startles him from a dream,
    The mountains now are bathed in evening sun.
15 In comfortable ease, he sits upon his ox
    And heads for home, playing his flute all the way.

Iwanami, p. 258. From *Kozan sensei ikō* (A Posthumous Text of Master Kozan's Works), 1816

☺ 135 Farewelling a Friend Who Is Returning to His Hometown

On the stone embankment we said our farewells,
Pacing back and forth till dusk had fallen.
Can the length of this vast flowing river of color
Be greater than the unending sadness of parting?

Iwanami, p. 259. From *Kozan sensei ikō*, 1816

2. An original Japanese monochrome painting of a cowherd astride an ox,
probably from the late Edo or Meiji period (1868-1912),
by an unidentified artist named Kakimata Hajime.

Shibano Ritsuzan, 1736-1807

One of the so-called "Three Great Savants" of the Kansei period, the other two
being *Bito Jishū and Koga Seiri (1750-1817), Shibano Ritsuzan is generally
better known today for his anti-heterodoxy legislation of the late-eighteenth
century than for his kanshi poetry, which was nonetheless masterful. Ritsuzan
was a native of Takamatsu in what is today Kagawa prefecture. He first learned
the fundamentals of Neo-Confucianism in Takamatsu with Gotō Shizan (1721-
1782). In his late teens he became a student of Nakamura Ranrin (1697-1761),
a disciple of *Muro Kyūsō, and later received instruction from Hayashi Ryūkō
(1681-1758). At age thirty he began to study Kokugaku (National Learning) in
Kyoto, and two years later became a scholar in the Awa domain, receiving a
salary of four hundred *koku*. He also tutored the heir apparent of the domain
lord.

Ritsuzan became a Shōheikō professor in 1788 and the same year received
an appointment as a major advisor to the shogunate. At the Shōheikō academy
he worked with Hayashi Kinpō (1733-1792) to reform the institution, endeavoring
to restore traditional Neo-Confucianism as its philosophical base while rejecting
a revival of Soraiism and various heterodoxies in the school.[1] Ritsuzan was the
prime mover behind the Kansei anti-heterodoxy laws (Kansei Igaku no Kin, 1790)
promulgated by Matsudaira Sadanobu, which outlawed instruction in Confucian
doctrine that did not fully conform to the Chu Hsi orthodoxy. With the
implementation of this law, a thorough grounding in Chu Hsi Confucianism
became the intellectual mainstay of shogunal and domainal schools as well as a
requirement for employment in shogunal posts.[2]

---

[1]Inoguchi, pp. 199-200.

[2]Maruyama, p. 280.

In his later years, when he served the shogunate in Edo, Ritsuzan was perhaps the most powerful and wealthy intellectual in the land, enjoying a sumptuous lifestyle.   He did not leave behind a large corpus of Chinese poetry—many of his poems may simply have been lost—but much of his surviving verse is of high quality.   If the first verse below is anything to judge by, Ritsuzan, despite his fortune and fame, appears to have been a modest man who had an insouciant disregard for the esteem in which others held his work.

☻ 136 In Reply to Persons Who Have Requested My Old Manuscripts

To you gentlemen who've asked me for old manuscripts and books:
These have been scattered by the wind and have turned into clouds.
Why don't you go and look for them on the clear waters of the River Lo?
The wind and the flowers, the clouds and moon—
    there's where you'll find my words!

Inoguchi, p. 204

Line three: A tributary of the Yellow River originating in China's Shensi province.

⏀ 137 Strolling in the Moonlight Beyond the Forbidden Wall

From the palace gardens the scent of cassia is borne on the wind from the west.
Beyond the Shōmeimon gate the moonlight appears like frost.
Who, I wonder, could it be, tonight in the Seiryōden,
Playing the melody "Feathered Jackets" and offering the emperor wine?

Inoguchi, p. 201

Title: The Forbidden Wall surrounds the imperial palace in Kyoto. Through this wall only high-ranking imperial retainers and important members of the nobility were allowed to pass.
Line one: The west wind is the autumn wind. The cassia blooms around this time, i.e, the lunar Eighth Month (September or October by the Gregorian calendar)—see our discussion of Ritsuzan's afterword, below, which dates this poem.
Line two: Shōmeimon: the central southern gate of the imperial palace.
Line three: The Seiryōden was a hall in the heart of the imperial palace just west of the Jijūden (Emperor's Sitting Room), where the emperor traditionally held court and made his residence. From the 1590s, it was used only for court ceremonies, a new residential building having been erected.
Line four: The full name of this Chinese melody was "Rainbow Skirts and Feathered Jackets." Yang Kuei-fei, the tragic consort of the Emperor Hsüan Tsung of the T'ang dynasty, is said to have danced to this song.

Ritsuzan wrote an afterword (for the text, see Inoguchi, p. 200) which explains the circumstances in which this verse was composed. It was evidently written on the sixteenth day of the Eighth Month, during the third watch on the day after the full moon, when Ritsuzan and his friend Minagawa Kien (1734-1807) were out strolling in the moonlight, which was as bright as day. The year was probably around 1766, which is when Ritsuzan went to Kyoto for two years to study Kokugaku. They were chilled to the bone by the freezing wind, and no one else was around. A beautiful, lustrous corona appeared around the moon, its light scattering across their sleeves. Only the first two lines of this poem were written by Ritsuzan; Kien added the next two upon hearing the clear sound of a flute piercing the cold evening air just outside the imperial palace. The entire effect was otherworldly, Ritsuzan tells us, and the poem itself took shape with a remarkable ease which Kien declared "divine."

☺ 138 Mount Fuji

Who took water from the Eastern Sea,
And washed this lovely lotus so clean?
The mountain bestrides three provinces,
A mound of eight petals piercing the skies.
Clouds and mist ring the great foothills like steam;
The sun and moon shun her central peak.
Alone she stands, ever without peer,
The grandest mountain of them all!

Sugano, p. 52; Inoguchi, p. 202. From *Ritsuzandō shishū* (Collected Poems from the Residence of Ritsuzan), 1841 (earliest extant text)

<u>Line two</u>: "Lovely lotus" is a reference to Mt. Fuji's conical shape.

Akamatsu Ranshitsu, 1743-1797

Akamatsu Ranshitsu was a native of Harima in modern Hyōgo prefecture and the son of an Akao domain scholar. He took lessons from his father, excelling in the composition of Chinese poetry. Ranshitsu later served as principal of the Hakubunkan academy, which he established as the domain school. He also had his own private school, as did many Edo kanshi poets. Ranshitsu was in his time considered one of the three great literary masters of his age, along with *Yabu Kozan and Kōno Josai (1743-1779).[1]

The first of the two poems below presents the bleak image of sleeplessness and isolation on a relentlessly stormy night. Little of the romance we commonly associate with descriptions of stormy weather in Japanese poetry is present here. While the images of rain pounding on the roof and the guttering candle are conventional in themselves, when combined with the poet's sleeplessness and the rather unusual added burden of caring for his child, they create a poignant tableau of human desolation. The second verse addresses the transience of life and the vanity of glory, both familiar philosophical themes in Chinese and Japanese verse. The poet seems resigned to his fate, determined to enjoy the pleasures of life in a manner reminiscent of the poets Li Po and Tu Fu.

---

[1] Iwanami, p. 481.

⏺ 139 Miscellaneous Thoughts

Dreary the rain that falls on the wooden roof.

Doleful the wind as it blows against the paper window.

All night I lie here, holding the baby,

With the dying lamp flickering at my side.

Iwanami, p. 264. From *Ranshitsu sensei shibunshū* (The Collected Poems and Writings of Master Ranshitsu), 1818

⏺ 140 Some Thoughts

Old graves are turned into paddy fields, and cedars and pines are cut down.

A lifetime of a hundred years is like dust before the wind.

What do wealth and rank and honor amount to in the end?

For now I'll finish my cup of wine while I am still alive!

Iwanami, p. 266. From *Ranshitsu sensei shibunshū*, 1818

Igata Reiu, 1745-1787

Igata Reiu was born into a farming family in the province of Higo, part of modern Kumamoto prefecture. He enrolled in the domain school, Jishūkan, when he was twenty-one. *Yabu Kozan, a professor at this school, was astounded by his poetic sensibilities, reportedly proclaiming on one occasion, "Li Po has been reborn!"[1] Reiu later went to Kyoto, where he received instruction in Kogaku from *Akiyama Gyokuzan, also studying Japanese poetry and the native classics with Shigeno Ikinkazu (1733-1781). In 1770, he returned to his home district to teach in a school he had founded, then accepted an appointment five years later as professor of the Jishūkan academy, where he had once been a student himself. A simple, unpretentious man, Reiu was content being among his fellow country folk, preferring his quiet, rustic surroundings to the hurly-burly world of the city. The two verses below are distinctive for their wild, almost epic, description of the awesome power of nature, portraying a rugged environment in which the poet seems to have felt fully at home.

◑ 141 Crossing Akamagaseki (Red Horse Pass) Straits

Through crashing waves and winds from afar my sailboat travels homeward.
Far in the distance, Akamagaseki, surrounded by azure waters.
Thirty-six perilous shoals we crossed, our journey nears its end;
Away on the skyline the mountains of Kyushu come into view at last.

Inoguchi, p. 173; Sugano, p. 50; Andō, p. 78. From *Rakuhan shū* (A Collection from the Shores of Pleasure), 1778

Line four: Akamagaseki is the old name for the Straits of Shimonoseki, north of the island of Kyushu. The poet's home was in Kumamoto in Kyushu.

---

[1]Inoguchi, p. 173.

◙ 142 Miscellaneous Thoughts

On Mt. Minami the trees stand alone,
Tall and stately, reaching the clouds.
A fierce wind blows unceasingly;
Mournful the sound as it breaks their branches.
They break, for pines and cedars by nature
Cannot be like willow trees.
Yet their delicate beauty should surely be loved,
And their lofty virtue is indeed hard to shake.

Inoguchi, p. 174. Probably from *Rakuhan shū*, 1778

Line one: Mt. Minami (unidentified), "South Mountain," may simply mean "southern hills" and not refer to any specific mountain.
Line eight: "Pines and cedars": symbols of steadfastness and fidelity in the Chinese tradition. In Japanese, moreover, *matsu* (pine) is homophonous with *matsu*, meaning "to wait," thus heightening the poetic associations with the notion of faithfulness.

Bitō Jishū [Seikiken], 1745-1813

The son of a boatman, Bitō Jishū, known also as Bitō Nishū, was born in Iyo, in what is now Ehime prefecture. He was a sickly child who became crippled with beriberi when he was only five. As a young man in his twenties, Jishū studied under Katayama Hokkai in Osaka, immersing himself in the discipline of Kogaku. In 1765, Hokkai formed the poetry coterie known as Kontonsha, which flourished through the 1780s. Jishū was an active member, as was Rai Shunsui, the father of the illustrious poet and historian *Rai San'yō. Jishū and Shunsui became friends first and later brothers-in-law by virtue of marrying into the same family.[1] Under the influence of Shunsui and Nakai Chikuzan, Jishū turned away from Kogaku to the more traditional Chu Hsi doctrine, championing the official orthodoxy. He became a shogunal Confucian official and a professor of the Shōheikō academy around 1790. His peers regarded him as one of the three greatest scholars of his time, the others being Koga Seiri and *Shibano Ritsuzan. Jishū was one of the chief architects of the anti-heterodoxy campaign of the Kansei period, having been recruited for this task by Matsudaira Sadanobu, chief senior councillor between 1787-1793.

Inoguchi writes that in prose composition, Jishū took Han Yü and Liu Tsung-yuan of the T'ang dynasty and Ou-yang Hsiu and Su Tung-p'o of the Sung as his models, and that in poetry he admired T'ao Yuan-ming and Liu Tsung-yuan. His own verse is characterized by plainness and simplicity. In his later years he came to enjoy the poetry of Po Chü-i and was rebuked for this interest by Koga Seiri, who disapproved of Po Chü-i's writings. *Shibano Ritsuzan tried to mediate the dispute that arose between them, but without success.

In the first of the three selections which follow, we encounter Jishū, the Confucian moralist, sternly admonishing his students to rid themselves of

---

[1]Inoguchi, p. 205.

"womanly ways" and develop strength of character. In Tokugawa society, the samurai class was gradually being converted into a civil bureaucracy. Consequently, the samurai were losing many of their martial ways and becoming corrupted by the material comforts of urban society. Jishū evidently found their dress and behavior too foppish for his liking and reminiscent of the affluent merchant class. Thus, he enjoined his disciples to return to the masculine values of frugality and asceticism. The second verse starts out as a fairly conventional nature poem and then surprises us with the farmer's act of blithe indifference to the beauty of nature, an act which leads the poet to sense a wide aesthetic gulf between himself and this peasant.

☯ 143 To My Students

1   If you wish to become a gentleman,
     First you must become a man.
     Men value firmness of principle:
     Such is the Way of Manliness.
5   Why is it that today's men
     All behave like young girls,
     Striving to be like them in speech and appearance,
     And feeling ashamed if they aren't?
     Men must behave in the proper manner—
10   Where is the shame in this?
     You must rid yourselves of your womanly ways;
     Learn quickly the meaning of "firmness of principle."
     We don't judge a horse by the color of its hair:
     A gentleman is a gentleman because of his character.

Sugano, p. 55. From *Seikiken shū* (The Seikiken Collection)

◎ **144 A Morning Walk after Rain; Following the
Rhymes of Old Master Ushiba**

Layers of scattered clouds are trailing across the peaks ahead.
With staff in hand I seek scenic spots, now that the rain has stopped.
The aged farmer doesn't realize he should cherish the beauty of spring.
He is plowing the fallen flowers under, deep into the ground.

Inoguchi, p. 207

Title: Old Master Ushiba remains unidentified.

◎ **145 An Impromptu Poem**

I sit alone beneath the eastern eaves;
A cool wind arises, bringing rain.
The insects in the grass cry unceasingly;
For whom do they grieve the whole night long?

Inoguchi, p. 207

Uragami Gyokudō, 1745-1820

Uragami Gyokudō was a renowned master of the *ch'in*, an ancient Chinese stringed instrument, as well as a renowned Nanga painter and kanshi poet. He was born in the town of Okayama in Bizen (modern Okayama prefecture), the fourth son of an Ikeda domain retainer. He is also known as Gyokudō Kinshi, "The *Ch'in* Master of Gyokudō (Jade Hall)," the "Gyokudō" being derived from the name of a Ming dynasty instrument which he purchased in 1779. Gyokudō was raised by parents who were older than normal—his father was fifty-four, and his mother forty when he was born. He was educated in the clan school, serving the Ikeda lord from the age of fifteen. Gyokudō at first performed guard duty in the lord's mansion hall but seven years later received a key appointment as shogunal administrator to the fief, at which time he took the name of his father, Heiemon, assuming his hereditary position at the same time.[1]

Around 1772, Gyokudō married a woman named Yasu, the daughter of a Bizen samurai. Her death in 1792 seems to have upset him deeply; now bereft of his wife, his parents, his brothers and sisters, and even his daimyo, he had no compelling reasons to remain in Ikeda, so he decided in 1794 to give up his domain post to travel the country with his two sons.[2] For the rest of his life Gyokudō pursued his poetry, art, and music exclusively, writing verses that show his love for nature, wine, music, and solitude. Everywhere he went, he held elegant drinking parties for his friends, his *ch'in* and brushes near him at all times.[3] In 1811, Gyokudō finally took up residence in Kyoto, where he consorted with the Nanga artist and potter Aoki Mokubei (1767-1833) and his

---

[1]Stephen Addiss, *Tall Mountains and Flowing Waters: The Arts of Uragami Gyokudō* (Honolulu: University of Hawaii Press, 1987), p. 5.

[2]Ibid., pp. 10-13.

[3]Roberts, p. 35.

group.[4] Among his other friends were *Tanomura Chikuden, Tani Bunchō (1763-1840), *Kan Sazan, and the aforementioned Minagawa Kien. Only in relatively recent times have his paintings, especially his monochrome landscapes, received the acclaim they deserve. Indeed, scholars credit him with bringing about the second flowering of the Nanga school.[5]

Much of Gyokudō's poetry is devoted to describing the pleasures of retirement in his remote cottage, a theme particularly reminiscent of *Ishikawa Jōzan. Few intellectual or philosophical concerns inform his poetry; instead we have a portrait of the consummate dilettante, a self-absorbed man of the arts whose life revolves around the solitary pastimes of writing poetry, enjoying nature, and playing the *ch'in*. Without even a lock on his door, he lives in a state of rustic seclusion, enjoying such simple pleasures as looking for mushrooms, watching the bats fly around in the eaves, and drinking pine wine. He receives visitors from time to time, yet he evinces little appreciation for their company. Indeed, his reference to their practice of carving their names in the moss near his hut leads us to wonder whether he was in fact pleased to have them there at all.

146 An Admonition

Coarse food is better than having an empty stomach,
A rough dwelling is preferable to the open spaces.
If in life you don't realize you have enough
When will your cravings ever cease?

Iriya, p. 111. From *Gyokudō Kinshi shū*, 1794

---

[4]Ibid.

[5]Ibid.

☺ 147 Retirement

1 Now that I'm retired, my remaining years are flying by.
  Poor is my health, and my mental powers are fading.
  Many long years I spent in study,
  And they laugh at me for buying this hill so late in life.
5 I have eight or nine willow trees of yellow and green,
  And on my temples hair black and white.
  New shoots of bamboo rise above the fence,
  But half my friends from the past have now grown old.
  Their money they spend on "virtue and sageliness";
10 Tired of books, they water their gardens and hedges.
  I have my *ch'in* and can enjoy it on my own—
  What need is there to wait for Chung Ch'i to come?

Iriya, p. 105. From *Gyokudō Kinshi shū* (The Collected Poems of Gyokudō, the *Ch'in* Master), 1794

Line nine: "Virtue and sageliness" was, according to the commentator, scholar's argot for clear and cloudy wines, that is, high and low quality wines, respectively (Iriya, p. 106).
Line twelve: Chung Ch'i is Chung Tzu-ch'i, a woodcutter-cum-connoisseur of music who, according to legend, became the companion of the illustrious lute player Po Ya of the Spring and Autumn period (722-468 B.C.). When Chung died, Po Ya destroyed his lute, never to play for anyone again.

☪ 148 Mountain Village on an Autumn Day

Autumn evening in the mountain village.

Leaves blow about in the chilly forest.

High in the pines, the nests of cranes.

The waters recede, a fishing islet appears.

The reeds are white, still bearing their coat of frost.

The maple leaves are red, radiant in the setting sun.

Where should I go to pick the mushrooms of the immortals?

Empty-handed, I shut the door of my house in the bamboo.

Iriya, p. 72. From *Gyokudō Kinshi shū*, 1794

Line seven: The mushroom is *reishi* or *mannentake* (*Fomes japonicus*), an edible bracket fungus which grows on dead trees and is said to promote longevity.

☪ 149

My old obsession only deepens, the colder grow the days.

I play my *ch'in* the whole day long, devoted as a priest.

At night if visitors come I gather greens from my garden at the back.

And ask my neighbor to give me a light to brew some bitter tea.

Iriya, p. 61. From *Gyokudō Kinshi shū*, 1794

Line one: He is referring to his obsession with playing the *ch'in*. Note that we see a somewhat different attitude toward the instrument in poem 152, below.

◙ 150-151 From a series titled "At Leisure in
My Mountain Abode: Nineteen Poems"

(No. 12)

Here in these hills all covered with snow, travellers are seldom seen.
Lovely valleys, beautiful trees—I close my cottage door.
My boy has poured me some pine-scented wine from an earthen pot.
Just this morning he came back home, bringing me some crabs.

Iriya, p. 91. From *Gyokudō Kinshi shū*, 1794

Line three: "Pine-scented wine," *shōshū*, is probably *shōrō*, a wine brewed using pine oil.
Line four: The subject here is not specified in the Chinese. It may instead have been Gyokudō
himself who brought back the crabs.

(No. 15)

No keyhole in the door to the cottage where I spend my days.
Rhododendron blossoms cover the ground and drift down onto my *ch'in*.
Now and then a barking dog wakes me from my dreams.
Day and night, bats fly about, up there in the eaves.

Iriya, p. 92

⏻ **152-153   From a series titled "Living as a Recluse: Ten Poems"**
(No. 4)

Morning dew moistens the flowered branches.
Bamboo shadows shift in the twilight.
Wisteria covers the door by my pine gate.
Grass buries the pond by the stone lanterns.
When I feel tired I call for wine.
After recovering I sometimes write poetry.
Playing the *ch'in* is actually wearisome;
To be idle is naturally best of all.

Iriya, p. 100. From *Gyokudō Kinshi shū*, 1794

Title: Only nine poems of the ten appear in the Iriya text of this series, which we have assumed
to be in the original sequence. It is apparently the tenth verse which is missing.

(No. 5)

At this tranquil place surrounded by mountains
The white clouds part as I roll up the blinds,
And high peaks appear, one upon the other.
My close friends trudge up here on foot.
In the morning they leave with the tame deer;
In the evening they return with my lean cows.
I only recently divined this site for my hut,
But already the green moss is covered with names.

Iriya, p. 101. From *Gyokudō Kinshi shū*, 1794

Line five: Deer are traditionally depicted in association with hermits and sages.
Line eight: It is unlikely that the poet took kindly to having his moss despoiled. Compare this
to poem 293 in which the poet indicates that he asks his guests to remove their wooden *geta*
sandals to avoid damaging the moss in his garden.

Murase Kōtei, 1746-1818

Murase Kōtei, a Kyoto native, studied with the Syncretic scholar Takeda Bairyū (1716-1766). Well-versed in the classics, Kōtei was an outstanding kanshi poet, writer of Chinese prose, and a noted painter as well. In 1783 he entered into the service of the Akita domain, helping found the Meidōkan school and drafting its charter. He retired to Kyoto to lecture in his declining years. Kōtei was a friend of *Priest Rikunyo. The first selection below is among Kōtei's best, vividly presenting the sights and sounds of an autumn evening in the countryside as experienced by a gentleman at leisure. The images of dew on the yam plants glistening in the moonlight and the pall of smoke from mosquito-fires hanging over the village are memorable, evoking with the richness of a painter's palette the tranquil bucolic beauty of the Japanese rural landscape which so captivated the artists and poets of the Edo period.

◙ 154 Evening Scene after Rain

A country riverbank wet with rain; verdant pagoda trees and willows.
After bathing I remove my head-wrap, chanting poems on the bank
    where the water-peppers grow.
On the wind comes the chirping of cicadas, cooling air descends.
A misty haze gathers on the hills, darkening as nighttime falls.
Bands of smoke hang over the huts as mosquito-fires burn,
And beneath the moon in the yam patches, dew is glistening like stars.
A child from the village appears from nowhere and walks along beside me.
He asks if he can borrow my fan so he can chase the fireflies.

Iwanami, p. 272. From *Kōtei shokō* (Kōtei's First Collection), 1783

☺ 155 Idle Amusements on a Winter's Day

I can't make out these fly-speck characters, reading by the lamp.
Glasses perch on the bridge of my nose to help me see more clearly.
I lunge to wipe my gummy eyes but cannot get at them.
My little grandson claps his hands and laughs at my careless haste.

Nakamura, p. 145. From *Kōtei nikō* (Kōtei's Second Collection), 1807

Priest Nichiken [Nikken, Chōshōan], 1746-1829

Priest Nichiken, a native of Osaka, was friends with *Kan Sazan and Rai Shunsui, and a great admirer of *Priest Gensei. He used the style name Chōshōan (Hut for Listening to the Pines), in reference to the cottage where he retired after serving as chief priest of Hōonji, a Nichiren temple in Izumo province, modern Shimane prefecture. It is perhaps this hut which provides the setting for the poems below. The images of buzzing insects, the sweat-soaked robe, and the burning heat in the first verse create a vividly oppressive summer atmosphere. Here, we begin to see the homey earthiness which was increasingly present in kanshi from the mid-eighteenth century onward. The second poem contrasts markedly with the first, showing a different side of summer, with the slanting rain, clean sky, and cool moon enhancing the poet's enjoyment of the nocturnal beauty of his surroundings.

◐ 156 An Impromptu Poem to Record a Sight

Midday cicadas buzzing around as I lie here in my hut.
Sweat has soaked my robe of hemp; I suddenly awake from a dream.
Young boys give no thought at all to escaping the summer heat.
They gather at my gate and call to each other, as dragonflies they catch.

Iwanami, p. 356. From *Chōshōan shishō* (A Book of Poems by Chōshōan)

◐ 157 The Summer Moon

A fierce gust of wind comes up; in a trice my window grows dark.
A slanting shower of driving rain soaks the wooded garden.
After a while the clouds disperse, the heavens now seem cleansed.
The cool moon, so lovely and remote, shines down upon my hut.

Iwanami, p. 357. From *Chōshōan shishō*

Akada Gagyū, 1747-1822

Akada Gagyū, a native of Hida province in what is today Gifu prefecture, was born into a sake-brewing family. Like so many of his merchant-class contemporaries he transcended his origins, becoming a Confucian scholar and kanshi poet of some note. He was a great admirer of the philosophical works of *Ogyū Sorai and *Dazai Shundai and enjoyed the poetry of *Hattori Nankaku. Gagyū was largely self-taught, but he studied for a period with *Emura Hokkai, later making his living by teaching the Confucian classics at his private school, called Seishūkan. He was a friend of the poet *Tachi Ryūwan.

Gagyū is not well known as a poet, but his work has considerable appeal nonetheless. Both verses below find the poet dwelling in rustic seclusion, writing poems in his proverbial scholar's hut as nighttime descends. The first of the poems shows the equanimity of a man who, although pleased to have visitors at his mountain retreat, is equally content in solitude with just the moon as his companion. The second verse captures with subtle precision the brooding atmosphere of an approaching storm, tracing the transition from dusk to darkness. Japanese poets show a particular fondness for autumn, with its brisk winds, driving rain, and falling leaves. The withering of the landscape in late autumn is an omnipresent reminder of the impermanence of human life, evoking melancholy emotions in both the poet and the reader alike. In the Chinese and Japanese eremitic tradition, the hut represents the most minimal buffer between man and nature. It is also the physical representation of the scholar's wish to live apart from the material trappings of civilization and escape its responsibilities.

◉ 158 My Mountain Dwelling

Outside my dwelling, high in the sky, a pale scar of a moon.
In the hills a myriad dots—plum blossoms all around.
At times I read aloud good verse while entertaining friends.
Nights I sit here drinking tea in the stillness of my window.

Iwanami, pp. 274-275. From *Gagyū shū* (The Collected Works of Gagyū), 1825

◉ 159 Autumn Rain at Night; I Was Assigned the Rhyme-Word "Rain"

Boundless are the autumn clouds, it's growing dark in my hut.
Leaves fall with a rustling sound, consigned to the dirt and dust.
The wind shakes the scattered trees—it looks as if someone's there.
So much rain, the Pashan rains, have fallen since last night.

Iwanami, p. 275. From *Gagyū shū*, 1825

Line four: Pashan (Mt. Pa) is located in China's Shensi province. This line alludes to a poem by the T'ang poet Li Shang-yin (813?-858), the first couplet of which reads, "You asked me when I would be coming back, but there is no certain date./The nighttime rains falling at Mt. Pa have caused the autumn ponds to rise...." (our translation). Thus, "the Pashan rains" came to be synonymous with heavy rain.

Kan Sazan, 1748-1827

The son of a prosperous farmer, Kan Sazan (also known as Kan Chazan), was a native of Kannabe in Bingo, part of modern Hiroshima prefecture. A scholar of the Teishugaku orthodoxy, he was considered in his time to be one of the most individualistic and renowned of all kanshi poets. As a young man he was trained in medicine and studied Neo-Confucianism under Naba Rodō of Kyoto. Rodō's other pupils included Nakai Chikuzan and *Nishiyama Sessai, who became Sazan's close friends. After completing his formal education, Sazan returned to his home district in 1781, opening a school which looked out at maple-covered hills and was appropriately named Kōyō Sekiyō Sonsha (The Country Cottage of Sunsets and Autumn Leaves). This institution acquired the highest reputation, attracting young men from all across the country, and later expanded to become the official village academy, receiving subsidies and book allowances from the domain. It was subsequently renamed Renjuku, and Sazan continued to serve as its head. He took care of the poet *Rai San'yō for a time during San'yō's years of semi-detention.

Despite his national fame, Kan Sazan kept a relatively low profile, remaining in his home district most of the time. In fact, Lord Abe of the Fukuyama domain, where Sazan resided, was unaware of his existence until quite late in Sazan's career. According to one story, once when Lord Abe was discussing poetry with the Confucian scholar Hayashi Jussai (1768-1841) in Edo, the latter mentioned Sazan, praising him as the finest poet in the land. Abe was reportedly amazed that such a distinguished literatus had been living in his domain for so long without his knowledge and promptly sought to employ him.[1] Sazan served first as an occasional advisor, from about 1800, and then later as the compiler of *The Chronicles of Fukuyama*, finally rising to the position of *daimetsuke* (senior

---

[1]Inoguchi, p. 223.

censor) in 1823. He died a few years later of a stomach ailment, at age eighty, having been preceded in death by his first and second wives and lacking any heirs.

Sazan was reportedly a large, rugged-looking man who had an imposing presence without being intimidating. Despite his fame, he was never pompous and reportedly behaved in a friendly manner toward all people, regardless of their status. Frugal yet generous, he periodically gave money to victims of natural disasters.[2] Sazan's poetry was in keeping with his unpretentious, magnanimous manner, being composed largely in the direct, realistic styles of the Sung dynasty. He used his everyday surroundings as poetic material, employing plain language that avoided empty ornamentalism. His style is often likened to that of Rikunyo, although the two men never met until 1794.[3] In Keene's words, Sazan was skilled at finding "a happy medium between the startling and the familiar," and in his opinion, Sazan may have been a better poet than Rikunyo,[4] although this point is debatable. Among his most appealing poems are those featuring scenes from the workaday lives of village folk—girls catching octopi on the seashore (poem 169) and deer-hunters returning home with their bounty (poem 170), for example—which provide a colorful picture of the graceful rhythm and dignity of life in the countryside.

---

[2]Ibid., pp. 223-224.

[3]*WWW*, p. 547.

[4]Ibid., p. 548.

⚫ **160 From a series titled "Miscellaneous Verses**
on Autumn: Twelve Poems"

(No. 1)

Warm sun shining at noon; dew still sparkling on the bush.

Withered flowers mingled together, purple and yellow their hues.

The praying mantis is used to seeing visitors at this spot;

Languidly it shifts from the flowering reeds to where the water-peppers grow.

Sazan, p. 16

Title: The original number of this verse and the next within the series cannot be determined from this edition. We have numbered these one and two for convenience only.

(No. 2)

Autumn colors in the country garden; cold and clear the day.

Crickets chirping in the hedge, even in broad daylight.

Bolls of cotton ready to burst, branches growing heavier.

Gourds near ripe and drooping down from their wooden frame.

Sazan, p. 16; Fujikawa, p. 36

⚫ **162 Plum Rains**

The plum rains have fallen day after day, the skies have yet to clear.

I delight in seeing the pillars of my house reflected in the newly-risen waters.

The dry spell of the previous year lasted well into autumn,

And the markets along the river rang with water-vendors' cries.

Hirano, p. 229

Line one: Plum rains refers to the yearly summer monsoon from around early June to early-mid July.

◑ 163 Reading on a Winter's Night

Snow surrounds my mountain dwelling, trees cast shadows deep.

The bell beneath the eaves hangs motionless, here in the dead of night.

I quietly tidy my scattered books and ponder points in doubt.

The pale blue plume of flame in my lamp illuminates the minds of the ancients.

Sugano, p. 60; Inoguchi, p. 227. From *Kōyō sekiyō sonsha shi* (Poems from the Country Cottage of Sunsets and Autumn Leaves), 1812 (1st ed.), 1823 (2nd ed.), and 1832 (posthumous ed.)

◑ 164 Ninth poem in a series titled "Miscellaneous Verses on Winter: Ten Poems"

Chilly birds chase one another into the scattered pines.

Across the valley at the lonely temple softly tolls a bell.

A mountain wind suddenly arises, whisking the dusk clouds away.

Snow has fallen on several peaks that rise southwest of here.

Iwanami, p. 283. From *Kōyō sekiyō sonsha shi*, 1812-1832

◑ 165

The air was filled with flakes of snow, my room was cold last night.

Bedding and curtains pierced by the chill; I didn't sleep well at all.

A friend of mine then happened to call, bearing a gift of new wine.

After one cup I was finally able to open the window and look out.

Sazan, p. 161

The winter of 1814-1815 brought much more snow than usual. This poem, like the next, was probably written in the Tenth or Eleventh Month of 1814, when Sazan was in Edo visiting friends, far from his home.

🌙 166

Old and feeble yet braving the cold, I stand in the shadows by the wall.
No need to search for inspiration and labor over my verse:
Although the snow falls in our province every single year,
Never before have I ever seen snow deeper than a foot!

Sazan, p. 152

This poem was written in 1814 on the eighth day of the lunar Eleventh Month when Sazan was visiting friends in Kanda, an area of Edo.

🌙 167

What hamlet isn't busy now with agricultural tasks?
Those who toil the hardest of all are right here in this village!
Torches of pine burn here and there, flickering in the dark.
Laughing and singing, the young girls sort the rice seedlings by night.

Sazan, p. 90

🌙 168

No rain for more than twenty days at the village by the river.
The rocky shallows and sandy shoals have started drying up.
Cicadas buzz in the noontime lanes from the shade of the locust trees.
A boy from the mountains is selling sweetfish, walking from house to house.

Fujikawa, p. 29

Line three: The locust (*Sophora japonica*) is a hard-wooded leguminous tree, also known variously as the Chinese scholar tree or the Japanese pagoda tree.

☺ 169 En Route to Kamogata

The fisherman are no longer rapping their boats, a faint mist hangs on the water.
Dewy reeds, breeze in the rushes, winds through the old burial ground.
The tide retreats and the evening shore is now a stretch of sand.
Girls are calling out to each other, catching octopi in the sea.

Fujikawa, pp. 29-30

Line one: Rapping the side of the boat was a traditional method of attracting fish to the lures.

☺ 170

Cold stars are twinkling brightly above my woodland hut.
Over the cedars a solitary cloud hangs frozen, motionless.
At the house next door noise and excitement—what's it all about?
Some villagers have caught a deer and brought it back on a pole.

Fujikawa, p. 30

☺ 171 On the Road

The twilight sun shines into the willow forest.
Evening has come, but the sandy bay is not yet dark.
A mother cow and her young calf
Are lowing at each other from opposite sides of the river.

Iwanami, pp. 284-285. From *Kōyō sekiyō sonsha shi*, 1812-1832

☾ 172   Written for a Wine Shop Customer Who
Asked Me to Write Something on His Fan

One cup of wine a man can drink;
Three cups of wine and the wine drinks him!
I've no idea whose words these are,
But we'd all do well to take note of them!

Inoguchi, p. 224

☾ 173   The Butterfly

A strong breeze blows through the flowering trees.
Blossoms fall, landing on the poet's bench.
A petal suddenly returns to the branch—
It turns out to be a butterfly!

Inoguchi, p. 225

☾ 174   On the Tamamizu Road

The mountains stretch in a green line from the northern to the southern capitals.
The Yodo River flows along, angling into the river Kasagi.
For years no horses with bells and yokes have travelled this abandoned road.
Angelica and paeonia now grow in profusion throughout these springtime fields.

Inoguchi, p. 230; Fujikawa, p. 40

Title: Tamamizu is a reference to the Idenotama River (Idenotamagawa) in Yamashiro province south of Kyoto. This verse was written in 1794 while the poet was en route to Ise from Yamato province.
Line one: The northern capital refers to Kyoto, the southern capital to Yoshino. Yoshino, southeast of Nara, was where Godaigo established a rival imperial court in 1336. The half-century (1336-1392) during which the Yoshino court existed is known as the period of the Northern and Southern Courts (Nanboku-chō). See also the notes to poem 200, below.

☺ 175 Travelling to Yoshino

Behold the sight of a thousand trees, their flowers all abloom.
A vast expanse of snowy white is all that I can see.
Nearby I hear some people talking but can't tell where they are—
The sound of their voices reaches me from within a fragrant cloud.

Inoguchi, p. 230

☺ 176 On the Seventeenth Anniversary of My Mother's Death

My dreams of the past are distant and hazy, now in the seventeenth spring.
Plum blossoms bloom in the drizzling rain, another fragrant day.
Before her grave I prostrate myself, my hair completely white—
I, who was once a babe in arms, nursing at her breast.

Inoguchi, p. 230; Hirano, p. 231

☺ 177 Written Impromptu One Summer Day

Here in the outskirts the clouds have dispersed, the evening sky is clear.
Overhead shines the Milky Way—it seems to have a voice.
The children next door are still awake, enjoying the evening cool.
They follow me, asking the names of the stars, as I stroll with my poet's stick,
    chanting verse.

Inoguchi, p. 231

208

☺ 178 The Road Ahead Is Hard

The Chiang and Han rivers still stir my emotions,

But I cannot navigate the waves of this world.

I can fathom the eclipses of the sun and the moon,

But I cannot understand your heart's inner workings.

The old well vows that in a hundred years its water will never turn choppy.

The road blocked by thorny brambles will be seen by the world no more.

If anyone were to shine a Ch'in mirror upon me,

They'd find that I, your wife, have a heart pure and true.

Inoguchi, p. 231

Lines five and six: The old well whose water remains placid is an image of fidelity, while the blocked road represents a woman living in seclusion, faithful to her husband.
Line seven: "Ch'in mirror" is literally "a Ch'in dynasty mirror for illuminating the internal organs." These were semi-mythical bronze mirrors, believed to have been cast during the Ch'in dynasty (221-207 B.C.) and supposedly endowed with magical properties, including the power to exorcise demons, cure illnesses, and, as seen here, reveal a person's true nature.

☺ 179 On the Kashiwadani Road

Tumbled rocks and gravel slips; I cannot find my way.

On the wind that blows through pines and cedars comes

    the crowing of cocks at noon.

Peace reigns within the Four Seas, no idle land to be found.

Farmland stretches up the mountains to the layers of clouds above.

Hirano, pp. 229-230, Inoguchi, p. 230

Title: This road has not been identified.

⬛ 180 Written on the Way to Visiting My Sick Sister

Late cherry blossoms have come into bloom, the early ones have withered.
A wind from the forest has blown all day, and yet it has not been cold.
The Second Month and the Third Month are the best times of the year,
But just how often in this life are we able to enjoy their beauty?

Hirano, p. 230

Line three: These months in the lunar calendar roughly correspond to March and April, that is,
early to mid-Spring.

Ichikawa Kansai, 1749-1820

An important Confucianist and eminent kanshi poet, Ichikawa Kansai was born in the Kanra district of Kōzuke in what is today Gunma prefecture, an area that produced relatively few scholars of Chinese studies.[1] He was taught by his father, Yamase Rantai, a retainer of the Kawagoe domain and former disciple of Hosoi Kōtaku (1658-1735). In his twenties Kansai briefly served with his older brother as a Kawagoe retainer in the domain's Edo residence. But he left without permission at the age of twenty-seven, adopted the surname Ichikawa for reasons that are unclear, and married the daughter of a scholar from Kōzuke in 1775, only to leave her the following year to return to Edo.[2]

Late in 1776, Kansai commenced studying under Hayashi Masayoshi in Edo. He served as secretary of the Shōheikō academy between 1783-1787 and then as a professor there before resigning in 1790, the year Sadanobu's Anti-Heterodoxy laws were passed.[3] Although Kansai claimed ill health, the intellectual oppression of the 1790 campaign was surely the precipitating factor in his resignation: his own monthly salary had apparently been cut in half as a penalty for reading "heterodox" literature.[4] In 1791, Kansai accepted an invitation to become a professor in the Toyama domain school, where he was to remain for more than twenty years. He continued to make visits to Edo during this period. The second poem below suggests that he endured a degree of material hardship in this outlying post.

---

[1]Some sources give his birthplace as Edo.

[2]Ōsone, p. 99.

[3]Reference to Kansai's position as secretary is found in Ōsone, ibid.; Inoguchi, p. 215, makes him the head of the school.

[4]*NKD*, p. 32; Ōsone, p. 99.

In his poetry, Kansai followed Sung models, which he preferred for their simple, unaffected language. While in Edo, he founded the prestigious Kōkosha poetry society, which met in the old Kanda-Otamagaike district and numbered *Kashiwagi Jotei, *Ōkubo Shibutsu, and *Kikuchi Gozan among its members. The poets in this club showed a particular interest in urban popular life, portraying, for example, scenes in the lives of geisha in the pleasures quarters of Yoshiwara in Edo, as seen below. In fact, we find among Kansai's works, and those of his peers, some of the earliest examples of urban genre poems. Kansai attracted hundreds of aspiring poets to his society from far and wide, his personal magnetism surely being a factor in the society's popularity. Indeed, he was famous for his warmth, sincerity, and kindness, but he also had a reputation as a man with grit and backbone. He would not tolerate misconduct on anyone's part, yet was always willing to help those in trouble.[5] Kansai enjoyed a stellar reputation rivalling that of *Kan Sazan, the other great poet of his day, who lived far away in Hiroshima prefecture.

Kansai's poems show the influence of the *seirei* style, and are highly varied in their subject matter and themes. Many are charming little vignettes of rural society, capturing scenes in the lives of the common folk with dignity and freshness while avoiding undue sentimentality. Mundane events in his own life—lunch being late when the firewood was soaked by rain, visits from old friends, and the like—are also depicted, often with humor and in the same matter-of-fact manner. In short, Kansai's verse subtlely conveys the rhythm, atmosphere, and colors of everyday life in Edo Japan with a vividness and originality seldom surpassed by other poets in this anthology.

---

[5]Andō, p. 93.

◉ 181 Waiting for the Ferry

A vast expanse of rolling waters brushed by a rosy sunset.
Folk heading homeward, anxious to cross, stand in the sandy shallows.
From the broad shoreline they call to the ferryman, but no reply is heard.
Smoke from evening cooking fires veils the houses by the willows.

Iwanami, p. 276. From Kansai sensei ikō (A Posthumous Text of Master Kansai's Works), 1821

◉ 182 Fourth poem in a series titled "Miscellaneous Verses Written after It Had Snowed: Five Poems"

The fifth-watch wind blows chilly air in through the torn paper screen.
This body of mine, eight *shaku* long, is curled up like a bow.
Several icicles hang from the eaves, reaching down to the ground.
The moon in the sky is glistening brightly beyond the crystal blinds.

Iwanami, p. 276. From *Kansai sensei ikō*, 1821

Title: These verses were written in the Eleventh or Twelfth Month of 1791 when the poet had just arrived at the Toyama fief to take up his appointment (Iwanami, p. 276).
Line one: The fifth watch was between 3:00 A.M. and 5:00 A.M.
Line two: He is curled up presumably to stay warm. A *shaku* was slightly less than a foot long. Kansai must have been speaking loosely here.
Line four: "Crystal blinds" means blinds covered in frost.

◉ 183 The Fisherman

On the clear river in the slanting sunlight he moors his solitary boat.
The water so pure that the fish swimming past will not take a hook.
He drains the wine in his earthenware flask, then falls into the deepest sleep.
A dragonfly lands silently atop his bamboo pole.

Iwanami, p. 277. From *Kansai sensei ikō*, 1821

◑ 184 A Temple after Rain

The wind has blown away the clouds, the showers have abated.
An autumn scene in a Zen garden, clear the evening sky.
The tall pines are shady and peaceful; no one passes by.
In the setting sun before the gate a priest stands sweeping leaves.

Iwanami, p. 278. From *Kansai sensei ikō*, 1821

◑ 185 On the Coolness of the Rain

A sudden shower brings cooling air, the night sky quickly clears.
Distant thunderbolts lost on the horizon, their sound still lingering on.
Plantain leaves hang heavily, the wind too weak to move them.
Bamboo and tree branches bending low; the moon has a special charm.
By the corner of the eaves a cloud of mosquitoes swarms around a burning torch.
In the middle of the pond a school of fish swim in the pristine waters.
The old men are feeling comfortable, wearing their summer robes,
Hands behind their backs at the Southern Pavilion, watching the Big Dipper sink.

Iwanami, p. 278. From *Kansai sensei ikō*, 1821

Line three: The leaves hang heavily because they are laden with moisture from the fallen rain.
Line eight: The Big Dipper, part of the Ursa Major, was moving to the northeast at this time (Iwanami, p. 279).

The poet composed this verse while living in Toyama (Iwanami, p. 279).

◑ 186 A Spring Jaunt

I amble slowly down a village path through the greenery.
Emerald willows, pink peach trees, water high against the banks.
I've barely left the town behind, but already my ears feel cleansed.
The cry of a wild pheasant fills the air as the sun begins to rise.

Iwanami, p. 279. From *Kansai sensei ikō*, 1821

214

187 When Seiryō Came to Visit from the Capital

When we met again there were gaps in our teeth, our heads already bald.
We had ten years' worth of stories to tell, the bitter and the sweet.
When my daughter heard that a guest from Kyoto had come to pay a visit,
She came and stole a peek at us, through the half-lowered blinds.

Nakamura, p. 146

Title: Seiryō is unidentified.

188 My Guests Have Departed

My guests have departed, the study is empty, now at the second watch.
I brew another pot of tea with water from the rocky spring.
The moon is low, the hour late; at last I can settle down.
Crickets are chirping everywhere amidst the autumn stillness.

Inoguchi, p. 217

Line one: The second watch was between 9:00 P.M. and 11:00 P.M.

189 A Word to My Child

Sunlight bakes my window; spring is in the air.
Reading makes me sleepy and I yawn and stretch.
Don't shout at the maid just because lunch is late!
Last night the firewood was badly soaked by rain.

Nakamura, p. 147

◙ 190

She's had a hangover since the night before, and today lies in bed
  as the flowers bloom.
Over and over she calls for a tonic to cure her drunken state.
The young maid goes down the stairs, and without even leaving the house,
Shouts repeatedly through the blinds to someone across the street.

Nakamura, p. 181. From *Hokuri no uta* (Poems from Hokuri [Yoshiwara])

Title: This poem and other verses in this group of individually untitled songs describe geisha from the district of Yoshiwara, a famous pleasure district in old Edo (modern Tokyo).
Line three: "Young maid" is *kamuro* (*kaburo*) in the original, a geisha in training, between the ages of six and fourteen, who assists a fully-fledged geisha.
Line four: Probably a medicine-seller.

Ryū Kinkei, 1752-1824

Ryū Kinkei was a native of Aki in modern Hiroshima prefecture. As a boy, he was educated at the Hiroshima domain school.[1] Kinkei took a special interest in Kobunjigaku and later studied this discipline under Fukuyama Hōshū (1724-1785). He eventually received a teaching appointment at a village school and established his own school in Aki, called Seibundō, also known as Seibunkan. Kinkei retired to Hirano-chō in modern Osaka-fu where he again opened a private academy. "Hearing Fulling Blocks," the second selection below, stands out as an archetypal travel poem, reflecting what was a favorite theme in kanshi. The pounding of fulling blocks was one of the few human sounds to be heard late at night in a village and often brought feelings of nostalgia for home to the sleepless traveller.

☻ 191 A Poem for the Cowherd

He plays his flute in the autumn wind to farewell the crows heading home.
Whip dangling down, in the gloaming he rides on a path
    that slants through the fields.
Astride his ox he lifts a hand and points at a spot in the distance:
"There in the village where smoke is rising—that's where you'll find
    my house!"

Iwanami, p. 282. From *Seibunkan shishū*, 1819

---

[1]One source gives Kinkei's teacher as Terada Rinsen, but this is clearly an impossibility since Rinsen died in 1744, almost a decade before Kinkei's birth. See *NKD*, p. 718.

⏻ 192 Hearing Fulling Blocks

Autumn descends upon the myriad houses.

The clear sound of fulling blocks is brought by the wind.

Their distant echoes reach the edge of the forest.

I listen to the noise as I lie on my pillow.

From chilly skies frost will soon appear;

Over dawn trees the moon still shines.

Here by my lone lamp with nothing to do

The nostalgia of the traveller grows ever deeper.

Iwanami, pp. 281-282. From *Seibunkan shishū* (A Collection of Poetry from the Seibunkan), 1819.

Line two: Fulling cloth entailed shrinking and thickening it with moisture, heat, and pressure. The Japanese used wooden blocks in this process.

⏻ 193 A Poem in Three-, Five-, and Seven-Character Lines

The dawn cocks crow,

The morning moon descends.

Yesterday can never be today.

New alliances replace the old.

If there were no partings or meetings during our hundred years on earth,

What need would there be for grief and happiness to play a part in our lives?

Iwanami, p. 281. From *Seibunkan shishū*, 1819

Title: This poem is irregular in form, beginning with a couplet of three-character lines, followed by a couplet of five, and ending with a couplet of seven. This triangular structure is somewhat apparent even in the English translation. The earliest known example of such a poem is one by Li Po (Iwanami, p. 445).

Rai Shunpū, 1753-1825

A member of a family of distinguished scholars, Rai Shunpū came from Takehara in Aki, in modern Hiroshima prefecture. He had two brothers: *Rai Kyōhei, his junior, and Rai Shunsui, the eldest of the brothers and the father of *Rai San'yō. Shunpū studied Confucianism with Shunsui and also trained as a doctor. He was active in the Kontonsha poetry society and served the Asano lord as an official in the Aki domain. The members of Kontonsha were said to have summed up the personalities and appearances of the brothers with shapes, calling Shunpū a circle, in that he was round in shape and mellow in personality, magnanimous, and a true gentleman. By contrast, his elder brother Shunsui was described as a square, because of his seriousness and his strict approach to Neo-Confucian doctrine.[1]

Shunpū wrote several highly-regarded historical works but was not prolific as a poet, writing only when the spirit moved him and having no particular ambition to accumulate a large body of work.[2] Fujikawa writes that his poetry lacks individuality,[3] but the verses below have a refreshingly down-to-earth quality that makes them most appealing. The second poem seems especially poignant, with Shunpū expressing quiet resignation over his old age and declining health.

---

[1]Fujikawa, p. 54.

[2]Ibid.

[3]Ibid.

◉ 194 On the Road to Meguro

Fragrant breezes outside the city, blowing for more than ten *ri*.
Noontime, and the roosters crow as I enter the farming village.
Rustic lads have gathered here—what could be going on?
The elders are seated at their desks, composing village documents.

Fujikawa, p. 56. From *Shunpūkan shishō* (A Book of Poems from the Academy of Shunpū), comp. 1803, pub. 1841 (date of preface). Shunpūkan may have been a style name of this poet.

Title: Meguro is a ward in modern Tokyo, old Edo. Shunpū was sojourning in Edo at the time.

◉ 195 Leisure Pursuits

Where should one go to stroll and chant verse?
To the forest and to where the river flows.
As the sun goes down the crows recognize their trees.
In the light rain the bamboos float in the mist.
The long days I spend immersed in poetry,
Gazing at the flowers and recalling my youth.
Now that I'm ill, I do very little else
Except brew my medicine with water from the spring in front.

Iwanami, p. 289; Fujikawa, p. 55. From *Shunpūkan shishō*, 1841

◉ 196

Just lately I hoed some barren land and made a little garden.
Tender willows and a patch of maples I planted with these hands.
The moon shines down on my bamboo gate where no guests come and knock.
Now and then the sounds of autumn join me as I mournfully chant.

Fujikawa, p. 55. From *Shunpūkan shishō*, 1841

Rai Kyōhei [Shunsō, Shunsōdō], 1756-1834

A Confucian scholar, kanshi poet, and domain official, Rai Kyōhei was a native of Takehara in Aki in modern Hiroshima prefecture. He was the youngest of the three Rai brothers (the eldest being Shunsui) and the uncle of *Rai San'yō. At eighteen (twenty-five according to another source), Kyōhei went with his brother Shunpū to Osaka to join Shunsui, receiving instruction in the Confucian classics before returning to Aki to serve in the domain. The most scholarly of the three brothers, he was active in Katayama Hokkai's Kontonsha coterie. In this circle he developed his scholastic poetic style, which displays individuality bordering on eccentricity, as well as erudition and eloquence. Apparently, his vocabulary was noted even in its day for its novelty and complexity.[1] Just as his brothers Shunpū and Shunsui were likened to a circle and a square, respectively, Kyōhei was described by his Kontonsha peers as a triangle,[2] a comparison that must somehow be related to the individuality of his poetic style.

Shunsui later took Kyōhei to Edo where he received instruction from Hattori Rissai (1736-1800), a scholar in the *Yamazaki Ansai tradition. In 1785, in what was a rare double appointment, Kyōhei was invited to lecture on Chu Hsi Confucianism in the Aki (Hiroshima) domain, joining Shunsui who had begun teaching there five years earlier. He later took over from Shunsui as tutor for the heir to the daimyo in the domain's Edo residence. He moved into various political administrative positions thereafter, building up a distinguished record of achievements. Kyōhei was finally allowed to retire in 1830, remaining in Aki and spending his final years communing with nature and writing his beloved Chinese poetry.

---

[1]Fujikawa, p. 57.

[2]Ibid., pp. 54, 57.

⬛ 197 A Miscellaneous Poem Written while Visiting Edo

Brightly shines the moon over Edo, city of eight hundred and eight roads.
The chirping of insects offered for sale fills the air as the autumn winds blow.
The well-born never realize that the sounds coming from the cages
Are the cries of longing for the wind and dew of the city's western outskirts.

Hirano, pp. 235, Inoguchi, p. 262. Probably from *Shunsōdō shishō* (A Book of Poems by Shunsōdō), 1833

⬛ 198 One rainy evening I spent the night in the Double-White Hall in Takehara. My elder brother Shunpū built it to receive my [other] elder brother Shunsui. Both brothers are now dead. For this reason the Hall is called "Double-White." In sadness I have written this poem.

Rain is dripping down from the eaves, making a dreary sound.
I've trimmed the snuff of the wick to the end, for I find I cannot sleep.
The Double-White Hall is empty now, nary a soul in sight.
But the rain still sounds the way it did those years we slept side by side.

Hirano, p. 236. Probably from *Shunsōdō shishō*, 1833

Title: White is a color associated with death.

⬛ 199 Paying a Visit to Kan Sazan at Kannabe Posthouse

At the posthouse gate I dismounted my horse, the sun had already set.
Yet I managed to recognize Sazan's cottage, there in the weeping willows.
The moment I saw him I was filled with delight for the old fellow looked so well,
With his ruddy face and his snowy hair, and his jacket made of white linen.

Iwanami, p. 291. From *Shunsōdō shishō*, 1833

Title: Kannabe, Sazan's hometown, is the modern village of the same name in Hiroshima prefecture. It was a post town along the San'yōdō circuit.
Line four: "White linen" is linen woven from plantain fibers, a very plain fabric.

◑ 200 Travelling to Yoshino

Multitudes of drunken folk have ruined the fragrant shrubs.

The deep emotions that I feel—are they shared by anyone else?

It grieves me that the last pink blossoms are drifting toward the North,

On the wind that blows o'er the Engen tomb, scattering all the flowers.

Sugano, p. 76; Iwanami, p. 292; Inoguchi, p. 258. From *Shunsōdō shishō*, 1833

Line two: "Deep emotions" refers to the poet's melancholy over the fate of Emperor Go-Daigo (r. 1319-38), who had been exiled from the Kyoto court to nearby Yoshino, near the city of Nara. Line four: The Engen tomb is the burial place of Emperor Go-Daigo. It is located in the temple Kongōbuji in Yoshino, where Go-Daigo established the Southern Court after being driven from Kyoto. During a sixty-year period in the fourteenth century this court was in competition with the so-called Northern Court, established by his elder brother Emperor Go-Fukakusa (1336-1392). Kyōhei laments that no one seems to remember the sad fate of Go-Daigo, whose Southern Court he and many others considered to be the legitimate one. Even the flowers blow northward, suggesting an affinity for the Northern Court of Kyoto, in an act of symbolic disloyalty. This verse was written in the Third Month of 1828 when the poet took his nephew *Rai San'yō to Yoshino (Inoguchi, p. 259).

◙ 201 Song of the Giant White Radish (*Daikon*)

1   Have you not seen
    The Mihara *daikon* that grow as big as your thigh?
    If you boil and eat them after frost, you'll find them as sweet as milk.
    Have you not seen
5   The Satō type? These are as thin as your finger!
    Several feet in length they grow, their taste delicious and mild.
    All things have their heaven-sent gifts, each has its special appeal.
    What can possess all virtues at once and be praised by all the world?
    Things that are plump we cannot discard, and the thin are good as well.
10 Flying Swallow, Jade Bracelet—who could dislike either of them?
    With all the different vegetables and fish the very same thing is true.
    Our only cause for regret would be if the chef hadn't made enough food!

Fujikawa, pp. 57-58. *Shunsōdō shishō*, 1833

Line ten: Flying Swallow (Fei Yen) was the name of the slender consort of Emperor Ch'eng of the Former Han dynasty, while Jade Bracelet (Yü Huan) was the nickname of Yang Kuei-fei, the plump favorite of Emperor Hsüan-tsung of the T'ang dynasty. This entire line is taken verbatim from a poem by Su Tung-p'o (1037-1101).

Priest Ryōkan, 1758-1831

One of the most translated of Japanese poets, Priest Ryōkan (original name Yamamoto Eizō) was a native of Izumozaki in Echigo, part of modern Niigata prefecture. A member of the Sōtō Zen sect, he was a master of Zen-style painting, a notable calligrapher, and a distinguished writer of both Chinese and Japanese verse. Ryōkan was the eldest son of Inan (1738-1795), a pro-imperial village headman, Shinto priest, and haikai poet who committed suicide in Kyoto in 1795, possibly, as Donald Keene speculates, because his activities in support of an imperial restoration had come to the attention of the shogunate.[1] At eleven, Ryōkan began receiving instruction from Ōmori Shiyō at Kyōsenjuku, his academy.[2] After a period of youthful dissipation, at eighteen he took his Buddhist vows at the nearby Kōshōji temple under the guidance of Priest Genjō Haryō.

Ryōkan next studied as a disciple of Dainin Kokusen at Entsūji, a temple located in Tamashima, in Bitchū province, modern Okayama prefecture. Ryōkan became a fully-fledged Zen priest, after which he remained in Tamashima for about a decade, doing itinerant begging (*takuhatsu*). For years, he declined to take charge of a temple of his own and lived largely on the income derived from begging, a lifestyle considered unusual for priests of his status.[3]

In 1791 Kokusen died, and Ryōkan set off on a five-year pilgrimage, sleeping outdoors or in humble lodgings and generally avoiding populated urban areas. We know little of his travels, but it is at least certain that he visited points in

---

[1] *WWW*, p. 494.

[2] See the notes to poem 203 for information concerning this teacher.

[3] Watson 1976, p. 88.

southern Shikoku as well as Kyoto.[4] Ryōkan eventually went back to Echigo. From 1797 to 1816 he lived almost continuously in a hut called Gogōan (The Five Measures of Rice Retreat), behind the Kokujōji temple on the slopes of Mt. Kugami.[5] At Gogōan he read the ancient verse of the eighth-century *Man'yōshū* anthology, as well as the poetry of the legendary T'ang poet Han-shan, major influences upon his Japanese and Chinese poetry, respectively.[6]

As Ryōkan grew older and more feeble, he found it increasingly difficult to climb up to his mountain hermitage, so in 1816 he came to live at Otogo Jinja, a Shinto shrine at the foot of the mountain.[7] In 1826, Ryōkan accepted an offer of accommodation in the home of a rich farmer and devout Buddhist named Kimura, who lived in Shimazaki.[8] The following year, he happened to meet and fall in love with Teishin, a thirty-year-old nun who was the daughter of a Nagaoka retainer named Okumura. Teishin remained Ryōkan's companion until his death at age seventy-four and in 1835 compiled an anthology titled *Hachisu no tsuyu* (Dew on the Lotus), which contained a number of Ryōkan's poems and some of hers as well. Ryōkan's grave is in the Ryūsenji temple, alongside that of his younger brother Yamamoto Yūshi, who had helped nurse him in his final days.

Ryōkan apparently disliked the poetry of many of his contemporaries, perhaps finding it too mannered. His own poetry is characterized by its direct expression of personal emotions, testimony to the influence of his *Man'yōshū* studies upon his writing. Ryōkan's verse has been praised for its *kotan* (unworldly, plain and simple) quality, which doubtless owes much to the influence of Han-shan.

---

[4]John Stevens, *Three Zen Masters: Ikkyū, Hakuin, Ryōkan* (Tokyo: Kodansha International, 1993), pp. 109-110.

[5]Ibid., p. 113.

[6]*WWW*, p. 494.

[7]Ōsone, p. 113.

[8]Ibid.

☼ 202　An Impromptu Poem

My footsteps followed the river's flow as I searched to discover its source.
Reaching the spot where the waters began, I was suddenly speechless with awe.
For it dawned on me that you cannot find the original source of things.
So with stick in hand I wandered about, dabbling in the rushing waters.

Inoguchi, p. 232

☼ 203　Visiting Master Shiyō's Grave

Where will I find that old grave,
This day in spring with the grass so long?
In former times to the River Seba
I travelled faithfully, time and again.
But my old friends there have gradually vanished
And the neighborhood's undergone many a change.
Life is indeed just like a dream:
I look back and find thirty years have now passed.

Iwanami, p. 367.　From *Ryōkan shishū* (The Collected Poems of Ryōkan), ca. 1845

Title:　Shiyō was Ryōkan's early teacher, Ōmori Kyōsen (?-1791), a scholar who studied Kobunjigaku in Edo.　His grave is in Manpukuji temple in Ōkōzu-mura in the Mishima district of Niigata prefecture (Iwanami, p. 366).　Ryōkan did not know the precise location of the grave site as he had been in Bitchū at the time of Shiyō's burial.
Line three:　The Seba River (Sebakawa) was evidently near his teacher's home, which was in Jizōdō-chō (modern Wakemizu-chō).　Ryōkan lived about a mile away in Izumosaki.　This river, called the Nishi River (Nishikawa) today, has changed course over the past few centuries, so its exact whereabouts at the time is not clear (Iwanami, p. 457).

◎ 204 In Praise of the Mid-Autumn Moon

The moon shines tonight with a pale brightness.
The startled cries of the magpies grow louder.
Their doleful sound makes me think of home;
Where can I find a place of solace?

Iwanami, pp. 367-368. From *Ryōkan shishū*, ca. 1845

Line two: They probably think it is nearly daybreak.

◎ 205 An Impromptu Poem

In the foothills of Mount Kugami I make my dwelling.
Coarse tea and plain rice are the things that sustain me.
All year long, no visitors with pierced ears.
Just folks gathering leaves in the empty forest.

Iwanami, pp. 368-369. From *Ryōkan shishū*, ca. 1845

Line three: "Pierced ears" is a reference to a high priest. The poet meets no one in the same calling as himself, in other words.

◎ 206 Long the Winter Nights

I often recall how when I was a boy
I used to read in an empty building.
Time and again I would fill the lamp,
Never bothered by the long winter nights!

Iwanami, p. 368. From *Ryōkan shishū*, ca. 1845

☾ 207 Looking at the Flowers on the Way to Tanomo Hermitage

Peach blossoms like rosy clouds bloom between the banks.

A springtime river of indigo winds its way through the village.

I follow the river's course, looking at the flowers;

There on the east bank is my old friend's home!

Iwanami, p. 369. From *Ryōkan shishū*, ca. 1845

Title: Tanomo Hermitage (Tanomoan) was the abode of the poet's close friend, Priest Yūgan (d. 1808), a resident of Ōshima-mura (modern Sanjō city) in old Echigo, now Niigata prefecture (Iwanami, p. 457). Besides being a Buddhist priest, Yūgan excelled in painting. Ryōkan wrote a number of poems about visiting this man.

☾ 208 Autumn Dusk

Bleak and dreary this autumn day!

As I go out the gate a frigid wind blows.

The solitary village is veiled in mist.

People headed home stand near a rustic bridge.

Crows are gathering on an ancient tree;

A slanting line of geese vanishes in the distance.

Only the dark-robed priest remains,

Lingering by the river as night descends.

Iwanami, pp. 369-370. From *Ryōkan shishū*, ca. 1845

Line two: The Iwanami commentator indicates that the place he was leaving was Kugamidera, a temple on Mt. Kugami, where he lived in a small hut for many years.
Line seven: Ryōkan himself.

⦿ 209 Descent from Kingfisher Peak

Carrying firewood, I descend from Kingfisher Peak.
The road leading down is bumpy and uneven.
I rest awhile beneath a giant pine,
Quietly listening to the birds of spring.

Ishikawa, p. 74

⦿ 210 In the Dead of Night

More than fifty years have passed in barely the wink of an eye.
The good and the bad that I've seen in the world all seem like a dream.
The Fifth Month now at my mountain hut, and the plum rains have arrived,
Soaking the windows of this empty room, driving down late in the night.

Ishikawa, p. 121

Line three: Plum rains refers to the summer monsoon season, which lasts about a month, starting in early- to mid-June (circa the Fifth Month by the old lunar calendar).

Priest Chiei [Dokkaku], 1762-1825

Priest Chiei was born in Sanuki province in what is today part of Kagawa prefecture. He was trained by the priests Kenjū and Chikan and became a distinguished scholar-priest of the Jōdō Shinshū Honganji sect. He served as resident priest of Kōryūji temple in Kyoto, which belonged to the Honganji sect. At the request of Hon'i (d. 1826), the nineteenth priest of Nishi Honganji temple in Kyoto, Priest Chiei helped with the compilation of a text for *shōmyō* (Sk. *sabda-vidyā*, the chanting of Buddhist hymns), which was published to commemorate the 550th anniversary of Shinran's death. He was also instrumental in the revival of *shōmyō*, which he had studied under Chikan. The first poem below conveys succinctly a sense of remoteness and desolation intensified by the darkness and cold of winter. The second typifies the thematic genre of poems celebrating the natural beauty of one's rural surroundings. A special oneness with nature is suggested by the mention of the wind tugging almost affectionately at his clothing, providing an appealing climax to this verse.

◉ **211 Nighttime Snowfall at the Village on the River**

Nighttime snow illuminates the cold river.
The beachside village has lost its road.
The dim and distant hundred-foot bridge
Is crossed by no one at all.

Iwanami, pp. 364-365. From *Dokkaku shishū* (The Lone Crane Poetry Collection), 1824

☪ 212 Wandering Alone at Nishiyama

In spring I always get up early,
Then I leave my simple hut.
Dawn in the countryside; the first orioles calling.
As the pond brightens up the roosting herons fly off.
A thousand peaks veiled in balmy clouds;
A myriad trees touched by morning sun.
In the village I pause beside a bridge
As a light breeze tugs at my clothing.

Iwanami, p. 364. From *Dokkaku shishū*, 1824

☪ 213 Returning from the Western Outskirts in the Evening

A rustic boat bobs in the water by the riverbank.
Village houses stand silent and forlorn, their doors shut.
The moon rises above a lone peak in the distant sky.
A priest heads home on a road through the pines.

Iwanami, p. 365. *Dokkaku shishū*, 1824

Tachi [Tate] Ryūwan, 1762-1844

The son of the owner of a commercial shipping agency, Tachi Ryūwan was from Echigo in modern Niigata prefecture. He studied in Edo under Kameda Hōsai (1752-1826), a Syncretic scholar who had rejected the teachings of Kobunjigaku. Ryūwan is best known for his poetry, although he also served as a shogunal official in a variety of clerical posts for most of his life. He is described as a conscientious, quiet, retiring man who never sought fame for himself nor ingratiated himself with others.[1] His contemporaries wrote that he was a man of few words who seldom laughed, and that his greatest pleasures in life were reading books and writing poetry.[2] Ryūwan spent his retirement years in the Mejirodai area of Edo and achieved an outstanding reputation as a poet, even though he wrote comparatively little. He was a close friend and colleague of *Matsuzaki Kōdō, who contributed prefaces for two of his works.

Ryūwan particularly admired the mid- to late-T'ang poets. He wrote in a style that Fujikawa describes as "romantic and full of artistic effect," particularly where his earlier verse was concerned.[3] Later, however, his poetry tended to be in the plainer, more realistic Sung style promoted by the Kōkosha society. These poems, rich in local color and atmosphere, often describe the pleasures of solitude in retirement and the everyday lives and folk customs of people living in the rural outskirts of Edo.

---

[1]Inoguchi, p. 273.

[2]Fujikawa, p. 136.

[3]Ibid.

◐ 214 An Impromptu Poem

A leisurely day at the southern window; I brush the dust from my bed.
Then chanting poems and sipping tea, I sit in the evening sun.
I've had my fill of worldly affairs, being poor has a charm of its own.
My mind has ceased all calculations—what's wrong with being dull?
Here in the country I have faint dreams of home, a thousand *ri* away.
In the moonlight breezes I quietly ponder poems deep in my memory.
I accept the lot that has come my way and feel deep satisfaction.
You never hear me telling folk I'm busy anymore.

Inoguchi, p. 274

◐ 215

Fresh frost on the vegetable patch and on the paths through the onion plots.
The Chinese citrons on the trees sport golden yellow hues.
Who says that village kitchens lack the flavors of the seasons?
Every morning my old wife makes me citron *miso* soup!

Fujikawa, p. 142

Line four: This soup is *kōshitō*, which is made with fermented bean paste and Chinese citron.

◐ 216

Alone, I lie by my mountain window, still feeling half-asleep.
Awake, I languidly read a book on how to preserve my health.
Prolonging life and avoiding old age—easy to talk about!
I smile as I take my medicinal bath made with shoots from the wolfberry vine.

Fujikawa, p. 143

Line four: The wolfberry vine (*Lysium chinense*) is also known as Chinese matrimony vine. The poet is smiling because he is skeptical that the herbal bath will do him any good.

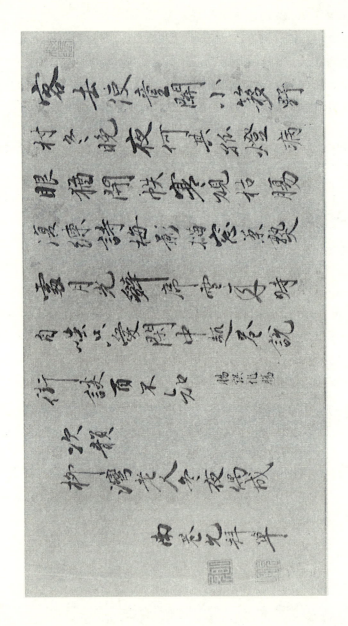

3. A handwritten piece of unknown provenance, probably early-nineteenth century, bearing an eight-line verse by Tachi Ryūwan (1762-1844), titled "An Impromptu Poem Written on a Winter's Night; Following the Rhymes of Another Verse" (poem 219).

◙ **217**

Hillside garden—half a *mou* of land I hoed myself.
Straggly hedge and melon vines encircling my hut.
No other tasks, this idle one has nothing else to do.
At the head of my bed a single book on cultivating trees.

Fujikawa, p. 143

Line one: This originally Chinese measurement amounted to about 120 square yards.

◙ **218   A Miscellaneous Poem on the Beginning of Spring**

Beautiful sunshine, breezes blowing, today, the first of the year.
Upon the red gate, bamboo and pine, veiled in springtime haze.
The young master of the household is in a room upstairs.
He has rolled up the pearl-embroidered blinds and is watching the paper kites.

Inoguchi, p. 274; Fujikawa, pp. 136-137

Line two: Decorations made of pine and bamboo sprigs were traditionally hung up at New Years. The expression "red gate" refers to the houses of the nobility.

◙ **219   An Impromptu Poem Written on a Winter's Night;
Following the Rhymes of Another Verse**

The guests have gone; I tell my boy to close the door of the porch.
Rustic hamlet on a winter's evening—what to do with the rest of the night?
A solitary lamp, my eyes are tired, but still I open my notebook.
A cold ink stone, my mind is exhausted, yet still I work on my poems.
Plum tree shadows play on my window, the leaves have now grown old.
The moonlight vanishes from my seat, once the clouds roll in.
I laugh at myself for only loving the joys that come from leisure.
I know nothing at all about village gossip and rumors heard on the streets.

From an early nineteenth-century manuscript copy of this verse owned by the translators.

☺ 220 The End of Autumn

Alarming how the months and years just quietly disappear.
Alone I sit in this silent house, my thoughts are somewhere else.
The gloom of old age is like the leaves—hard to sweep away.
Their rustling sound is all around as another autumn passes.

Inoguchi, p. 273; Fujikawa, p. 144

This verse is said to have been a particular favorite of the modern writer Nagai Kafū (1879-1959) (Fujikawa, p. 144).

Kashiwagi Jotei, 1763-1819

Kashiwagi Jotei, an Edo native, was the son of a well-to-do shogunal carpenter who died when Jotei was young. Jotei himself worked as a carpenter for the shogunate until about the age of thirty. During his twenties, he used up the family's fortune on a life of dissipation, so at thirty-four he decided to entrust all family affairs to his younger brother, continuing himself to lead an unsettled, Bohemian life. Jotei never married. Lacking familial ties, he wandered the countryside restlessly for years. Wherever he went, he managed to support himself at a subsistence level by selling his artistic and literary creations, with a portion of the proceeds going to women in the pleasure quarters. In his mid-fifties Jotei died of exhaustion in a disused temple in the eastern hills of Kyoto, where he had spent his final years.

He was much admired by *Yanagawa Seigan and *Rai San'yō, who reportedly raised the money needed to give him a proper burial and publish his works following his death. After Jotei's burial, Seigan wrote a beautiful kanshi eulogy for his friend containing the following lines:

> You only loved songbirds and flowers, and never craved office.
> In vain you prided yourself on the grandeur of your poetic soul,
>   your intransigence.
> Could you endure the poverty, the traveler's thin clothes?[1]

Burton Watson writes that Rai San'yō, in his own preface to the posthumous Jotei collection he had compiled with Seigan, observed,

> If Jotei had only been willing to compromise a little and pay some attention to appearances, he, like Ichikawa Kansai and other poets of the time, might have enjoyed a life of ease...consorting with persons of wealth and position, instead of living and dying in poverty.[2]

---

[1] Trans. by Donald Keene in *WWW*, pp. 554-555.

[2] Paraphrased in Watson 1990, pp. 65-66; the original text is cited in Inoguchi, p. 212.

However, there is no evidence in his poetry or elsewhere that Jotei was disaffected with his nomadic life of obscurity and penury, although in rhapsodizing about the Shinano buckwheat and other simple fare in poem 225, he may have been simply making a virtue of necessity.

A thick, holographic manuscript bearing the title *Jotei Sanjin shishū* (A Collection of Jotei's Poems) was discovered in the Shinshū area in the early 1940s by an unidentified man named Suzuki, but the whereabouts of this rare manuscript are today unknown. The work reportedly contained many verses about life in the pleasure quarters.[3]

Jotei studied under *Ichizawa Kansai and was on close terms with two of Kansai's disciples, *Ōkubo Shibutsu and *Kikuchi Gozan. Under Kansai's influence, Jotei had at first drawn inspiration from the Sung poets, but he was later attracted to the T'ang masters, whose works he came to prefer.[4] Jotei was a central figure in Kansai's Kōkosha society and in 1797 founded his own group, known as Bansei Ginsha (Fair-Weather Evening Poetry-Reading Society), in which he was active for about a year before going off to Niigata. His poetry is sincere, rich in lyricism, and full of freshness and local color. Jotei is particularly distinguished for his poems describing scenes from the daily lives of merchants, geisha, and other urban folk.

---

[3]Inoguchi, p. 212.

[4]Watson 1990, p. 65.

◐ 221 An Impromptu Poem Written on a Winter's Night

I was searching for just the right turn of phrase, then couldn't contain my joy.
Braving the cold, I threw off my covers, anxious to jot down the words.
It was then that I noticed a group of priests on the other side of the road,
Chanting the *nenbutsu*, walking along, in the heavy fog of dawn.

Nakamura, p. 136. From *Bokkō shū* (The Carpenter's Collection), 1793

Line four: The *nenbutsu* was a popular Amidist Buddhist invocation.

◐ 222 A Poem Recited from My Pillow on New Year's Day

The noisy hubbub out on the streets went on until the fifth watch.
By dawn the people had quietened down and I was nearly asleep,
When a peddler came to the house next door, crying out "Fans for sale!"
These words I heard were the very first sounds of the New Year now arrived.

Nakamura, p. 136. From *Bokkō shū*, 1793

Line one: The fifth watch: the period between 3:00 A.M. and 5:00 A.M.

◐ 223 Mokuboji Temple

Crowds of people in scented robes go walking past the willows.
Sober folk come here and weep, while drunkards come to sing.
At sunset a shower of rain comes down and soaks the fragrant plants,
Seeming to fall most heavily upon the young lord's grave.

Hirano, pp. 238-239; Andō, p. 94

Line four: To the poet, the rain seems to be "weeping" in sympathy for Umewakamaro, the young boy buried here, who became the subject of various legends. Umewakamaro is said to have lost his father when he was five and at seven was sent to Enryakuji temple to practice Buddhist austerities. One day, he slipped out of the temple and got lost, ending up in Ōtsu. He was then abducted by thieves and taken to the Sumida River in Musashi province, where he took ill and died. Local people were moved by the boy's sad plight and buried him at Mokuboji, a Tendai temple located in Mukōjima, modern Tokyo, on the Sumida River. They planted willows to mark his grave.

☝ 224 My Reply

Returning to farming is all very well, but what if I have no land?
Vainly I've searched in other parts, for years and years on end.
I'd like to find a place to plant an orchard of three hundred plums:
A quiet spot among lakes and hills—I'd be Lord of the Flowers there!

Inoguchi, p. 214

☝ 225

Edo, the capital of our land, a paradise on earth!
What might the mouth and stomach seek that cannot be found in this city?
Fresh fish, vegetables, lavish delicacies—these are what people prize!
At their banquets they vie to outdo one another, presenting each dish
    like an edict.
Those ladies and gentlemen, so serene, have never a care in the world.
They feast at vast tables on sumptuous spreads, acting like nobles and lords.
But nothing at all compares to the buckwheat that comes from Shinano province.
And for fish from Sagami or Suruga eggplants, I'd hatch a hundred schemes!

Nakamura, p. 98. From *Shihonzō* (Poetic Materia Medica), 1818

☝ 226 Flowers Reflected in the Water

Flowers in profusion like flames of fire ready to burn my boat,
Then plunged deep down beneath the water, under the glassy flow.
Plying my pole, I watch amazed as the redness suddenly breaks up.
I hadn't realized that trees were growing upon the riverbank!

Nakamura, pp. 104-105. From *Jotei hakuzetsu* (One Hundred Quatrains by Jotei), 1815

☾ 227

Over and over the clappers are struck; still the night is young.

The young man and the young lady with him are facing one another.

Their emotions so deep they do not speak,

    for they're shy in each other's presence.

The incense stick beside the pillow has burned completely down.

Nakamura, p. 184. From *Yoshiwara shi* (Yoshiwara Poems)

<u>Line four</u>: The young man appears to be a customer in a brothel. The incense stick was used to keep time.

This series of poems, originally thirty in all, record Jotei's experiences as a young man in the pleasure quarters of Yoshiwara in Edo. The manuscript of these thirty poems was lost during Jotei's lifetime, and he is said to have reconstructed as many as he could recall from memory. He was only able to remember twenty. See Nakamura, p. 183.

☾ 228 After Parting

Long ago the seeds of love were sowed in the fields of my heart.

Since we parted I've been unable to sleep, alone in my empty bed.

I take the love letter you sent to me and unfold it all the way.

Here by the lamp with the rain outside, the night feels like a year.

Nakamura, p. 185. From *Jotei Sanjin kō* (A Text of Jotei's Works), 1810

Ōta Kinjō, 1765-1825

Descended from one of Toyotomi Hideyoshi's senior retainers, Ōta Kinjō was a native of Kaga in what is today Ishikawa prefecture. The youngest of eight children, he was the son of a skilled herbalist who was also an expert in On'yōdō divination. Kinjō was considered a child prodigy. He began to read at five, wrote poetry proficiently by age eleven, and lectured on the Confucian classics at thirteen. Having decided not to pursue the family trade, Kinjō left his village to study in Kyoto under Minagawa Kien. It appears, however, that he did not remain there long. He next proceeded to Edo, intending this time to work with the *seirei* poet Yamamoto Hokuzan, but his affiliation with the latter was apparently also rather brief, due to problems in their relationship.

At this point Kinjō resolved to teach himself, using the classics as his teacher. By dint of determined study, he eventually became one of the most respected Confucian scholars of his time. Kinjō was rather eclectic in his approach to Confucianism, being oriented more toward Setchūgaku than to orthodox Chu Hsi studies. He was particularly concerned about what he considered the low standards of certain Confucian scholars who blindly maintained the waning traditions of the Sorai school in the late-eighteenth to early-nineteenth century. In his view, they were bent on the frivolous, decadent pursuit of the literary and fine arts rather than serious scholarship. "Upright and prudent men dislike [them]," he wrote during the Bunsei period (1818-1830), "as they dislike gamblers and pederasts."[1] Kinjō, like other eclectic academicians, hoped to fill what he considered to be a moral and philosophical vacuum, although, as Maruyama concludes, "Eclecticism is eclecticism and implies little creativity, so they contributed very little that was theoretically new."[2]

---

[1]Maruyama, p. 140.

[2]Ibid., p. 141.

Kinjō went on to establish a school which had its own distinct academic orientation, placing emphasis upon close textual exegesis and the use of Chinese commentaries from all periods. He was renowned for his eloquence as a lecturer, and in 1811, he became employed by the Matsudaira family of the Yoshida domain in Toyohashi. He also helped found Jishūkan, the domain school, serving as a professor there himself. In 1822, Kinjō was lured back to his native Kaga province to work as a Confucian scholar, lecturing in the Meirindō for three years and drawing the large salary of three hundred *koku*. Following the death of his lord, he returned to Edo, where he died at age sixty-one.

Kinjō's poetry is characterized by a simple, austere beauty, as is well illustrated by the two verses which follow. The first poem in particular is remarkable for its sparing depiction of *sabi*, with the withered beauty of water-peppers and the nearly dried-up river set against the utter stillness of the landscape. No human presence disturbs the peace of the natural setting, allowing the reader to focus all the more clearly on the aesthetic and symbolic qualities inherent in the description of the scenery itself.

◐ 229 Autumn River

The water-pepper flowers have passed their prime on the rustic autumn banks.
On this empty river the water is low; motionless, flowing no more.
At a fisherman's hut by the river ford, the glow of approaching dusk.
Two snowy herons are standing guard upon an unmanned boat.

Sugano, p. 59; Inoguchi, pp. 217-218. From *Kinjō shikō* (A Book of Poems by Kinjō), 1817

◘ 230 Setting off from Mishima at Dawn

The sky is filled with wind and dew, clear the light of dawn.
The waning moon shines down on the hut, the cocks have yet to crow.
The road we travel is lonely and deserted amidst the autumn grass.
We stop the litter several times to hear the insects chirp.

Inoguchi, p. 219

Oike Tōyō, 1765-1834

Oike Tōyō was a native of Sanuki in modern Kagawa prefecture. He studied with Nakai Chikuzan as a youth, was a friend of *Kan Sazan, and, as is evident from the second verse below, clearly admired Rai Shunsui. The latter's son, the poet *Rai San'yō, thought highly of Tōyō's work, his *kotai* (old style) poems in particular. The first selection below is novel for its whimsical notion of a man racing a cloud up a mountain and points to the special affinity between man and nature, a theme so prevalent in Japanese poetry.

☺ 231 Hiking in the Mountains

I scrambled halfway up the hill
Then rested briefly on my bamboo stick.
A drifting cloud swept past my feet
And beat me to the top!

Iwanami, p. 320. From *Kokuji shū* (A Collection of Grain), 1854. *Kokuji*, which literally means "like grain," was possibly one of the poet's style names.

⏻ 232 A Poem Sent to Master Shunsui

Those extra lectures you give on the Classics are elegant and refined.
Your poetry outclasses the sages of T'ang, your brushwork, the masters of Chin.
In age and virtue you rank above the most venerable elders of our times.
Three thousand students now take their places beyond your red silk curtain.

Iwanami, p. 321. From *Kokuji shū*, 1854

Title: Rai Shunsui (d. 1816), a famous Confucian scholar, poet, and the father of the Japanese historian and kanshi poet *Rai San'yō.
Line four: "Red silk curtain" is a conventional reference to a teacher's seat, harking back to the red silk curtain behind which Ma Jung (79-166), a scholar and official of the Han dynasty, is said to have taught.

Ōkubo Shibutsu, 1767-1837

The son of a doctor named Muneharu, Ōkubo Shibutsu was a native of Hitachi, part of modern Ibaragi prefecture, an area not famous for producing Chinese scholars. Nonetheless, Shibutsu was to distinguish himself as a scholar and poet, being ranked with *Kikuchi Gozan, *Kashiwagi Jotei, and *Ichikawa Kansai as one of the four most important Edo-area poets of his day. As a young man, Shibutsu moved to Edo and set up practice as a pediatrician, taking instruction from the poet Yamamoto Hokuzan on the side. He later studied Chinese poetic composition with Ichikawa Kansai and showed such promise that he abandoned his medical practice to become a full-time poet. He was a prominent member of Kansai's Kōkosha (The River and Lake Society), a coterie whose membership and level of activity had fallen off considerably by the beginning of the nineteenth century. Shibutsu had by this time become involved in running another literary society with *Kashiwagi Jotei, called Nisō Shisha (The Double-Thin Poetry Society), established in 1792. Its name was an allusion to style names used by Shibutsu and Jotei, "Thin Plum" (Nibai) and "Thin as Bamboo" (Sōchiku), respectively. This new group, which had about one hundred members, sought to pursue poetic spiritualism and restore vitality to kanshi.

Around 1804, Shibutsu established a small school in the Otamagaike area of Kanda, naming it Shiseidō (The Hall of the Sage of Poetry), a reference to Tu Fu. This building, which housed a statue of Tu Fu, served as the center of Shibutsu's poetic activities until it burned down in 1829.[1] As Burton Watson notes, "Owing to these efforts, the school of kanshi founded by Ichikawa Kansai and the poetic theories it propounded were restored to their former position of importance in Edo literary circles."[2] A reputable artist and calligrapher as well,

---

[1]Inoguchi, p. 288.

[2]Watson 1990, p. 90.

Shibutsu was considered a specialist in the painting of monochrome bamboo and enjoyed a close friendship with the eminent artist Tani Bunchō. It is said that Shibutsu once journeyed to the province of Kōzuke where he impersonated Bunchō, painting under his name. Thus, some of the Bunchō paintings surviving from this area could be the work of Shibutsu.[3]

Shibutsu loved to travel and did so extensively, particularly in his later years. He also served a short stint as a Confucian functionary in the Akita domain and taught at the domain's residence school in Edo. Shibutsu was famous as a host, entertaining guests from all walks of life almost daily with lavish banquets. He even had a special map printed to guide guests to his home.[4] A hint of these epicurean tastes can be found in the first verse below describing the pleasures of seasonal delicacies.

In the second verse, an ordinary fireworks display is seen as more than mere entertainment. Filtered through Shibutsu's imaginative sensibilities it turns into an almost supernatural experience, its brilliance and force recreated by a startling barrage of dramatic, quasi-mythological images. We know of no other such treatments of fireworks in Japanese poetry.

---

[3]Roberts, p. 145.

[4]Nakamura, p. 126.

◙ 233 Bonito

When special delicacies come into season and are offered for sale in the shops,
Folks fight to buy them at any price, although they're as costly as pearls.
The people of Wu like to brag about the tastiness of their perch,
But would any among them pawn his clothes to purchase one of these?

Nakamura, p. 131

Line three: "The people of Wu" is a reference to people from the modern province of Chiangsu in China.

◙ 234 The Firework Display

Above the river in the vast heavens the rosy sunset has faded.
Now the noise of fire-crackers frightens the roosting crows.
Cold stars suddenly descend like rain over half of the sky.
Trees of fire burst wide open, coming into bloom.
Their force rolls back the incoming tide, sending the water-rats scurrying;
Their brilliance strikes the shifting clouds, scattering the snakes of gold.
The night wears on, the display is over; everyone goes back home.
The banks of the river now chilly and bleak, veiled in a pall of smoke.

Nakamura, p. 130

Line six: "Snakes of gold," a metaphor for lightning.

Matsuzaki Kōdō, 1771-1844

The son of a farmer, Matsuzaki Kōdō was a native of Higo, in modern Kumamoto prefecture. A precocious child, he became a Buddhist priest at age ten to please his father, but at fifteen he decided to become a Confucian scholar instead. He ran away to Edo, planning to stay with relatives there, but, unable to find them, wandered south to Musashino and Sagami, where he was attacked by robbers who stole all his money.[1] Kōdō eventually made his way to Mishima in Izu and presented himself at a temple, where he was provided with a letter of introduction to a priest at a temple in Asakusa in Edo. Genmon, the priest in Asakusa, encouraged him to return to the priesthood, but Kōdō insisted that he had his heart set on becoming a Confucian scholar. Deciding not to interfere with his ambitions, Genmon gave him money and sent him off to study at Shōheikō in Edo, where he excelled in all his scholarly endeavors.[2] Before long, Kōdō was teaching in one of the Hayashi family's private academies in Edo.

An unfortunate incident occurred during Kōdō's tenure as a teacher, in 1796. Inoguchi Atsushi relates that a student named Hirazawa took out an unauthorized loan, using Hayashi Kanjun's books as collateral and having Kōdō act as the guarantor. When Hirazawa defaulted on the loan, Hayashi dismissed Kōdō from the school and refused to recommend him for a domainal appointment. Kōdō fled the academy and went to Bōsō Peninsula, across modern Tokyo Harbor, spending the next three years in poverty, lying low. It may have been during this difficult period that he wrote the second poem below, which alludes to chronic illness and his consequent inability to visit his mother.

---

[1]Inoguchi, p. 275.

[2]Ibid.

While Kōdō was in hiding, his parents mounted a frantic search for him, having heard a variety of rumors, including one that he had stolen his teacher's entire library and another that he was dead. Both parents themselves soon died, worn down by stress and humiliation, without ever seeing their son again. Kōdō finally returned to Edo and was reinstated in the Hayashi school after about a year. The news of his parents' death remained a source of bitter regret for the rest of his life. Inoguchi notes that Kōdō never apologized to his teacher or otherwise explained himself; nor did he ever publicly blame Hirazawa for what had happened.[3]

At thirty-two Kōdō was appointed as a Confucian scholar in the Kakegawa domain in Tōtōmi province. Rising steadily through the ranks, he served a succession of daimyo there. The lord of Higo, Kōdō's home domain, repeatedly coaxed him to return and take up an appointment, but Kōdō declined, feeling an obligation to the daimyo he was currently serving and perhaps a lingering sense of shame as well, on account of the Hirazawa scandal. In 1815, at the age of forty-four, Kōdō retired on grounds of ill health, going off to live in a retreat which he had built in the Nishi-Hanezawa area of Edo. He was to reside there for the remaining twenty-three years of his life, never once returning to his native Higo.[4]

Kōdō was known for his broad erudition and command of the classics, being considered one of the most important Confucian scholars of his time. He was a leader in the field of Han-T'ang studies in Japan, specializing in Han dynasty stone-inscribed texts of the classics. An ardent advocate of Kogaku, he repeatedly emphasized the importance of "using the text to comment on the text," rather than relying upon notes and commentaries, which he viewed as extraneous. He campaigned tirelessly for the pardon of his disciple *Watanabe Kazan following the Bansha no Goku inquisition of the late 1830s, the first attempt by the shogunate to suppress pro-Western activism. During this campaign, Kazan,

---

[3]Ibid.

[4]Ibid., pp. 275-276.

Takano Chōei (1804-1850), and other members of the Rangaku (Dutch Learning, i.e., Western studies) movement were punished for criticizing the exclusionary policies of the shogunate. After his release from prison, Kazan sent Kōdō a letter expressing his deep gratitude.[5]

In his declining years Kōdō was sent a miniature pine from Higo, which he cultivated faithfully. On his deathbed, he apparently asked his students to sprinkle some soil from the pot onto his feet, whereupon he said, "Now I have walked again upon the land of my parents." So saying, he breathed his last.[6]

235 Enjoying the Cool in the Marketplace at Night

Evening is here, my bathing done, I go out to enjoy the breezes.
I stroll about through the lantern market, wandering east and west.
The autumn season has yet to arrive, but autumn seems already here.
The streets are full of the colors of night and cages of insects for sale.

Nakamura, p. 133

236 Thoughts while Lying Ill in Bed One Autumn Day

When will I be able to return to my village to visit my mother dear?
I've been so ill for many a year, unable to go where I please.
Three thousand *ri* away, off in the clouds—I dream of that place hard to reach.
Flocks of geese fly through autumn skies, but for me they fly in vain.

Inoguchi, p. 277

Line one: The poet's mother lived in the village of Kikura in Higo, Kōdō's birthplace. The birds migrating south reminded him of his own wished-for journey, one that he in fact never managed to make. Kōdō left home at fifteen and never returned.

---

[5]Ibid., p. 276.

[6]Ibid.

☪ 237 A Poem Written while Drunk about the Slender Bamboo Grown By Kawasaki Yoshifuku

Bamboo by nature stands up straight,
But when the wind blows, it bends.
Today in the world in which we live
Everyone acts this way.

Inoguchi, p. 277

Title: Another reading of this name is Kawasaki Kichifuku; unidentified.

Kikuchi Gozan, 1772-1855

Kikuchi Gozan, who enjoyed a great reputation as a calligrapher and kanshi poet in the *seirei* style, was born in the town of Takamatsu in Sanuki province, part of modern Kagawa prefecture. He began his Confucian training in the Takamatsu domain with Gotō Shizan, later going to Kyoto to study with *Shibano Ritsuzan and then to Edo to become a pupil of *Ichikawa Kansai. Gozan made his home in Edo and gave private instruction from his school in the Hongō Itchōme district near what is present-day Tokyo University. He was inspired by Kansai's poems on the pleasure-quarters to write verse on the same subject, a knowledge of which he had personally acquired as a youth in the Fukagawa district in Edo. Gozan eventually returned to Takamatsu to take up a post as a scribe.

◉ 238

Down on her luck, she has recently moved away from the Northern Quarter.
All she need do is look at the mirror to know that her beauty has faded.
Even when she has made up her eyebrows, done up her hair as well,
She's still afraid she'll be seen by people who know her from former times.

Nakamura, pp. 190-191. From *Suitō chikushi shi* (Bamboo Branch Songs from East of the River), 1797

Line one: Northern Quarter (Hokuri): a reference to Yoshiwara, the famous pleasure-quarters in the old Asakusa-Yamadani area in Edo. The geisha in the poem had evidently moved from Yoshiwara to Fukagawa in Edo, on the banks of the Sumida River between Sendai-Horikawa and Horikawa—see Nakamura, p. 191.
   A note attached by the poet to the end of the collection containing this poem states that in the summer of 1797 he stayed on the east bank of the Sumida River. Having time to spare, Gozan composed these poems about the world of the geisha for his own amusement. Later, they fell into someone else's hands and were circulated, which led to his being criticized as frivolous for having written such verse (Nakamura, p. 191).

☯ 239

Through the reeds a stiff wind blows, the weather cool as autumn.
At the prow of a boat a young geisha stands, learning how to fish.
Her graceful fingers haven't quite got the knack; she jerks the rod too soon.
All she can say is, "Silly fish! They just won't take the hook!"

Nakamura, p. 189. From *Suitō chikushi shi*

☯ 240

All across the twilight river densely hangs the fog.
Boats coming in at times encounter boats going the other way.
Through the blinds it seems to be her face—so hard it is to see.
And then I recognize her voice, as softly she calls to me.

Nakamura, p. 190. From *Suitō chikushi shi*

Line one: The river is the Sumida in Edo, modern Tokyo.

Priest Tokuryū, 1772-1858

A priest-scholar of the Shinshū Ōtani sect, Priest Tokuryū [style name Fusōshitsu] was born in Mizuhara in Echigo province, part of modern Niigata prefecture. The second son of a priest in charge of the Muishinji temple, Tokuryū was considered a child prodigy, acquiring a remarkably thorough knowledge of the Chinese classics and Japanese history at an early age. Tokuryū studied Pure Land Buddhism at the Takakura Gakuryō academy, which was attached to the Higashi Honganji temple, the center of the Pure Land sect, and became a teacher there in 1847. He never married. Remarkably, it appears that the only extant poems by Priest Tokuryū were written when he was between the ages of nine and twelve.[1] These are contained in his *Hokuzan shishū*, the introduction to which was written by his teacher, *Shibano Ritsuzan. Although these are by no means distinguished poems, we have included them as examples of kanshi written by a child poet.

◖ 241 Gazing at the River on an Autumn Evening

Autumn dusk; chanting poems, I gaze at the river.
Rosy clouds are reflected in the cerulean waters.
Beneath an isolated patch of willow trees
A fisherman is mooring his little punt.

Iwanami, p. 360. From *Hokuzan shishū* (The North Hills Poetry Collection)

---

[1] Iwanami, p. 490.

☪ 242 Gazing at the Sea on an Autumn Day

The autumn wind whips up waves by the cliffs;
The sea spray is cold as it wets my clothes.
Where the color of the tide touches the sky
A lone wild goose flies across the sunset.

Iwanami, p. 361. From *Hokuzan shishū*

Nomura Kōen, 1775-1843

Little is known about the life and career of the Confucian scholar Nomura Kōen. A native of the Osaka area who studied with Koga Seiri and later became a Shōheikō scholar, he was considered a specialist in *tenshi* (Ch. *t'ien-tz'u*, "filling in words"), a variety of *tz'u* poetry employed in the composition of lyrics for songs set to specific tune patterns.[1] The Teishu scholar Koga Tōan (1788-1847) described Kōen and his versification as follows:

> He is honest and mild-mannered and possesses the mind and will of a true gentleman, being stern, thorough, and precise. He borrows his technique from the T'ang, exhibiting breadth of learning and excellence. His material he collects from the *Ssu-k'u* encyclopedia....Artifice and substance are in perfect balance [in his verse] with nothing lacking, nor is any trace of coarseness present.[2]

His collected verse amounts to twenty *maki*, some of it of very high quality. The first two verses below are archetypal treatments of two stock subjects in kanshi: the fisherman and the herdsman, who are traditionally depicted as leisured and carefree figures.

---

[1]Kang-i Sun Chang writes that there were 825 tunes in all and more than 1,670 forms when the variants of each pattern were included. See *The Evolution of Chinese Tz'u Poetry*, p. 2. The genre flourished in the Sung, after having first been introduced by the T'ang poet Liu Yü-hsi (772-842). See Chang, p. 13n.

[2]Cited in Shimonaka Kunihiko, ed., *Nihon jinmei daijiten*, vol. 5 of 7 vols. (Tokyo: Heibonsha, 1979), p. 84.

243 The Old Fisherman

Autumn all around at the seaside village; vast the misty waves.
The fisherman has hauled in his line and moored his boat in the shallows.
Lying drunk on the bank among flowering reeds, he wistfully stares at the moon.
When he awakes, his raincoat of straw is covered with drifts of snow.

Iwanami, p. 312. From *Kōen shishō* (A Book of Poems by Kōen)

Line four: "Drifts of snow," the fluffy, down-like seeds of the reed.

244 Inscription for a Picture

By morning he travels a grassy path, pushing through dense greenery.
At dusk he passes a flowery bank, trampling fallen pink petals.
He rides through the spring village ten *ri* long, secure upon his ox.
The music of his flute is cut off by the wind, blowing in the evening sun.

Iwanami, pp. 312-313. From *Kōen shishō*

Line three: A *ri* (Ch. *li*) was approximately one-third of a mile, but this distance was probably not intended to be taken literally.

245 Plantains

A hundred feet along the eaves the silken greenery extends.
Shadowy leaves flutter to and fro as the season's first coolness arrives.
Here in my solitude I feel content, listening to the fresh evening rain,
As it drives against my poetry window, rousing me from my sleep.

Iwanami, pp. 313-314. From *Kōen shishō*

Tanomura Chikuden, 1777-1835

Tanomura Chikuden was a native of Takeda in Bungo, part of modern Ōita prefecture. His family had for generations served the Oka domain as physicians. Chikuden was both a celebrated kanshi poet and a highly regarded Nanga painter in the literati style. His aptitude for poetry was noticed early on, and at the age of eleven he entered the domain school, Yūgakkan, where his achievements soon outstripped those of the other students. In Bungo he studied painting techniques under Watanabe Hōtō while training as a doctor, his original intention being to follow in his father's footsteps. But he abandoned medicine when he was still in his early twenties and went on to serve the Oka domain as a Confucian scholar. In 1801 Chikuden went to Edo for a year to take painting lessons from Tani Bunchō and to read Kogaku scholarship under the guidance of Furuya Sekiyō (1734-1806) and Ōtake Tōkai (1735-1803). His visit to Edo was also for the purpose of doing research for a Bungo domain history which he was compiling.

In 1805 or 1806 he went to Kyoto to study poetry with *Murase Kōtei and Minagawa Kien, living during this period in the Amidadera temple. While in Kyoto, he became friendly with such prominent poets as *Nakajima Sōin, *Uragami Gyokudō, and Shinozaki Shōchiku (1781-1851), as well as the novelist Ueda Akinari (1734-1809), from whom he acquired a love of the tea ceremony. He next returned to Bungo, where he taught ethics and history at the domain school, rising to become its principal. In 1811 Chikuden met *Rai San'yō, who was deeply impressed by his literary skill and came to regard him as one of the two finest living poets, the other being *Hirose Tansō. "There are only two poets in western Japan worth talking about—you and Chikuden," he later told Tansō while visiting him in 1818.[1]

---

[1]Inoguchi, p. 265.

In the wake of a peasant uprising in 1811, Chikuden submitted a petition urging reform of various administrative abuses to improve the lives of the peasants. His advice went unheeded, and around 1812 he resigned his post and returned to his hometown of Takeda to live. Like San'yō, however, he travelled extensively, visiting his many artist and poet friends. Chikuden devoted the rest of his life to poetry and painting. His art has been characterized as somewhat uneven in quality, although he is nonetheless ranked among the best Nanga painters in the Japanese tradition.[2] Chikuden's paintings, which Roberts describes as "notable for [their] fine lines, light colors, [and] calm and harmonious composition," were always given to friends and never sold.[3] A well-rounded aesthete, he was also a master of the tea ceremony, flower-arranging, and incense-mixing.

246 A Miscellaneous Poem

My guests sit and drink wine beneath the plum blossoms.
The first signs of spring have come to the mountain garden.
Fish are swimming upstream in the river;
Wild geese are flying across the rosy horizon.
The day is mild, the plants are turning green.
Still quite chilly, but it's no trouble to put on more clothes.
The third watch, and the party is ending.
Plum fragrance on our clothes, we return along a secluded road.

Iriya, p. 147

---

[2]Roberts, p. 13.

[3]Ibid.

◑ **247 Returning in the Evening**

I walk along a road west of the mountains.
Hungry birds fly about and chirp.
I should take this road when I journey back;
The setting sun will still be shining.

Inoguchi, p. 267

◑ **248 Autumn Evening**

The crickets have started coming indoors, now that the nights are cold.
Once again, it's that time of the year for wearing cotton clothes.
Not only has the spring disappeared, autumn has gone as well.
I already see flowers flying about, flying leaves as well.
I ought to don my raincoat of straw and join the fellow who fishes on the banks.
But you cannot fish for merit and fame from the rocks amongst the grass.
I clearly recall a dream I had last night as I lay by my lamp:
A pine tree had sprouted inside my stomach—was this real or imagined?

Iriya, pp. 187-188

Line two: Linen was worn in summer, padded or lined cotton garments in the colder months.
Line eight: This line harks back to a passage in *Chuang Tzu* from the chapter entitled "Chih-lo pien" (Supreme Happiness). Here a man finds that a willow tree is sprouting from his left elbow. When asked by a companion if he is upset by this, he replies that he is not, explaining: "You and I came to watch the process of change, and now change has caught up with me. Why would I have anything to resent?" (quoted from Watson, *Chuang Tzu: Basic Writings*, p. 114). In Chuang Tzu's philosophy, people are encouraged to accept with equanimity whatever befalls them, regarding change as part of the natural workings of the universe, even if this means turning into a tree. According to Chuang Tzu, there is no distinction between dreams and reality; life itself can be seen as a dream. The poet's uncertainty about whether or not a pine tree was growing in his body is a reflection of this Taoist notion so characteristic of Chuang Tzu.

◨ 249 Travelling in the Mountains

Beneath the lofty towering pines
I sit with my koto in the twilight.
The cool breeze brings me boundless pleasure
As it blows through my coarse cloth robes.

Inoguchi, p. 266

Line four: His robe is made of woven *heira*, a coarse material created out of fibers from the spindle tree and wisteria vine. A *heira* robe is a conventional symbol of the recluse.

Hitta Shōtō, 1779-1833

Relatively little is known about the life of Hitta Shōtō. A native of Edo and a senior official of the Akita domain in northern Honshu, he was highly respected for his cultural refinement. He once brought the illustrious Confucian scholars *Murase Kōtei and Yamamoto Hokuzan to Akita in an attempt to reinvigorate the academic atmosphere of the domain. In his later years, he provided succor to the renowned poet and scholar *Ōkubo Shibutsu, who had fallen on hard times after years of living the good life.

The collection of love poems from which the selections below are taken has interesting origins. Nakamura Shinichirō relates that Shōtō was sick in bed in the Edo residence of the Akita daimyo one day when he overheard some young retainers telling lewd stories, believing he was not awake. Feigning sleep, Shōtō listened intently and the next morning set himself to the task of recording the essence of their tales in verse form. When he presented these poems, some thirty in all, to the young men and informed them of the circumstances of their composition, they were reportedly shocked and embarrassed.[1] The collection soon became well known and was eventually published, giving rise to all manner of discussion as to how such a high-ranking political figure could have acquired the first-hand knowledge necessary to compose poetry in such dubious popular taste. However, as another Akita scholar named Seya Dōsai explained in defense of Shōtō in a preface to the collection, "One can surely understand what it is like to be a fish without ever having been one himself."[2]

---

[1]Nakamura, p. 194.

[2]Ibid., p. 195.

☺ 250

Wispy tresses disheveled and in wild disarray.
Jewelled hairpins lying on the floor, pearls scattered about.
With skin so soft, nothing should come between them.
Her fancy clothes, now flung aside, dangle from a screen.

Nakamura, p. 196. From *Chōtei chikushi shi* (Bamboo Branch Songs from the Long Riverbank),
1814 (date of preface)

☺ 251

Spring at its height, but behind the blue screen our pleasure has yet to peak.
Make-up mingled with perspiration drips down on my lady's bed.
I raise her up but she falls back down, unable to hold herself up.
Then barely lifting her pretty head, she calls to summon her maid.

Nakamura, p. 197. From *Chōtei chikushi shi*, 1814

☺ 252

Leaning on her lover, she stumbles from the bedroom,
Opens the red curtains and takes a small box.
She ponders awhile, then pokes the silver brazier,
And burns up the old letters from her other men.

Nakamura, pp. 197-198. From *Chōtei chikushi shi*, 1814

☯ 253

They say that the room on the western side has seen many a strange occurrence.
Night after night an angry ghost has been giving the little ones nightmares.
The light of the lamp is dim and fading, and also it's raining outside.
She makes her lover stay the night, unwilling to let him leave.

Nakamura, p. 198. From *Chōtei chikushi shi*, 1814

Line two: "Little ones" is probably a reference to *kamuro*, young maids acting as attendants of geisha. "Angry ghost" (*enkon*) denotes the spirit of a man executed for a crime he did not commit.

☯ 254

The wind brings a shamisen's noisy sounds; midday and she's all in a flurry.
She puts her bronze mirror in just the right place and touches up her makeup.
Last night's hangover not yet gone, she has dark shadows under her eyes.
So she pours herself a drink of warm water, adding a bit of white sugar.

Nakamura, p. 199. From *Chōtei chikushi shi*, 1814

☯ 255

Down on my luck, I would still die for love, but not for the sake of gain.
Even if given a peck of pearls, I'd turn my back on royalty.
My pretty face would be willing to endure the spittle of my sweetheart.
Quietly taking my thin gauze robe, I hide the traces of my tears.

From *Chōtei chikushi shi*, 1814

Line three: "Spittle of my sweetheart" suggests a jealous lover.

Nakajima Sōin, 1779-1855

Best known for his genre poems depicting urban life, Nakajima Sōin was born in Kyoto to the family of a Confucian official. In his earlier years, Sōin was trained in the scholarly tradition of *Itō Jinsai, having studied first with his father. He lived in Edo for about a decade before returning in 1814 to Kyoto, where he studied for a period under *Murase Kōtei. Sōin showed promise in the composition of kanshi, but was particularly fond of light literature of all kinds and became a popular kyōshi poet whose works were widely read especially during the 1820s. He turned his hand to composing waka and writing novels, and his calligraphy was highly regarded as well. Sōin was known in kyōshi circles as Ankutsu Dōjin, "The Priest of Peaceful Hollow." He may also have written humorous Chinese kyōshi verse under the pseudonym of *Sūkatan.

Sōin led a dissolute, Bohemian life in the manner of *Kashiwagi Jotei. He moved many times and even when he lived in Kyoto, he was fond of moving from neighborhood to neighborhood—Kyoto Nijō, Okazaki, Sanpongi, and so on—as if wanting to get a taste of life in various areas and gather as much new poetic material as possible. His collection of verse depicting scenes from Kyoto's Gion pleasure quarters, titled *Ōtō shiji zasshi*, was inspired by the *chikushi* poems of *Ichikawa Kansai and received great public acclaim, establishing his reputation as one of the leading aesthetes of the day.[1] Several verses from this work are among the selections which follow.

---

[1]Nakamura, p. 208.

◲ **256-259   From a series titled *Ōtō shiji zasshi* (Miscellaneous Verses on the Four Seasons East of the Kamo River): 120 Poems**

(No. 1)

No lotuses grow upon this river; no boats can float on its waters.

Two-story buildings stand in a row along the eastern bank.

Imagine all that liquid lip-rouge—countless gallons in all.

If one were to pour every last drop out, it would flow forth like a river!

Hirano, p. 240. From *Ōtō shiji zasshi*, 1814. The first sixty-five poems in this long series were originally published under a slightly different title.

Title: The original sequence of these four verses is not known. We have provided our own numbers for convenience only. The series is set in Kyoto's Gion district, a famous pleasure district on the eastern bank of the Kamo River, where the traditional arts of the geisha still flourish. These verses depict urban scenes in each of the four seasons, centering on the Kamogawa Shijō area and the district immediately to its east, taking in neighborhood shrines, temples, and famous scenic spots.

(No. 2)

The red lanterns shed no light, the night is still and silent.

High above the willow trees there hangs a wisp of a moon.

The little maiden, just thirteen, is used to being with guests:

Undaunted by the wind and dew, she sees them across the bridge.

Hirano, p. 241. From *Ōtō shiji zasshi*, 1814

(No. 3)

Chop goes the knife plied by delicate hands used to being busy.

Against the red of the shopkeeper's apron the bean curd glistens white.

The cubes are all so daintily skewered, the corners perfectly square.

Inside an oven three feet high they will bake this fragrant snow.

Hirano, p. 241. From *Ōtō shiji zasshi*, 1814

(No. 4)

They're both dead drunk, so how could they know that dawn is close at hand?
Both asleep beneath the quilt, her makeup oily and smeared.
If the truth be told, men at play are like butterflies perched on flowers.
When they penetrate that fragrant center, it's not just happenstance!

Nakamura, p. 210. From *Ōtō shiji zasshi*, 1814

<u>Line three</u>: "Men at play" refers to the male clients of prostitutes.

◑ 260-261 Mourning for My Lady: Two Poems
(No. 1)

Poem after poem I wrote last year about the fallen flowers.
How could I know that the flowers portended the loss of the one I love?
I shall always remember those nights at the inn beside the Amida Temple.
There she'd grind my ink for me, as the incense burned.

Nakamura, p. 215. From *Sōin-ken nishū* (The Second Collection from the Residence of Sōin),
1828

(No. 2)

I've grown old living as a writer, like Master Po himself.
How foolish to yearn for the springtime winds—they only broke my heart.
I couldn't bear to brush against the willows, so I went upstairs at the inn.
They made me remember just how thin her slender waist had grown.

Nakamura, p. 216. From *Sōin-ken ni shū*, 1828

<u>Lines one and two</u>: Master Po is Po Chü-i, the renowned T'ang poet.
<u>Line four</u>: Lines three and four of the original have been reversed in the translation for the sake
of clarity.

Rai San'yō, 1780-1832

The illustrious historian and kanshi poet Rai San'yō was born in Osaka, but his family moved to Takehara in Aki (now part of modern Hiroshima prefecture) when he was two years old. In Takehara, San'yō's father Shunsui held a post as a scholar-official in the Aki domain school. San'yō, Shunsui's only surviving son, had a turbulent childhood. Bright but temperamental, at seven he developed epilepsy, which plagued him periodically throughout his life and caused his parents endless worry. They spoiled him by making too much fuss over his health, and San'yō was often more than his mother Baishi could handle, particularly from about the age of ten.

Considered a child prodigy, San'yō began his Confucian education at the age of six, being tutored by his uncle *Rai Kyōhei. At twelve, he possessed sufficient insight into his own interests to compose an essay in which he expressed his idealistic ambition to "develop the land and save the people." His father was a worthy role model, being an exceptional poet and teacher in his own right and an orthodox follower of the teachings of Chu Hsi. San'yō never showed much enthusiasm for traditional Confucian studies, however, and was much more interested in history and Chinese literature. Already highly ambitious by the age of fourteen, he revealed a desire to go down in history in his poem entitled "Reflections," below, which was written at that age. At seventeen he was taken by Kyōhei to Edo to enrol in the Shōheikō academy where he was to study with his maternal uncle *Bitō Jishū. San'yō remained there only for a year, but while in Edo he was advised by Akasaki Kaimon (1739-1802) to study history if he wanted to advance in the world. Kaimon suggested that he start with the monumental history of China *T'ung-chien kang-mu* (A Comprehensive Mirror: Text and Commentary), advice which San'yō evidently took to heart.[1]

---

[1] Inoguchi, p. 234.

In his late teens, San'yō had a recurrence of his epilepsy, then left Edo for reasons that remain unclear. Inoguchi suggests that he may have been chafing under the strict control and supervision of his uncle, Jishū,[2] while Watson speculates that a sexual indiscretion might have been the reason for his departure.[3] Throughout his life San'yō suffered from bouts of depression and at times displayed behavior that was impulsive and unpredictable. After his return to Aki from Edo, his parents decided that marriage might improve him, so it was arranged that he would marry Misono Junko, a girl of fourteen who was the daughter of a domain physician. The marriage took place but eventually ended in failure. Their son Itsuan (Yoichi) had to be raised by San'yō's father after Junko had a mental breakdown.[4] An excerpt from a long poem, below, describes San'yō's tearful parting with Itsuan after a brief visit.

In the Ninth Month of 1800, when he was twenty-one, San'yō announced that he was leaving to attend his paternal great-uncle's funeral in Takehara, representing his father. Instead he absconded to Osaka, neglecting to obtain the domain's permission, which was a criminal offense in those days. In Osaka he led a life of dissipation for several months before being finally escorted back to Aki.[5] After his return, he divorced Junko, then was kept in confinement at home for the next three years, until the Twelfth Month of 1803. This was a lesser punishment than might have been meted out had his parents not pleaded for leniency on the grounds of their son's mental instability.

In 1804, San'yō's father disinherited him, making his cousin the official family heir. San'yō's only real consolation at this point was his fondness for study. He was fortunate enough to be allowed to continue his work while under house arrest, and several works appeared after his release from detention. In 1807, he completed the first draft of *Nihon gaishi*, an unofficial history of Japan

---

[2]Ibid.

[3]Watson 1976, p. 121.

[4]Ibid.

[5]Inoguchi, p. 235.

written in Chinese which turned out to be the most highly-acclaimed work on this subject ever written.

When San'yō was thirty, his father arranged for him to study with *Kan Sazan, a close friend. At Renjuku, Sazan's school in Kannabe, San'yō read widely and taught Chinese composition as an assistant for about two years, before going next to Osaka and then Kyoto in 1811 to teach. Scholars consider the period in Kannabe to be a critically important one in San'yō's development as a poet. Sazan was so taken with his prodigious talent that he treated San'yō as his own son and even considered trying to adopt him. However, San'yō did not fully appreciate Sazan's solicitude and soon became disaffected with the rusticity of the place. Moreover, he was unimpressed with the students and at times even showed disrespect for his mentor, whom he apparently used to refer to as "Bald Head."[6]

Although San'yō often went home to Takehara to visit his mother, he spent the remainder of his life in Kyoto, never holding an official post. In Kyoto he opened an academy in the Shinmachi Marutamachi district. Concerned that he was out of favor with Kazan on account of his poor behavior while at Renjuku, he wrote to his old teacher frequently, trying to mend fences and regain his approval. His conduct at Renjuku was not the only reason why he feared he had earned Kazan's displeasure. In Kyoto, San'yō had reverted to his former dissolute ways, paying frequent visits to the geisha quarters, which angered Kazan. San'yō's familiarity with, and interest in, life in the pleasure quarters is apparent from the "Songs of Nagasaki" selections, below. Throughout this period, San'yō remained extremely successful in his teaching, partly because he had few rivals other than *Murase Kōtei (d. 1818), who was already old by this time, and *Nakajima Sōin.[7] As San'yō's fame as a kanshi poet, historian, and amateur painter grew, he attracted increasing numbers of pupils and enjoyed reasonable prosperity. San'yō married his second wife, Hikita Rie, in 1815,

---

[6]Donald Keene, *Some Japanese Portraits* (Tokyo, New York and San Francisco: Kodansha International, 1983), p. 124.

[7]Inoguchi, pp. 235-236.

when he was thirty-six, but he was actually in love with a fellow poet named *Ema Saikō, and two of the selections below deal with their relationship. Rie eventually bore him a daughter and three sons: one of these sons, Tatsuzō, who died in early childhood, is the child described in poem 270, below, as having "skin like newly-fallen pomegranate petals." The other two were Matajirō and Mikisaburō. Tragically, Mikisaburō, a pro-imperial activist, was beheaded in the Great Ansei Purge (Ansei no Taigoku) of 1858.

The year after San'yō married Rie, his father died, which made San'yō regret that he had not been a more filial son. As if to expiate his feelings of guilt, he started showing more devotion to Baishi, his mother. Several of the following poems reveal his attachment to her and describe his many long journeys on foot to visit his mother at her home or to escort her to and from Kyoto. Baishi lived on in good health until 1843, outliving San'yō by eleven years. On the third anniversary of his father's death, San'yō returned to Takehara to be with his mother. From there, he left for an extended visit to Kyushu, which included a three-month sojourn in Nagasaki, where he wrote a number of Chinese poems on the subject of the Dutch and Chinese merchants. Two of these poems have been included below.

In 1827, when San'yō was forty-eight, his *Nihon gaishi* (An Unofficial History of Japan) was finally published. Written with literary style and color in a free-wheeling, naturalized variety of Chinese, it became one of the most popular works of its day and was so widely circulated that demand outstripped supply. San'yō even started printing *Nihon gaishi* himself to alleviate the shortage. It is estimated that a third of the three million literate Japanese of the day came to possess this book, and San'yō's fame skyrocketed after the publication of this, his master work. Despite his popularity, San'yō never became completely integrated into Kyoto's kanshi world, in part because he often found fault with the poems of his contemporaries.[8] *Hirose Tansō was critical of his arrogance and over-confidence and noted that few could abide San'yō's conceited personality, although he clearly considered him a remarkable talent

---

[8]*WWW*, p. 552.

nonetheless.[9] It was in this later period that San'yō began to write historical verse, often patriotic or moralistic in sentiment, at a time when, as Donald Keene points out, it was perilous to express such sentiments openly.[10] In his final years, San'yō made his living purely through writing rather than by teaching. He died of lung disease on the twenty-third day of the Ninth Month of 1832 at age fifty-three, working on his manuscripts until the very end.

◑ 262 Reflections

Thirteen springs and thirteen autumns
Have flowed past like the waters of a stream.
Though heaven and earth have no beginning or end,
For us there is life and death.
Would that I could be ranked with the ancients,
Remembered forever in the annals of history.

Sugano, p. 65; Inoguchi, p. 243. From *San'yō shishō* (A Book of Poems by San'yō), 1832

This verse was written when poet was fourteen years old.

---

[9]Ibid.

[10]Ibid., p. 551.

◎ 263 Year's End

Another year has passed since I left my village.

What news of my beloved parents?

A snow storm in the capital has deprived me of companionship,

So tonight I'll trim the cold lamp and read by myself.

Iwanami, pp. 293-294. From *San'yō shishō*, 1832

Line one: It was the end of 1812, San'yō's second New Year's Eve since coming to Kyoto early
in 1811 (Iwanami, p. 293).
Line three: This line has one character too few, in the middle. The other lines all have seven
characters.

◎ 264

. . . .

My boy sobbed as he tied up my sandals.

Angrily, I bade him to make haste.

One of us weeping, the other scolding, yet both of us felt the same.

As I turned and looked behind me, the mountains and ocean seemed blurred.

Nakamura, p. 150. From *San'yō shishō*, 1832

Line four: The blurring was probably due to his tears.

This poem, excerpted from a long verse in five-character lines, was written in 1813, just after
San'yō had parted for a second time from his small son Yoichi (later called Itsuan), the only child
born to Junko, his first wife, from whom San'yō was divorced. The child had been left in the
care of San'yō's ailing father, Shunsui, because San'yō was mentally unstable at the time.

◉ 265 Leaving Ōgaki for Kuwana by Boat

The Kiso River flows on and on, all the way to the sea.
The sound of oars and the cries of geese bring feelings of nostalgia for home.
In this faraway place we journey alone as the year draws to a close,
Travelling through Mino in our covered boat, braving the wind and snow.

Inoguchi, p. 241; Andō, p. 106

Title: In 1813, San'yō travelled with two artist friends to Mino, Owari, Ōmi, and Ise, leaving
on the ninth day of the Tenth Month and returning to Kyoto around the end of the year. On the
way back they boated down the Kiso River, from Ōgaki to Kuwana. This poem was written en
route.

◉ 266 Mooring on the Sea of Amakusa

Are those clouds or mountains over there? Is that Wu or Yueh?
The ocean waters meet the sky in a slender thread of blue.
I moor my boat in the Amakusa Sea, having journeyed from afar.
Mist beyond the curtained window; the sun is gradually setting.
I catch a glimpse of a giant fish leaping amongst the waves,
As the light of Venus, bright as the moon, shines down upon my boat.

Sugano, p. 66; Inoguchi, pp. 244-245. From *San'yō shishō*, 1832

Title: The sea of Amakusa refers to the ocean expanse stretching between Amakusajima Island
in Kumamoto prefecture (Kyushu) and the Shimabara Peninsula in Nagasaki prefecture. This
poem was written in the Eighth Month of 1818, when the poet was thirty-nine. He was
journeying along the coast of Kyushu at the time and had stopped for the night on the sea of
Amakusa.
Line one: Wu and Yueh were ancient coastal states in China. Commentators concur that China
would not, in fact, have been visible from this place.

☾ 267 Encountering Rain after Crossing into Satsuma Province

1   Autumn rain, falling endlessly;
    Autumn winds that can knock you down.
    The journey is long; I lament that the days are short.
    Time and again I ask the way.
5   I have already crossed the Hirei passes
    And travel along the Satsuma coast.
    Darkness falls at a lonely village;
    Few hoof prints and wheel ruts mark the road.
    Ties fluttering, my hat rises from my head;
10 The sleeves of my bamboo cloak are soaked to my skin.
    I pick up my feet and trudge through the mud
    Over jagged rocks that block my way.
    In darkness I travel till I reach a checkpoint
    Where the officer on duty scolds me roundly.
15 I beg for lodgings at a villager's house,
    Falling to my knees and kneeling on the ground.
    The tumble-down stove yields no smoke;
    My pine torch lights up layers of dust.
    I stretch out like a dead man but cannot sleep,
20 So I sit up and chant poems all by myself.
    How many posthouses since leaving my province?
    When I look around, is there anyone I know?
    The mulberry bow decreed I would follow my heart,
    So there is no use speaking of hardship and pain.
25 Restless, I'm ever possessed by wanderlust,
    For in the northern room lives my aged mother.
    She counts the days, awaiting my return,
    And yet I am already twenty days late.
    What possesses me to travel like this,
30 Now, when the hair on my temples is greying?

278

I wish I were able to turn back midway,

But I'm just like a man on the back of a tiger.

I knew in advance that the trip would be hard.

So what's the use of having second thoughts?

35 I struggle out of bed and wrap up my feet,

For the crows have announced the arrival of dawn.

Iriya, pp. 227-229

Title: This poem was probably written during the poet's journey to Kyushu in the spring of 1818.
Line five: These are located between Kumamoto and Kagoshima along the sea of Yatsushiro (Iriya, p. 229).
Line thirteen: On checkpoints, see the notes to poem 75.
Line twenty-three: In ancient China, it was customary after the birth of a son to shoot artemisia (or jujube) arrows into the air, using a mulberry wood bow. The arrows were shot in all directions to drive away evil spirits and supposedly to secure the future success of the child. San'yō had always loved to travel and seems to have felt that being born a male (as symbolized here by the mulberry bow) had destined him to follow his heart.
Line twenty-six: "Northern room" is a conventional term for women's living quarters.
Line thirty-five: In preparation for travel.

☺ 268-269   From a series titled "Eight Satsuma Poems," 1818
(No. 2)

On the road I met some Koreans, descendants of prisoners of war.

They make their living with a potter's kiln and live in a village of their own.

I feel moved when I think of them digging up clay, here in this land of ours,

And making it into Koguli ware, renowned from ages past.

Fujikawa, p. 218

Line one: The original prisoners, some eighty potters, were among a group of war captives brought back to Japan with the returning armies of Toyotomi Hideyoshi and his generals in the last decade of the sixteenth century, following an attempted conquest of Korea. The potters founded a major kiln in Satsuma (in the western part of modern Kagoshima prefecture, Kyushu), which later produced the now-famous Satsuma ware.

(No. 3)

I met some folk who were from the South in the local marketplace.

Their raucous tongue was the strangest blend of Chinese and Ryukyuan.

They knew the cost of imperial ink and brushes from Peking,

And boasted of having been to that city on two occasions before.

Fujikawa, p. 218

Line one: "From the South": a reference to the Ryukyu islands, from which traders came in great numbers to Satsuma in San'yō's day.

270 Not long after getting married I had to go into mourning. I now have a baby son. I wrote these poems to record my happiness.

Fists like the half-opened fiddleheads of a fern,

Skin like newly-fallen pomegranate petals.

All you do is howl and seek your mother's breast;

Your lovely eyes still don't recognize your father's face!

Nakamura, p. 159

The poet went into mourning after his father Shunsui died in 1816. Tatsuzō, the subject of this poem, was born on the seventh day of the Tenth Month of 1820 but died of smallpox in the Third Month of 1825. This is the third of six poems written on the birth of Tatsuzō.

271

Late in life and wasted by illness, I begat a beloved son.

It greatly pains me to think that my father never saw your face.

Don't take after your father, my son; be like your grandfather instead.

I secretly rejoice that *he* is the one whom this child of mine takes after.

Nakamura, p. 160

Line one: The baby son appears to be Tatsuzō, seen also in the previous poem. San'yō would have been about thirty-nine or forty at the time of his birth.

◧ **272** **The Fisherman's Song**

My fishing is done, and the autumn wind blows through the reeds on the bank.
Beyond the shadows of the water-peppers the evening sun still shines.
My son is warming some wine; my wife is boiling the fish.
This place where I have moored my boat is where I make my home.

pp. 294-295. From *San'yō shishō*, 1832

Line three: This line has only six characters instead of the expected seven.

◧ **273** **Inscription for a Painting in Fushiki Temple**
 Depicting the Attack on Kizan

Crisp and harsh the sound of their whips as they crossed the river by night.
At dawn the thousand-strong force could be seen, with the general's flag aloft.
A pity it was that for ten long years he had kept his sword so sharp,
Only to see that great snake vanish, in a flash like a falling star!

Ishikawa, p. 170

Title: Kizan was one of the battle sites in the Kawanakashima wars, which were fought from
1553 to 1563 between Takeda Shingen (1521-1573) and Uesugi Kenshin (1530-1578) in Shinano.
Neither side won a decisive victory.
Line three: "He" is Kenshin, referred to in the previous note.
Line four: The "great snake" is Shingen.

◧ **274**

Past the mansions of the fan-shaped island our boat is slowly rowed.
Under red lanterns that hang from green railings wine glasses sparkle like jewels.
I lean out the window to attract the attention of some women whom I see.
They were the ones who had served the foreigners at that banquet the other night.

Nakamura, p. 203. From "Nagasaki yō" (Songs of Nagasaki)

Line one: Nagasaki's Dejima island, official ghetto for the Dutch during the Edo period.

⊙ **275**

She offers him tea and lights some incense, gesturing with her chin.

Both pairs of eyes are doing the talking, no trouble being understood.

Once in the bedroom no need at all for someone to interpret their words.

They are able to convey their feelings with ease, just as you'd expect.

Nakamura, p. 204. From "Nagasaki yō"

This poem describes an imaginary meeting between a prostitute from the Maruyama pleasure quarters and a foreigner.

⊙ **276 Chuang Tzu's Dream of Being a Butterfly**

Chuang Chou or a butterfly—which is really me?

Laboring to prove that all things are one is a waste of mental energy.

Would that the dream could last forever and that I'd never awake.

I'd be landing on blossoms and entering flowers, flying wherever I pleased.

Inoguchi, pp. 257-258

Line one: Chuang Chou is Chuang Tzu, the famous Chinese Taoist philosopher credited with having written *Chuang Tzu*. In one of the later chapters of this work, the philosopher writes that he once dreamed he was a butterfly. After waking up, he was unsure which of these two states—his existence as Chuang Tzu or as the butterfly—was reality and which was the dream.
Line two: In the chapter of *Chuang Tzu* titled "Ch'i-wu lun" (Discussion on Making All Things Equal), Chuang Tzu argues that all distinctions between the different phenomena and categories in the universe are man-made and relative, hence, invalid. The true sage forms no value judgments and just accepts things for what they are. Chuang Tzu tells us that all philosophical discussion is a waste of time and energy, and San'yō seems to be implying that Chuang Tzu was guilty of the very thing he criticized in other thinkers.

☾ 277 A Letter from Home

Alone, I unfold the letter from home and trim the wick of the lamp.

I can almost hear her endless chatter, pouring forth in torrents.

She wanted to write down all her memories of every day that had passed:

How the mid-autumn moon looked in all kinds of weather she described
    in minute detail.

Nakamura, p. 152

Line one: This letter, which Sanyō received while in Shimonoseki, was from *Ema Saikō, his lover, who was in Kyoto at the time (Nakamura, p. 152). San'yō had been involved with her since his early thirties. Following his divorce in 1813, he had proposed to Saikō, but her father would not give his consent to the marriage. In 1815, San'yō ended up marrying Hikita Rie instead, after losing all hope of winning Saikō's hand. It seems, however, that he continued to love Saikō no less ardently.

🌙 278 Saying Goodbye to Saikō in the Rain from a Window

In the parlor by the candle's waning light, let us tarry awhile and make merry.

Fresh mud lies on the road leading home; we should wait until it dries.

The clouds over the peaks beyond the river have finally dispersed.

At the house next door, shamisen and singing continue as the night wears on.

Since this spring has an extra month, you, my dear guest, should stay on,

Though the rain last night was merciless, and the flowers have all been spoiled.

Nōshū, where you're headed for, is not so far away.

And yet I fear that now I'm old we'll have trouble meeting often.

Iwanami, p. 298. From *San'yō ikō* (A Posthumous Text of San'yō's Works), 1841

Line three: San'yō is using the weather as an excuse to make Saikō stay longer. The dispersal of the clouds is seen as a sign that the weather will soon improve, allowing the mud on the roads to harden. The river was the Kamo; the mountains were the Eastern Hills (Higashiyama) to the east of Kyoto, which Saikō would have had to cross to reach the road to Mino beyond Lake Biwa.
Line five: The extra month is an intercalary month, the intercalary Third Month, which happened between the Third and the Fourth months. The phenomenon of intercalation occurred about seven times in a period of nineteen years and was intended to make up for the incongruity between the solar and the lunar years. This verse was written on the ninth day of the intercalary Third Month, 1830. Saikō had arrived in Kyoto to visit San'yō on the twenty-second day of the Third Month, just over two weeks earlier. San'yō was fifty-one at the time, Saikō forty-four (Iwanami, pp. 298, 449).
Line seven: Nōshū is a reference to Mino province, Saikō's home province.

🌙 279 Thinking of Mother

Chilly autumn wind that blows against me,

Putting to flight the leaves on the trees:

When you reach the trees in my village,

Don't interfere with my dear mother's robes!

Iwanami, p. 298. From *San'yō ikō*, 1841

☉ 280 On the Road

Sunset, and a wind is blowing through the trees that mark the miles.
The rice I bought at the station inn is tainted by dust and grit.
Nine times in the past ten years I've travelled the San'yō Road,
Only because my aged parents are still alive in my hometown.

Iwanami, p. 296. From *San'yō ikō*, 1841

Line one: The trees marking the miles are *enoki* (hackberry). These were planted on mounds on both sides of the road at prescribed intervals of one *ri* to mark distance.
Line three: The San'yō Road was the major highway through the San'yōdō (the San'yō circuit), which was a major territorial division composed of eight provinces: Harima, Mimasaka, Bizen, Bitchū, Bingo, Aki, Suō, and Nagato, all in southwest Honshu. Together with the eight provinces of the San'indō, this circuit formed the region known as Chūgoku, the "middle provinces."
Line four: The poet's hometown was in modern Takehara in Hiroshima prefecture. After settling in Kyoto in 1811, San'yō made many trips back, including ones in 1816, 1818, and 1819 (Iwanami, p. 449). This poem was probably written in the decade following his move to Kyoto.

☉ 281 Waiting on Mother on a Moonless Night in Mid-Autumn

Since last we spent this eve together thirteen years have passed.
I am able to offer her wine once more as the winds of autumn blow.
No moonlight shines upon our cups, but this I don't regret,
For it means that Mother cannot see the grey hair on my temples.

Hirano, p. 244

Title: It was the fifteenth day of the Eighth Month (Hirano, p. 244).

⬡ 282 A Short Poem Written on the Road while Escorting My Mother

1 The east wind greeted my mother when she arrived.
 The north wind farewelled her when she returned.
 When she came, the roadside plants were fragrant,
 But soon they were frozen by the frost and snow.
5 When I heard the cock crow, I wrapped my feet,
 Then hobbled along behind her litter,
 Never complaining that my feet were sore,
 Only concerned that she journey in comfort.
 I offered my mother a cup of tea, then drank a cup myself.
10 The teashop was filled with the sunlight of dawn,
    the frost had disappeared.
 For a son of fifty to have a mother seventy years of age—
 Fortune like this is rarely seen in this world of ours!
 People were travelling north and south, like the threads of silk on a loom;
 Yet who among them could possibly be as happy as this mother and son?

Sugano, p. 67; Iwanami, p. 297; Inoguchi, p. 257. From *San'yō ikō*, 1841

Lines one and two: The east wind is the spring wind; the north wind, the wind of winter.
Line nine: Beginning here, the poetic meter changes from five to seven characters per line.

⏻ 283 Waiting on Mother in Her Litter

1   When her litter moved, I would move;
And when it stopped, I stopped, too.
On our journey we never ceased talking, mother in her litter.
Often I pointed out mountains and rivers we passed along the way.
5   From time to time I stooped to tie my laces which had come undone.
Mother would call out, "Hurry up, son!" and I would answer yes.
I've traveled ten times back and forth along the San'yō Road,
But every time I've gone back home my visits have been brief.
Could this old man attending her litter have dared to admit fatigue?
10   Whether on boats or at mountain posthouses all was like home to me.
We were travelling a road that I knew well, but for mother all was new.
So I always set my gaze upon the sights that met her eyes.

Nakamura, p. 155

Lines one and two: The first two lines of this poem have only five words each, as opposed to seven in the others.

◐ **284 I had inquired about old Kan [Sazan]'s illness, but he died before I could be there. With this poem I record my grief.**

When I heard he was ill I ran a thousand *ri*.

But on the way I learned that he had died.

Unable to help them carry his coffin

I regretted having set off so late.

At his old house the willows looked blurry and dim;

In his empty room a light burned brightly.

I was grieved by words he'd said near the end—

Awaiting my arrival, he'd left me his papers.

Iwanami, pp. 295-296. From *San'yō ikō*, 1841

Title: Sazan died of a stomach ailment on the thirteenth day of the Eighth Month of 1827 (Iwanami, p. 448).
Line five: Sazan's willows appeared blurry perhaps because they were seen through tears.
Line six: The light is most likely a memorial candle at the Buddhist altar.
Line eight: That is, Sazan had left his literary manuscripts to the care of San'yō.

◐ 285 Written while Ill

1 Who says that illness is cause for concern?
  My illness is really not grave at all.
  A chronic ailment may afflict me,
  But my vision at least has not declined.
5 The nights are long; I wake early each morning.
  When it's light outside I hear frozen sparrows.
  Someone announces that the congee is ready;
  Hunger sated, my stomach feels calm.
  Wrapped up in blankets, I sit and read.
10 Having my faculties is reason for joy.
  That my old friends grow distant bothers me not,
  For my best friends still comfort me now that I'm ill.
  The span of my life is determined by Heaven;
  Good health or bad—it's out of our hands.
15 Knowledge alone is without any limits,
  And does not submit to the Creator's control.

Iriya, p. 232

◐ 286 A Conversation with Seigan before Parting

The lamp stands next to some yellow flowers, the middle of the night approaches.
When morning comes you will be gone, travelling through the Shinshū clouds.
Even though the wine pot is empty, please don't get up yet!
Why must we part at a time like this, when I'm sick and near to death?

Iwanami, p. 299. From *San'yō ikō*, 1841

Line one: The flowers were chrysanthemums, an autumn flower symbolizing longevity common
in Chinese eremitic poetry. San'yō's wife had bought these for her husband on the ninth day of
the Ninth Month of 1832, as he was ill at the time. This poem was written eight days later when
San'yō, still ailing, was visited by the poet *Yanagawa Seigan prior to the latter's departure for
Edo. San'yō had started coughing up blood in the Sixth Month of that year and died on the
twenty-third day of the Ninth Month at age fifty-three, less than a week after bidding farewell to
his friend. See Iwanami, p. 449.

Priest Kaiun, fl. ca. 1815

Priest Kaiun was the chief cleric of Undōan, a temple in Ueda in old Echigo, part of modern Niigata prefecture. Little is known of Kaiun's life and career except that he was influenced in his early years by the kanshi poet Hattori Hakuhi (1714-1767) of Osaka, the foster son of *Hattori Nankaku. In the first selection below, we find the poet moved by the sight of the solitary old man returning home from the fields, perhaps seeing in this lonesome figure his own self. The second verse evokes the chilly, crystalline beauty associated with *hie*, an aesthetic quality championed by the renga poet Shinkei (1406-1475) and seen also in the haiku poetry of Bashō. The forest seems all the more frigid due to the lonely remoteness of the poet's vantage point as he observes the panorama in tranquil isolation, no other person in sight.

☽ 287 Misty Rain in the Paddy Fields

The outskirts are shrouded in misty rain.
Through the haze I see the setting sun.
An old man in a straw cloak comes into view.
Hoe on his shoulder, heading home through the paddies.

Iwanami, p. 363. From *Kunshū shū* (A Collection of Selected Poems), 1816

☽ 288 Evening Bells at a Secluded Temple

Like silk brocade the frosted forest stretches beyond the river.
The slanting light of the setting sun illuminates the Brahma tower.
Clouds descend from the heavens above and all is hidden for a while.
Nothing left but the evening bells, drifting in from across the water.

Iwanami, p. 363. From *Kunshū shū*, 1816

Oka Kunshō, fl. ca. 1814

A Teishugaku scholar, Oka Kunshō was a native of Awa in what is today Tokushima prefecture. Little is known about him except that he flourished around 1814 and lived in Namihana (modern Osaka-fu) in his youth.[1] It is also known that he belonged to Kontonsha, the society whose members included some of Edo Japan's finest kanshi poets, such as *Shibano Ritsuzan, *Bitō Jishū, Koga Seiri, Rai Shunsui, and *Emura Hokkai. Some of these fellow poets may have been among the merry band who accompanied him on the epic-like drinking expedition described in the first poem. Kunshō eventually went back to his village and concentrated on writing verse. His poetry collection, published in 1817, has a preface by Rai Shunsui.

---

[1]Iwanami, p. 485.

☾ 289 A Little Drinking Party aboard a Boat:
A Poem Using the Rhyme Category "Tō" (East)

Clear flowing water—fine for beating the heat!
We gathered, poet travellers, two or three,
And spirits high, sailed off on Wings of Blue.
Wine in bamboo tubes helped keep us cool.
Through a gap in the reeds the evening moon appeared.
Over the duckweed a chilly breeze did blow.
Once in our cups we wrote a poem or two,
And cared not whether they were good or bad.

Iwanami, pp. 261-262. From *Hankan'en ikō* (A Posthumous Text from the Garden of the Half-Room Retreat), 1817

Line three: "Wings of Blue" refers to a type of boat which had a blue figurehead carved in the shape of a bird.

☾ 290 The Old Battlefield

In ancient times this was a battlefield.
But now it is a place where birds lament.
Mournful winds blow across the bleached bones
As the setting sun shines down on the green moss.
The country temple was ravaged by the fires of war;
The ancient castle was reduced to dirt and ash.
What's left to see amidst this desolation?
Just the moon moving back and forth in the chilly trees.

Iwanami, p. 261. *Hankan'en ikō*, 1817

Hirose Tansō, 1782-1856

Hirose Tansō, known in his day as the "Poet-Sage of the Western Seas," was one of the foremost kanshi poets and teachers of the Edo period. A native of Bungo in modern Ōita prefecture, he was the son of a prosperous merchant. Although sickly as a child, Tansō was highly precocious, and by the age of eight he had read *The Classic of Filial Piety* and *The Four Books*. At sixteen he studied for about three years under Kamei Nanmei (1743-1814) and Nanmei's son Shōyō (1773-1836) in Hakata, northern Kyushu. Nanmei faithfully corrected his poetry, while Shōyō supervised his prose writing, both appreciating his talents. Tansō was particularly ill between the ages of eighteen and twenty-one and was even forced to return home, but eventually managed to recover. On account of Tansō's continuing health problems, one of his younger brothers took over the family business, freeing him to pursue a teaching career and live quietly in his beloved home, which he poetically named Enshirō (The Chamber of Faraway Thoughts).

As a scholar, Tansō was associated with Setchūgaku. At twenty-four, he opened a school in rented space within Chōfukuji temple in his native village of Hita. Two years later, in 1807, he opened Keirinsō (The Cassia Forest Retreat, also known as Keirin'en), admitting all capable students regardless of their social status, although as their numbers increased, he came to need larger teaching facilities. Thus, in 1817 he founded yet another academy, called Kangien (The Garden where All Are Proper), in Horita. Tansō had more than three thousand pupils over the years, some of whom became distinguished figures in their own right. These included the Dutch Studies scholar Takano Chōei and the military strategist Ōmura Masujirō (1825-1869).

In 1842 Tansō received an outstanding service award from the shogunate together with a surname and sword. He was a kind and sincere person with a reputation for being demanding and methodical as a teacher. As Inoguchi relates,

Tansō established grade levels in his school and each month evaluated his pupils' levels of attainment. But the same scrutiny was also directed at himself. From the age of eighteen, he kept a strict daily record of his own good deeds and failings, hoping to accumulate ten thousand meritorious acts in the course of his lifetime. This activity was inspired by a Ming work he had read in his late teens called *Yin chih-lu* (Record of Secret Acts of Benevolence), written by Yuan Liao-fan.[1]

The first poem, below, is one of the best known and loved of kanshi verses. It sees Tansō lending heart to his homesick pupils and endeavoring to forge a sense of camaraderie among them. The second and third poems, on the theme of his study, show the poet at his best. The images of dense incense smoke hanging in the indoor air and shoe-marks scoring the moss outside his study door provide us with two memorable scenes from his immediate environment.

291 Second poem in a series titled "Miscellaneous Verses to Instruct Students at The Cassia Forest Retreat: Four Poems"

Don't say that life in a different village is filled with suffering and toil.
Comrades, you have friends here and will naturally form close ties.
At dawn when we leave our brushwood huts the frost will be just like snow.
You'll fetch water from the river, and I will gather the firewood.

Andō, p. 116; Iwanami, p. 316; Kudō, p. 41. From *Enshirō shishō* (A Book of Poems from The Chamber of Faraway Thoughts), pt. one, 1837; pt. two, 1849

Title: The Cassia Forest Retreat (Keirinsō) was a prestigious academy which Tansō established in 1807 when he was twenty-six.

---

[1]Inoguchi, p. 314.

⊙ **292-293** **From a series titled "Five Tansō Poems"**
(No. 2)

Desolate and bleak, so desolate and bleak!
I burn incense as light rain drizzles down.
A column of smoke sinks beneath the humid air,
Unwilling to push its way out the latticed window.

Kudō, pp. 50-51. From *Enshirō shishō*, 1837, 1849

This verse and the next were written between the summer and autumn of 1826.

(No. 5)

After walking down a path that leads through pines,
They look for a gate among bamboo.
Visitors here do not wear *geta*,
Lest they leave marks and harm the green moss.

Kudō, p. 56. From *Enshirō shishō*, 1837, 1849

Line three: *Geta* are high-platform wooden sandals with thongs that rest on two horizontal slats
for soles.

⊙ **294** **A Village by the River**

A scattering of homes with brushwood fences, east and west of the river.
Reed spikes and bush clover wave in the wind now that the rain has passed.
The sun has set and the fisherman has already gone away.
But his fishing pole is still standing there, wedged between the rocks.

Iwanami, pp. 317; Inoguchi, p. 317. From *Enshirō shishō*, 1837, 1849

⊙ 295 A Poem for Master Gofū Who Entertained Me
with Wine near the Naka River

Fragrant plants are now appearing before the Sumiyoshi Shrine.

Beside the riverbed, hand in hand, we slowly strolled along.

With pride I'll tell the village folk after I return

Of the noodle-fish we cooked and ate in the shade of the willow trees.

Kudō, p. 68. From *Kaikyū rō hikki* (Notes from The Chamber of Ancient Remembrances)

Title: Master Gofū (Gofū Shujin), also known as Komeya Seizō, was a friend of Tansō's who
lived in Hakata (in northern Kyushu), the setting for this poem. Tansō wrote this verse to thank
Seizō for treating him and four others to boiled whitebait and sake at a shop on the Naka River
(also known as the Sumiyoshi River), which flowed through Hakata (Kudō, p. 69).
Line one: The Sumiyoshi Shrine was located about one kilometer to the west of
Hakata posthouse.
Line four: "Noodle-fish," an old Chinese word for whitebait.

⊙ 296-297 From a series titled "Miscellaneous Verses on the
Kuma River: Five Poems"

(No. 1)

Clear river ten miles long, bluer than indigo its waters.

Here and there along its banks stand houses built over the water.

A young boy who hasn't yet learned how to work the rudder of a boat

Is leaning against a wooden railing, learning how to fish.

Inoguchi, p. 320; also Kudō, p. 30. From *Enshirō shishō*, 1837, 1849

Title: The Kumagawa, also called Mikumagawa, is a river which flowed east to west through
Tansō's hometown of Hita (Tansō, p. 30). Tansō is believed to have written these five poems at
around age thirty.

(No. 2)

A young lady, enjoying the spring, leans on a painted railing.
Why does she face the wind as she plays her melancholy koto?
A traveller on the river pauses in his poling to listen to her voice so pure,
Unaware that his boat is drifting toward the rocky shoals.

Kudō, p. 32. From *Enshirō shishō*, 1837, 1849

Ema Saikō [Shōmu], 1787-1861

One of the few well-known female Edo poets, Ema Saikō was a native of the town of Ōgaki in Mino, modern Gifu prefecture, and the daughter of Ema Ransai (1747-1838), who was a distinguished Dutch Studies scholar and physician in the Ōgaki domain. Her style name, Saikō, meaning "delicate scent," evokes the subtle, almost aromatic quality present in many of her poems. She was also known as Shōmu (Dreams of the River Hsiang), which similarly conjures up a romantic aura. Saikō excelled in Chinese poetry and letters, as well as in Nanga-style painting. Among Nanga artists, she is regarded as one of the most skillful, flowers being her area of particular expertise. She learned painting under Nakabayashi Chikudō, Uragami Shunkin, and Yamamoto Baiitsu.

Saikō acquired the fundamental techniques of writing Chinese poetry with *Rai San'yō, who courted her for many years. San'yō had been in love with her since his early thirties and proposed marriage to her in 1813, more than a decade after he had divorced his first wife, Junko, but Saikō's father would not give his consent. San'yō ended up marrying Hikita Rie instead, in 1815, after losing all hope of winning Saikō's hand. It seems, however, that he remained in love with her for the rest of his life. Saikō never married, and although she lived a fully independent life, she remained in spirit San'yō's devoted companion. Their relationship was well known in society at large, and people seeking an introduction to San'yō would often approach Saikō first. When San'yō's mother, Baishi, visited from Hiroshima, she brought gifts for Saikō that were no less substantial than those she gave to Rie, her daughter-in-law.[1]

Saikō was a member of a coterie called Hakuōsha (The White Sea Gull Poetry Society, est. 1818), which met monthly in Ōgaki over a period of about twelve years. She kept company with such eminent poets as *Yanagawa Seigan

---

[1]Nakamura, p. 223.

and Murase Tōjō (1791-1853). Her poems are contained in the two-volume work *Shōmu ikō* (A Posthumous Text of Shōmu's Works, ca. 1871). The first two verses which follow possess a delicate sensibility characteristic of Saikō's poetry in general, mingling color with light and scent with scent. In the second poem in particular we see a degree of sensitivity toward the interaction of light and color seldom matched in Japanese poetry. The final two poems are passionate and despairing, the bitter frankness with which she describes her solitary drinking being especially poignant. As these two verses suggest, her physical separation from San'yō cannot have been an easy burden to bear.

◙ 298 A Summer Evening

The rain has ended, gusts of wind blow through the garden bamboo.
A new moon shaped like an eyebrow casts a pale and slanting light.
Late at night, to enjoy the cool I leave the windows open.
From out of the darkness the scent of silk blossoms mingles with the perfume
   on my pillow.

Iwanami, p. 339. From *Shōmu ikō* (A Posthumous Text of Shōmu's Works), ca. 1871

Line four: Blossoms from the silk tree (*Albizzia julibrissin*) actually produce a flower with a very weak scent. The tree is six to ten meters in height.

◙ 299 Walking in the Moonlight by the Plum Trees

Moonlit plum trees, enchantingly lovely—how should I spend this evening?
Softly chanting verse, I wander through the crisscrossing shadows of the trees.
My body is dappled with patterns of light as distinct as water is clear.
I can only perceive the subtle fragrance and cannot see the blossoms.

Iwanami, p. 339. From *Shōmu ikō*, ca. 1871

◑ 300 Parting from Master San'yō under the Pine Tree at Karasaki

I am standing upon the bank, you are on the boat.

From the boat, from the bank, we gaze at each other,

    bound by the sadness of parting.

As your form grows smaller and smaller, away on the misty lake,

I curse the wind because it has made the sails of your boat so full.

I tarry awhile beneath the pines and cannot bear to leave,

Though the boundless expanse of cerulean waves is a vast and empty void.

Seven times we've farewelled each other during the past twenty years.

But never before has there been a parting as hard to describe as this.

Iwanami, p. 340. From *Shōmu ikō*, ca. 1871

Title: Master San'yō is Rai San'yō, her lover. The tree at Karasaki was a Lake Biwa landmark. See notes accompanying poem 81. This parting occurred in 1832, sometime before the twenty-third day of the Ninth Month, when San'yō died, but the exact date is unknown.

◑ 301 Picking Lotus Seeds and Throwing Them at the Mandarin Ducks

The two of you floating and swimming there, on the green and rippling waters,

Unaware that in the human world there is parting and separation.

For fun I take some lotus seeds and throw them into the pond.

"As you both fly off in opposite directions, may you feel a moment of longing!"

Nakamura, p. 225. From *Shōmu ikō*, ca. 1871

Line four: Mandarin ducks are a symbol of conjugal love and fidelity; thus, seeing their happiness evokes envy in Saikō, reminding her of her own deprivation. She was in love with Rai San'yō but had been unable to marry him because of her father's opposition. Unlike San'yō, she never married but continued to see him to the end of his life.

◔ 302 An Impromptu Poem

Lonely by the spring window, daylight slowly breaking.

Drunk on wine, my senses dulled, feeling as dead as ashes.

I haven't tended the kitchen fire for three whole days on end.

In bed I listen to the morning rain as it drizzles on the fallen flowers.

Nakamura, p. 226. From *Shōmu ikō*, ca. 1871

Line three: In the original language, "kitchen fire" is literally "duck fire," a phrase whose meaning is unclear.

◔ 303 An Impromptu Poem

Few are the things that bring me pleasure, and my temple hair is thinning.

Now I'm only intimate with my shallow goblet of jade.

I am constantly drunk on wine these days, but place no blame on me:

I want to feel that I'm young again, if only for a while.

Nakamura, pp. 228-229. From *Shōmu ikō*, ca. 1871

Kusaba Haisen, 1788-1867

A kanshi poet of note, Kusaba Haisen was the eldest son of a Saga domain retainer in Hizen, modern Saga prefecture, in northern Kyushu. At eighteen, he entered Kōdōkan, the Saga domain school, and later took lessons in Chinese in Nagasaki. Haisen went to Edo at twenty-three with his daimyo, Nabeshima, and studied Teishugaku there with Koga Seiri. Trained in poetics by *Yanagawa Seigan and Shinozaki Shōchiku, he is known to have written upwards of twenty thousand kanshi. Haisen subsequently returned to Hizen to serve as a teacher in a local village school. His enthusiasm for learning and his eagerness to convey this spirit to his students is evident in the first poem below.

Haisen was also famous as a Nanga artist and waka poet. While the depiction of bamboo in monochrome ink was one of his particular strengths, his poems are anything but monochromatic in their imagery. The last two selections below seem to stimulate all the senses at once. "Autumn Evening on a Mountain Road" places the poet amidst a profusion of flowers and tiny insects, suggesting a richness of colors which are not explicitly identified. As Ōoka Makoto reminds us, this use of natural objects to suggest individual colors is a distinctive characteristic of the Japanese poetic tradition and indicative of a highly refined sensory awareness.[1]

---

[1]Ōoka, p. 332.

🔘 304 A Poem for My Fellow Students Composed while Walking in the Mountains

The road becomes steep and winding, and I slip on the mossy rocks.
From below my feet a wind arises, blowing the clouds about.
Mountain climbing is exactly like the endeavors of a student:
With every upward step you take the brighter the vista before you.

Sugano, p. 100. From *Haisen shishō* (A Book of Poems by Haisen), 1849

Line three: This notion is derived from a passage in *Chung yung* (The Doctrine of the Mean) which states that learning is like climbing a mountain (Sugano, p. 100). Motoori Norinaga's essay *Uiyamabumi* (First Steps Up the Mountain, 1798) has a similar passage.

🔘 305 The Pleasures of Spring

Butterflies chase each other—why are they so wild?
I've searched for flowers here and there, my sleeves now bear their scent.
Home again, I feel like sleeping; several cups and it's time for bed.
The spring moon, so laden with sentiment, shines into my rustic room.

Fujikawa, p. 168

🔘 306 On the Outskirts of Town

Clear one minute, then it's cloudy; springtime, fallen flowers.
Everywhere smoke from kitchen fires; new growth upon the trees.
Along the road wet fields of rice, flat and stretching forever.
A chorus of croaking frogs escorts the evening traveller home.

Fujikawa, pp. 168-169

◙ 307 Autumn Evening on a Mountain Road

Bellflowers, bush clover, crickets;

Little bugs and tiny shrubs whose names I do not know.

This evening as I follow a road through the autumn mountains

Flowers of every sort are in bloom, all kinds of creatures are chirping.

Iwanami, p. 319. From *Haisen shishō*, 1849

Yanagawa Seigan, 1789-1858

The son of a prosperous farmer, Yanagawa Seigan came from Sone village in Mino, which is now incorporated within Ōgaki-city in modern Gifu prefecture. Seigan is ranked with *Rai San'yō as being among the foremost nineteenth-century kanshi poets. Some say that San'yō was the better prose writer, Seigan the better poet. A precocious and bookish child, Seigan was orphaned at twelve, losing both his father and mother within the space of three months. After his parents died, he went to live with a wealthy cousin, Inazu Nagayoshi. When Seigan was eighteen, the family decided that his younger brother would become heir to the family estate, freeing Seigan to pursue scholarship, his preferred career. Seigan went to Edo in 1806. After trying unsuccessfully to enter Shōheikō, he instead became a student of Yamamoto Hokuzan. In time, Seigan came to be appreciated as a master of his craft, winning the respect of some of the leading poets of his day, including *Ōkubo Shibutsu and *Kikuchi Gozan. In Edo, Seigan also acquired a reputation for dissipation, frequenting brothels and going into debt, before returning to Kyoto in 1809 and deciding to turn over a new leaf. He was by this time twenty years old.

Emblematic of this change of heart was his taking of Buddhist vows and adoption of a new style name: Shizen, meaning "Zen Poet." At age twenty-two, he returned to Hokuzan's academy in Edo and achieved distinction as one of the top students in the school. Between 1814 and 1820, Seigan travelled extensively, becoming famous for his insatiable wanderlust. In 1817 he found time to establish a school in his village, naming it Rika Sonsha (Pear-Blossom Country Cottage). When *Kashiwagi Jotei died in 1819, Seigan visited Kyoto to put Jotei's papers in order. There, he became acquainted with *Rai San'yō; they met at a lodging house in Kamogawa and became life-long friends. A year later, Seigan married Inazu Kōran (*Yanagawa Kōran), the seventeen-year old daughter of Inazu Nagayoshi, the cousin who had taken care of him after he was orphaned.

It was a happy marriage, and the couple were inseparable. In 1822, Seigan and Kōran departed on an extended journey together, leaving from the area around Yokkaichi and Kuwana and proceeding to Ise and Ueno. From there it seems they went to Kyoto, Osaka, Okayama, and Hiroshima, visiting famous poets along the way, including *Kan Sazan and *Rai Kyōhei. They travelled for five years, during which time Seigan wrote a large body of verse, despite periods of illness. The couple settled for a short time in Kyoto in 1827 but continued to travel widely as before, visiting their vast network of friends.

Seigan moved his family to Edo in 1832 and two years later established Gyokuchi Ginsha (The Jewelled Pond Poetic Recitation Society) in Kanda. This society attracted as many as a thousand poets from all across the land and remained in existence until 1845, serving as an important locus for poetic activity in Edo. Gyokuchi Ginsha was to occupy most of Seigan's time over the next decade, bringing him national renown. But in 1846, the peripatetic Seigan moved yet again, this time back to Kyoto after a short stint in Mino province. By this time he had become an ardent pro-imperial loyalist, and Donald Keene speculates that the rationale for this final relocation was to be nearer to the emperor.[1] Inoguchi offers a different explanation, suggesting that Seigan was simply trying to put a safe distance between himself and the shogunate because of his imperial sympathies.[2]

Seigan's belief in activism as opposed to merely holding philosophical views without putting them into practice may well have stemmed from his knowledge of the proactive teachings of the Yōmeigaku school. He became politically involved with the distinguished poet and Confucianist Umeda Unpin (1816-1859), *Rai San'yō's son Mikisaburō (1825-1859), and with *Priest Gesshō, all of whom campaigned for the overthrow of the shogunate and plotted against the repressive policies of Ii Naosuke, whose notorious Great Ansei Purge had brought imprisonment or death to many imperial loyalists. Although Seigan's earlier

---

[1] *WWW*, p. 556.

[2] Inoguchi, p. 323.

works are in a romantic vein, many of his later poems are highly critical of the shogunate. He would eventually have been imprisoned himself had cholera not claimed him first. Seigan's "timely" death led to the oft-quoted saying to the effect that "Seigan was clever where both sorts of *shi* were concerned," the word *shi* meaning both poetry and dying.[3] Shortly before his death, Seigan had his beloved Kōran removed to another room, explaining that "men do not die in the arms of women."[4] Kōran was briefly imprisoned following his death but managed to regain her freedom, claiming that, being a woman, she had not been privy to her husband's affairs.

Seigan's poetry was his greatest legacy. Although an eclectic in style, he was inspired by the poetry of the T'ang in particular, excelling in both regulated verse (*lü-shih*) and the quatrain (*chüeh-chü*). His most important collection of verse is the *Seigan shū* (The Seigan Collection, 1841-1856). The following selections demonstrate the thematic variety and overall strength of his corpus.

☉ **308 Inscription for a Picture of Tokiwa Holding Her Baby**

Snow on the brim of her bamboo hat, the wind is lifting her skirts.
Her baby howls, demanding milk—how must he be feeling?
Years later, from the lofty cliffs, high on Mount Tekkai,
He roared loudly at those three armies, making the very same noise!

Ishikawa, p. 172; Andō, p. 134. From *Seigan shū* (The Seigan Collection), 1841-1856

Line two: The baby is Minamoto no Yoshitsune (1159-1189), who later distinguished himself in the Genpei Wars.
Line three: It was here upon Tekkai at the Hyodori-goe Pass near modern Kobe that Yoshitsune defeated the armies of the Taira. The year was 1184.

---

[3]Andō, p. 135.

[4]Inoguchi, p. 324.

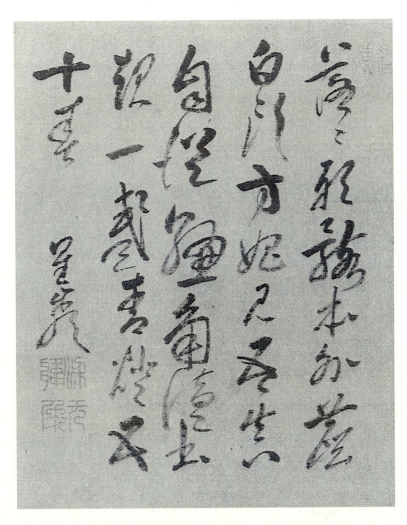

4. A holographic text of an untitled kanshi quatrain, written and signed by
Yanagawa Seigan (1789-1858). (Translated in the List of Illustrations.)

308

309 Dreaming I Was Going Home while on a Boat One Night

Autumn, and at a crossroads we stood, with a pot of cloudy wine.
My big brother poured my younger brother wine, I saw them toast each other.
Then my dream was suddenly shattered by the crash of rain on the window.
I was on a boat on the Tone River, journeying ten thousand *ri*.

Hirano, pp. 261-262

310 An Impromptu Poem on the New Spring Season

The wind from the east blows fiercely, filling the city with dust.
Limitless are the self-seekers inhabiting this world.
Justice is only found in abundance where plums and willows grow:
The red gates and the white roofs alike all share the very same spring.

Hirano, p. 260

Line one: The eastern wind is a spring wind; dust is synonymous with worldly cares and attachments, the tainted world of men.
Line four: "Red gates" refers to the rich; "white roofs" to the poor.

⏾ 311 A Miscellaneous Poem

1   I leave my village to visit the burial mounds.
　　One grave upon the other—why so many?
　　In these graves rest the bones of the wealthy,
　　Their bleached skulls covered with creeping vines.
5   While they lived, their days were joyful.
　　They dwelled in opulent, lofty mansions,
　　Surrounded by throngs of famous beauties,
　　Who plucked their instruments and sang with clear voices.
　　The lives of the poor are miserable and hard,
10 But in death they lie buried near the mounds of the rich.
　　The rich and the poor are no different in the end,
　　Having neither joys nor cares.
　　To all young men these words I send:
　　Seek nothing more than to cultivate yourselves.
15 And if in your lives you do nought but good deeds,
　　Posterity will revere you for a thousand autumns.

Iwanami, p. 301. From *Seigan shū*, 1841-1856

☾ 312 Written on a Wall

Cold weather comes, the heat disappears, one season yields to another.

These eyes of mine have now grown dim, my temple hair is like silk.

Good and bad fortune don't come uninvited—it is we who invite them in.

Life and death are determined by Fate; why should I have any doubts?

The ancient pine tree, standing so high, can live for a thousand years.

But the flowers of the hibiscus bloom for just the briefest time.

If this tiny room were my entire world, I'd wish for nothing more,

For the time would pass at such a slow pace, here in my "heaven-in-a-pot."

Iwanami, pp. 303-304. From *Seigan shū*, 1841-1856

Title: This is the fourth of four wall poems written in Kyoto around the Ninth Month of 1851.
Line eight: The poet is alluding to the legend of the immortal known as Hu Kung, "Lord Pot,"
who is said to have lived during the Latter Han dynasty in a vessel suspended from his ceiling.
According to legend, he used to go to the market of Chunan to sell medicine, and when the
market closed he would fly back to his pot (Iwanami, p. 450).

☾ 313

Her morning makeup at last in place, she emerges late from her room.

The water clock drips lethargically as the hour of noon approaches.

A parrot, cleverly mimicking the Madam of the brothel,

Calls to the girl in a cackling voice from the other side of the blinds.

Nakamura, p. 206. From "Niura Zatsuei" (Miscellaneous Poems from Niura), a collection of
Nagasaki *chikushi* contained in *Seisei shū* (The Western Travels Collection), 1822-1826

☪ 314

A new moon, high in the sky, reflected in the evening ripples.
A covered boat has come to this place to take in the evening cool.
Barbarian wine, a thousand jugs, its color lapis blue.
The scent of jasmine fills the air as they sing their songs of love.

Nakamura, p. 207. From "Niura zatsuei," in *Seisei shū*, 1822-1826

Line four: "Songs of love," literally *chikushi*, defined in note accompanying poem 91, above.

☪ 315 Spring Evening: A Quatrain

Here in Kainan once again I've heard cuckoo's cry.
Wind and rain, wind and rain, a time of falling flowers.
I clearly recall a dream I had, of a river near my home:
A three-inch sweetfish landed on our boat as we were drinking wine.

Hirano, p. 261

Line one: Kainan, part of old Ise, which occupied much of what is now Wakayama prefecture.
Line three: Seigan's home was in Mino; the river was the Nagaragawa, where cormorant fishing for *ayu* (sweetfish) is still practiced.

Asaka Gonsai (1790-1860)

Asaka Gonsai, a native of Iwashiro in modern Fukushima prefecture, was gifted as a child, amusing himself by reading *bukan* (military appointment rosters) before he had even entered school. At seven, he was able to write competent Chinese, amazing his teachers, and by twelve could compose Chinese poetry. Gonsai apparently had a countrified, unprepossessing appearance, with a dark complexion, crossed eyes, and disheveled hair. He was briefly married in his teens, but his wife reportedly grew to dislike his physical attributes and bookish ways.[1]

Gonsai left his wife at seventeen and fled in a penniless state to Edo to study with Satō Issai (1772-1859). At twenty, he entered the school of Hayashi Jussai (1768-1841), determined to become a scholar and free himself from his life of unbearable poverty. In his mid-twenties, Gonsai opened his own school in Surugadai, Edo and contented himself with living as a teacher, however penurious he still remained. He married again sometime prior to 1823, and his first son was born in 1826. A decade later, he became employed as a Confucian scholar for the Nihonmatsu domain, in the Adachi district of Mutsu, receiving a stipend of 150 *koku*. Gonsai was appointed as a professor in the domain school, Keigakkan, some seven years later. Around the year 1850, he became a shogunal official and the principal of Shōheikō, succeeding Issai and maintaining the prestige the school had built for itself. He lived for a period in lodgings within the school after his home was destroyed by the Edo earthquake of 1855.

Gonsai is described as a modest, endearing man who never flaunted his erudition, treating both superiors and inferiors with equal warmth and courtesy. Generous and encouraging to his students, it is said he would praise the paper their verses were written on if the poems themselves were mediocre or the

---

[1]Inoguchi, p. 361.

calligraphy commonplace.[2] The first of the two verses below adopts a didactic tone. Here, Gonsai admonishes his young disciples to adhere to their studies and avoid being distracted by women, reminding them of the risks such dalliance entailed. The second verse shows a man who has so completely detached himself from the mundane world that he can no longer bear listening to talk of worldly affairs. In true Taoist fashion, he celebrates the joys of idleness and freedom from responsibilities, a theme frequent in the poetry of scholar-officials in retirement.

316 Instructions to Students

I warn you never to gaze at the blossoms beside the Sumida River,
For the beautiful women you'll find there make the blossoms pale by comparison.
I warn you never to gaze at the moon above the Sumida River,
For the young women there beneath the moon are so lovely they put it to shame.
The sages of yore begrudged their time, so devoted were they to their studies.
What time have you to gad about, lost in the pleasures of the blossoms
    and the moon?
I've been observing all these students of mine for the past thirty years:
Many with promise have thrown it all away, just for the blossoms and the moon.

Inoguchi, p. 367

Line six: "The pleasures of the blossoms and the moon" are the pleasures of the flesh.
Line eight: "Promise" is more literally, "goals and accomplishments," in the original language.

---

[2]Ibid., p. 362.

314

☺ 317 A Sudden Recollection

Content being useless I lie about, here at my simple cottage,
Where blossoms fall, birds sing, and the spring days are spent in idleness.
Once a visitor came to my house and talked about worldly affairs.
Smiling at him, I said nothing at all, then rose to look at the mountains.

Inoguchi, p. 363. From *Gonsai shiryaku* (Selected Poems by Gonsai), 1853

Title: Titled "Late Spring" in one source.

Majima Shōnan, 1791-1839

A poet and painter of some renown, Majima Shōnan was born in Kyoto, the eldest of ten children. His father was a doctor, but Shōnan himself had no interest in taking over his father's practice, particularly since he had a younger brother who was willing to do this. Inoguchi Atsushi relates various anecdotes concerning these early years which point to Shōnan's devotion to his family and his love of study. According to one such story, Shōnan's relatives once advised him that if he failed to pursue a career in medicine and became a scholar rather than a doctor, he would have to endure financial hardship. Convinced, however, that scholarship was his true vocation, Shōnan replied that he was willing to endure poverty so long as he did not die of hunger, citing the precedent set by *Itō Jinsai, who likewise had been encouraged to become a doctor but instead went on to become the greatest scholar of his age. "Am I not still the same man, whether I am a doctor or a scholar?" Shōnan is reported to have said.[1]

Shōnan's father supported him in his chosen career, having him study with the scholars Igai Keisho (1761-1845) and Wakatsuki Kisai (1744-1826). Shōnan's father died leaving little property, which was a problem since there were eight daughters, all of whom had yet to marry. Shōnan scrimped on food and clothing and sold off many of the family's treasured possessions so that each sister could be provided with a dowry. Curiously, he also canceled various debts that people owed his father, apparently believing that none of them was capable of repaying his debt.[2] He then began teaching and gradually acquired a large following, his reputation spreading far and wide.

Serious and sedate, and somewhat self-abasing, Shōnan never curried favor with people in high office and was unconcerned about the niceties relating to

---

[1] Inoguchi, p. 268.

[2] Ibid.

social hierarchy. In the poem immediately below, Shōnan expresses contempt for people in official service, likening their obsequious nodding to the head-bobbing of a snap-beetle and asserting that he would rather be a silverfish himself, spending his life devouring books. This love of books is alluded to again in the second verse. His main preoccupation apart from his research was attending to his mother and siblings, whose interests, as we have seen, he placed before all else.

In general, Shōnan can be classified as an adherent of the Chu Hsi school, although he was not blindly wedded to the orthodoxy. Inoguchi writes that his prose was "rich and beautiful, but not effete," his poetry "special, with an enduring appeal yet never dominated by passing trends."[3] He is said to have written easily and quickly, without laboring over his compositions. He died after an illness of ten days' duration while a messenger from the daimyo was still on the road, coming to bring him good wishes for a speedy recovery.

◙ 318 On Silverfish

To piles of books they entrust their tiny bodies,
Forever keeping company with reclusive scholars.
They enjoy the flavor of challenging prose,
Never acting like those head-bobbing beetles!

Inoguchi, p. 268

Line four: This species of beetle is the *kome-tsukimushi* (head-knocker), also called *nukazuki-mushi* (snap-beetle), a kind of elaterid. A small insect a mere centimeter in length, it can flip itself over if placed on its back, and when held down it will knock its head on the ground repeatedly, the head movements resembling the actions of a person pounding rice or bowing. The poet, who naturally identifies with the book-loving silverfish, is alluding here to people in official service—complaisant, fawning, and bowing obsequiously even when oppressed.

---

[3]Ibid.

◙ 319 An Impromptu Poem Written at Year's End

My chosen path has never been the way to get ahead in life.
But I cannot escape from worldly affairs, I grow busier all the time.
In the brightness beneath my window there lie a thousand books,
While a radiance as bright as the sun and moon glows within my breast.

Inoguchi, p. 270

◙ 320 Enjoying Ourselves Together and Thinking about the Past

Mournfully I gaze at the spring grass, growing in such profusion.
No one about, just the fragrant trees that guard the ruined walls.
The creaking noise of looms can be heard as the light of the setting sun fades,
While dreams of departed souls we weave beside the flowering peach.

Inoguchi, p. 270

◙ 321

Whence will the autumn winds arise to console the brave spirits here entombed?
Over ancient grave mounds a steamy mist hangs; the rain has left a frowsy scent.
The beacon-fires have burned themselves out, their ashes have all grown cold.
In the scattered shadows of the pine trees Buddhist lamps cast a bluish glow.

Inoguchi, p. 270

◙ 322 Passing Hirosawa

Cold ripples across the pond, the purple caltrops now withered.

Frosty maples here and there brighten the autumn paths.

An old man from the village bows, and then he says to me:

"That clump of pines in the clouds over there is the site of the Emperor's tomb."

Inoguchi, p. 269

<u>Title</u>: Hirosawa is probably Hirosawa Pond in western Kyoto, a place famous for its cherry blossoms. The pond was created in the mid-Heian period and measures 1.3 kilometers in circumference.
<u>Line two</u>: "Paths" is more literally, "footpaths through the rice paddies."

Tomono Kashū, 1792-1849

Tomono Kashū, a minor kanshi poet and Confucian scholar of the Teishugaku pursuasion, was born in Edo and studied with Kawai Tōkai and *Nomura Kōen, eventually becoming a professor at the prestigious Shōheikō in 1842. The following year he was appointed as principal of a school in Kōfu (in modern Yamanashi prefecture). Kashū's published works include *Kashū sensei shishū* (The Collected Poems of Master Kashū) and *Kashū ginkan* (Kashū's Verses for Recitation). In the first poem below, we see the poet ruing the passage of time and the loss of his friends, a familiar theme. The second verse is a beautiful evocation of a summer's evening.

◙ **323 An Impromptu Poem Written in Early**
    Spring to Express My Thoughts

I've been alive for fifty years
Yet I still don't grasp my past mistakes.
This frail body bears no afflictions,
But my precious friends have gradually grown scarce.
Though the cold lingered on and snow seemed likely,
It has suddenly warmed up, bringing brilliant spring light.
The scattered shadows of a lone plum tree
Mingle with the mist that guards my wooden gate.

Iwanami, pp. 323-324. From *Kashū sensei shishū* (The Collected Poems of Master Kashū)

◉ 324 Rain on a Summer Evening

Slanting rays from the crescent moon, pale the Milky Way.
A refreshing breeze fills the trees, the sound of rain approaches.
The water is rippled like a fine bamboo mat; cool air rises from its surface.
Lying down, I watch the fireflies darting around on the moss.

Iwanami, p. 322. From *Kashū sensei shishū*

Aizawa Nanjō, 1792-1860

Aizawa Nanjō was a native of Echigo in modern Niigata prefecture. He made his livelihood by lecturing and considered himself a scholar in the Setchūgaku tradition, which sought to create a synthesis of Teishugaku, Kogaku, and Yōmeigaku.[1]   In 1820, he returned to his village in Echigo to enlarge his family's school, Nanyōdō (The Three Extra Rooms Academy), where he taught more than two thousand students over the next forty years. He wrote numerous scholarly commentaries on the classical texts and was a poet of some distinction. The two verses below have a whimsical quality and, as is typical of much of the kanshi written during the latter half of the Edo period, focus on mundane subjects rather than lofty themes.

◖ 325 Buckwheat Noodles

The man from the mountains makes his noodles
With even more skill than the old noodle seller.
Wrapped around chopsticks they droop three feet,
The ends still coiled in the bottom of the bowl!

Iwanami, p. 325. From *Nanjō sanyo shū* (Three Additional Collections of Nanjō's Poems)

---

[1]According to two sources (Iwanami, p. 480, and *NKD*, p. 1) Nanjō was a disciple of the renowned Syncretic scholar Katayama Kenzan (1730-1782) in Edo, but this seems unlikely, given both men's dates. It is of course conceivable that Nanjō was born some years earlier than is generally accepted and could thus have studied with Kenzan.

◐ 326 Autumn Evening at the Farmhouse

The last of the wheat has all been harvested, dusk is now approaching.
The sickle moon reclines in the heavens and then returns to the West.
Who's that fellow standing there, wearing a raincoat of straw?
An old scarecrow in the empty fields, guarding them all alone!

Iwanami, p. 326. From *Nanjō sanyo shū*

Watanabe Kazan, 1793-1841

An outstanding artist, scholar, and patriot, Watanabe Kazan was born in Edo, the eldest son of a senior official in the Tawara domain in Mikawa province, part of modern Aichi prefecture. Kazan started out as a pupil of the Tawara scholar Takami Seikō (1750-1811), and later studied with Satō Issai. Although he hoped to be able to support himself as a scholar, he remained quite poor, so he decided he could better provide for his family as an artist. He studied art with Hiraya Bunkyō, Sō Shizan, and, somewhat later, with Tani Bunchō and Kaneko Kinryō. He received training in Western painting as well. Meanwhile, he continued to immerse himself in the important texts of Confucianism, receiving instruction from *Matsuzaki Kōdō, beginning in 1820. Kazan went on to serve the Tawara domain from 1832 as a chief retainer, accumulating a fine record of achievements which included the revitalization of Seishōkan, the domain school.

Kazan also undertook the study of European subjects, working with some of the leading Dutch Learning scholars of his day with whom he formed a group called Shōshikai (The Society for the Respect of the Aged) around 1832. Shōshikai was concerned with Rangaku research and with promoting the exchange of views on political and economic matters. Kazan was a vocal critic of the shogunate's conservative foreign policy and advocated opening the country to foreign commerce, while at the same time insisting on the need to build adequate coastal defenses. Kazan's outspoken beliefs soon earned him the disfavor of Torii Yōzō, the shogunal censor. In 1839, the Shōshikai society was ordered to disband and Kazan was imprisoned. This anti-Rangaku repression was part of the so-called Bansha no Goku purge. Kazan was condemned to death, but his sentence was commuted and he was returned to Tawara to be placed under house arrest.

While in confinement Kazan was caught illicitly exchanging letters with a disciple, who had been selling Kazan's paintings in Edo to provide his teacher with a modest income. To Kazan's mortification, the shogunate thereupon censored the Tawara daimyo for allowing this happen. Believing that his actions had caused his lord to lose face, Kazan decided to commit suicide. He left behind a large-character epitaph on paper which read, "Watanabe Noboru, the Unfaithful, the Unfilial." In Inoguchi's view, he wrote this as an apology to his mother to whom he was deeply devoted.[1]

The first selection below has an element of surprise, with the unusual image of the rustic's gate buried in mud after three lines of conventional description. Kazan's perception of himself as a man of honor and uncompromisingly high moral principles is revealed in the second of the selections. The wily rat in the third poem seems designed to remind us of the constant uncertainty of life, a reflection, no doubt, of Kazan's own situation. His strength of character and indomitable spirit in the face of these difficulties comes through in the fifth verse. In the moon reference, Kazan seems to be saying that since the natural world has inherent imperfections, we must also expect to find human society less than perfect and should persevere in our lives whatever the odds against us.

🔘 327 A Poetic Inscription for a Landscape Painting

Rainy skies clearing over foreground hills; a village among trees and bamboo.
The flowing waters of the rocky stream are carrying silt and mud.
A barefoot rustic is heading home, like a bird going back to its roost,
Unconcerned that the gate to his house lies half-buried under deep mud.

Iriya, p. 239

---

[1]Inoguchi, p. 271.

☽ 328 A Poem Written for My Monochrome Painting of Bamboo

Old Cheng painted lotuses but didn't show them growing in the earth.

Certain things an accomplished man will never stoop to do.

When I'm drunk and paint bamboo, my leaves are like the leaves of reeds.

But you'll never find me drawing bamboo that, like Ou Po, has no joints!

Inoguchi, pp. 270-271; Andō, p. 120

Line one: Cheng Ssu-hsiao was a patriotic scholar who flourished in the late-thirteenth century. He was a skillful painter of lotuses. After the Sung dynasty fell, he no longer painted lotuses growing in the earth, because he believed that all of China's soil had been "stolen" by the barbarians. He fled south into retirement and reputedly always sat facing south from this time on, symbolically turning his back on the disdained Yuan conquerors to show his loyalty to the old dynasty.
Line four: "Joints" is a play on words, since the character means both bamboo nodes and human integrity. Ou Po (Sea Gull Waves) was the name of the family residence of Chao Tzu-ang (Chao Meng-fu, 1254-1322) and by extension stands for the man himself. Chao was a hereditary official, calligrapher, and painter. After the fall of the Sung, which had been founded by his ancestors, he was recalled to office in 1286 by the Mongol Yuan court, only to be criticized later for serving an alien dynasty. Chao subsequently wrote poems in which he expressed regret at having, in effect, betrayed the dynasty of his forefathers.

☽ 329 A Poetic Inscription for a Painting of a Wily Rat Eating Grapes

The wily creature eyes the cornucopia of fruit,

Then spirits it away, to the farmer's distress.

The workings of Heaven are hard to predict—

We must make provision for the unexpected.

Iriya, p. 24

☾ 330-332 Living as a Recluse: Three Poems

(No. 1)

The plum rains have washed away the dirt and the dust.

The entire valley is bathed in moonlight,

Brighter than on any night before.

How could one wish for a mid-autumn moon?

I lie in the cold grass, casting no shadow,

As the aging insects in the frost drone on.

Anyone coming here would be fraught with sorrow;

How much the more one as mournful as I!

Iriya, p. 251

Line six: The presence of frost in summer suggests that the poet may have been living at a high elevation.

(No. 2)

Amid the noisy hubbub of the world

The recluse wanders in the chilly mist.

No friends from afar come here to visit,

But the moon in the Ninth Heaven offers me solace.

At night my thoughts grow more distant and forlorn,

But in the face of adversity my will only strengthens.

Cease your talk about the world of dust:

The cold moon itself is not fully round.

Iriya, p. 252

Line four: The Ninth Heaven is the highest of the heavens.
Line eight: Here the poet seems to be saying that one is not justified in pointing to the imperfections of the human world when nature itself is subject to imperfection.

(No. 3)

With my stick I wander through my hidden garden;
Back inside I sit by my low lantern.
In the empty shadows stands frosty bamboo.
The garden is filled with the chirp of cold crickets.
Water from the Milky Way drips onto my ink stone.
The spirit of the Jade Hare enters my poetry.
A life of tranquility has brought me all this.
Looking back, I laugh at those dusty tassels.

Iriya, pp. 252-253

Line five: Water here means dew.
Line six: "Jade Hare" is an allusion to the moon, which, like the Milky Way, is a source of inspiration for the poet.
Line eight: "Dusty tassels" is a pejorative reference to ambitious officials, as tassels are a feature of the headgear worn by officials.

Saitō Setsudō, 1797-1865

The son of a retainer of the Tsu domain in Ise province (modern Mie prefecture), Saitō Setsudō was born in the domain residence in Edo. As a young man he was educated at the Shōheikō academy by Koga Seiri, specializing in the Japanese classics. Setsudō moved back to Tsu in 1820 to teach at Yōzōkan, the newly-opened domain academy, eventually becoming its head in his late forties. Setsudō is remembered for his efforts to raise academic standards in the domain, bringing new talent to the academy, enlarging library collections, and publishing hundreds of academic texts. Not only did he add Rangaku (Dutch studies) to the curriculum of the academy, he also initiated the public health measure of administering smallpox immunizations. His own face was scarred from smallpox, which may explain why he took up this cause. Although a man of many official accomplishments, he declined to accept a post in Shogun Iesada's administration in 1855, when he was fifty-eight. At the same time, he resigned from his post as head of Yōzōkan on grounds of illness and retired to Sama Sansō (The Tea-Mortar Mountain Retreat).

Setsudō is described in a contemporary account as a forthright man with an intimidating manner, someone who never hesitated to criticize a person's faults. He had distractingly large ears and tended to glare wide-eyed at people whenever his speech became animated.[1] Nevertheless, he was quick to recognize and praise the talent of others wherever he found it. Although usually labeled as a Chu Hsi Neo-Confucianist, Setsudō in fact endeavored to synthesize the ideas of several different philosophical schools. His poetry, which *Rai San'yō (an unusually harsh critic) admired greatly, was influenced primarily by T'ang models, although he experimented with styles from other periods as well. Like many of the best kanshi poets of his day, Setsudō chose folksy, original subjects

---

[1]Fujikawa, p. 230.

and themes that were thoroughly grounded in the native culture. The whale-hunt seen in poem 333, below, is a good example of this fresh poetic material and a measure of the extent to which the genre had adapted itself to the Japanese environment.

333

A whale big enough to feed seven villages!
With pride, the fishermen boast of their catch,
Celebrating New Year in the depths of winter,
Dancing and carousing drunkenly, as if gone mad.

Fujikawa, p. 234

Line three: "The depths of winter" refers here to the period near the end of the lunar year, which came in January or February by our Gregorian calendar. The fishermen were so pleased with their winter catch that they felt as if the bounties of the New Year had come early. The geographic setting for the poem may be the Wakayama area (Fujikawa, p. 234).

334 A poem from a series titled "Miscellaneous Poems Written En Route to Kumano"

Day and night beside the bay she awaits her husband's return.
There she stands against the railing, while the rice is steamed.
The hazy fog is thick and dense, the sky has not yet cleared.
The white sail of his boat with its tangerine cargo comes in and out of view.

Fujikawa, p. 233

◔ 335 Passing the Forbidden Gates of the Imperial Palace

The Golden Palace, tall and stately, rises into rosy clouds.
The water in the moat goes rushing past over the clean gravel below.
The spring breeze does not distinguish between the immortal
    and mundane worlds,
Blowing flowers over from the Imperial Gardens that land
    upon my clothes.

Hirano, p. 269

Sakai Kozan, 1798-1850

The son of Sakai Tōha, an Aki domain scholar-official and Kokugaku specialist, Sakai Kozan was tutored by his father as a boy. He was regarded as a child prodigy of great promise and reportedly spent little time sleeping, taking just the occasional doze over his books. He first lectured on the Chinese classics at age thirteen, stunning the academic community.[1] Later, he became a pupil of Rai Shunsui in the domain school and took up a teaching post there himself in 1825, following in his father's footsteps. He was on close terms with *Matsuzaki Kōdō, *Rai San'yō, Shinozaki Shōchiku, and Satō Issai, all of whom considered him a literary virtuoso. Known also for his patriotism, he had among his pupils the influential pro-imperial activist and distinguished kanshi poet *Priest Gesshō.

◎ 336 Sengakuji Temple

Though the mountain peaks may tumble down and the ocean be overturned,
The souls of the forty-seven retainers will never fade away.
Moist the grass and moss that are growing there before the grave—
All the result of tears that were shed by later generations.

Sugano, p. 78; Inoguchi, 283; Andō, p. 122. From *Kozan shikō* (A Book of Poems by Kozan), 1849 (earliest extant text)

<u>Title</u>: For information on this temple and the story of the forty-seven loyal retainers buried in its precincts, see the notes to poem 107.

---

[1]Inoguchi, p. 282.

☾ 337 The Old Flower Seller

1 The old flower seller makes his home on the eastern side of the city.
His bamboo door is tumble-down, his sideburns are disheveled.
He's been growing flowers since his youth, and now he's seventy,
Carrying on the cultivating skills passed down within his family.
5 Although he's good at growing flowers, he's poor at making a living,
Yet has no choice but to walk the streets, crying out his wares.
When the sun has set he goes back home, sighing to himself,
For his entire stock is not even worth a single flask of wine.
He toils away at growing flowers, but never looks at them himself;
10 He leaves it to others to be smitten by their beautiful springtime colors.
Alas! All things in this world of ours appear to be this way.
Yet the old man isn't the only one for whom we should feel pity:
The woman raising silkworms has no clothes,
    the house of the carpenter leaks.
And the men who were once the rulers of our land
    now grow old in obscurity.

Inoguchi, p. 285

Hara Saihin, 1798-1859

Hara Saihin, one of the better-known female poets of the Edo period, was a native of Chikuzen, part of modern Fukuoka prefecture in Kyushu. She was the daughter of Hara Kosho (1767-1827), a Kobunjigaku scholar from the Akizuki domain. Saihin's verse was praised by *Rai San'yō and *Yanagawa Seigan in commentaries they wrote for her small collection of verse titled *Saihin shishū* (The Collected Poems of Saihin). She opened a private academy in Asakusa, Edo, but later returned to her hometown to teach and take care of her mother. After her mother's death, when Saihin was fifty-five, she travelled extensively throughout Kyushu. Open-hearted, spirited, and renowned for her love of wine, Saihin often carried a sword and appeared in public without makeup.[1] While her personality seems to have been far from conventional, her poetry is very much in the mainstream of Edo kanshi poets, as the following examples, pleasant albeit unremarkable, illustrate.

◙ 338 An Impromptu Poem

The chopping sound of trees being cut has ceased.
Mountain clouds send down a shower of rain.
The woodsman tries to find a short-cut home,
Returning alone, his firewood soaked by rain.

Iwanami, pp. 335-336. From *Saihin shishū* (The Collected Poems of Saihin)

---

[1]Inoguchi, *Josei to kanshi*, p. 300.

☾ 339 Spring Rain

Rising clouds waft gently upwards;
Slanting rain drizzles lightly down.
Warm mist hangs over the willow inlet,
Springtime trees enclose the houses.
Water babbles as it flows from a spring.
The banks of the pond grow ever more verdant.
How many branches will be bearing flowers
By the time the spring rains come to an end?

Iwanami, p. 335. From *Saihin shishū*

Noda Tekiho, 1799-1859

Noda Tekiho was a native of Tanabe in Tango, near Kyoto. At thirteen, he went to Edo to study with Koga Seiri, and in his twenties became a pupil of Koga Tōan at the Shōheikō academy. His family was very poor and could scarcely afford to send him to school, but eventually his tuition expenses were met by his daimyo, who was moved by the family's plight and believed that Tekiho was a rising star of great promise.

Tekiho was a fluent speaker of Chinese and one of the best known poets and prose writers of his day. He became famous across the land in 1826 when, at the request of his teacher Tōan, he spent about two months exchanging poems and stories with some poetry-loving Chinese merchants from a commercial ship in Nagasaki. The Chinese were reportedly amazed at Tekiho's literary erudition and mastery of poetry, and the material they exchanged was enough to fill two large volumes.[1] In a work edited by the poet *Priest Gesshō, Tekiho was rated with *Saitō Setsudō, Shinozaki Shōchiku, and *Sakai Kozan as one of the four literary giants of western Japan.[2] Tekiho lectured in Edo for a period, then in 1850 returned to his village and became an important official in the Tanabe domain, working to advance domainal education and administering the local academy. In his declining years, he asked several times to be allowed to retire but was turned down. Tekiho's verse, much of which remains unpublished, is characterized by a tendency toward unusual subject matter (as seen in the first two poems) and the use of plain, slightly quirky language.

---

[1] Inoguchi, p. 337.

[2] Ibid., p. 338.

◐ 340   A Poem for a Painting of a Skull

In this world where we live
People view the heart as the body's keeper.
But nothing can compare to this dry old skull:
This part has the pleasure of ruling it all!

Inoguchi, p. 340

Line four: "Ruling it all" is literally "looking south" in the language of the original, an expression which denotes rulership, since the Chinese emperor traditionally sat facing the south. The skull similarly rules the body, "looking south," i.e., downward.

◐ 341   A Poem for a Painting of Hsiao Chiao

The makeup she wears has stained her book, so the book now shares her beauty.
Seated beside the springtime window, she has read to the chapter on fire-attacks.
A shower of pink petals blown about by a gust of springtime wind
Makes her recall that year when her husband set those rebels ablaze.

Inoguchi, p. 341

Title: Hsiao Chiao was the wife of the military leader Chou Yü (174-218). Chou served the state of Wu during the Three Kingdoms period (220-265). At the Battle of Red Cliffs in 208, he led the attack which burned the fleet of the rival commander Ts'ao Ts'ao, thus inflicting heavy losses upon the latter's forces. This is the event to which the poet alludes in the last line of the verse.
Line two: The lady appears to have been reading Sun Tzu's sixth-century B.C. classic, *Sun Tzu ping-fa* (Sun Tzu's Art of War), China's most famous work on military strategy.

☾ 342 Taking the Cool Night Air on Shōhei Bridge

Summer clouds like shreds of cotton, the moon casts a bright and slanting light.

My thin hemp robe is caught by the wind as I lightly step along.

Watch-fires burning here and there in the marketplace over the bridge,

Where cages of insects hang from vendor's poles—for sale, the sounds

    of autumn!

Inoguchi, p. 340

Title: This bridge is located in Tokyo near the east entrance of Ochanomizu station about one hundred meters from Hijiribashi, a bridge spanning the Kanda River. One source gives the title as "Summer Night" (Inoguchi, p. 339).

☾ 343 Autumn Dawn

The light of my solitary lamp is fading, smaller than a firefly its glow.

The tangled bamboo taps against my window; dawn, and sounds can be heard.

I haven't finished my dreaming yet, early still the hour.

Lines of autumn geese fly past, through the starry skies.

Inoguchi, p. 341

Nakajima Beika, 1801-1834

The eldest son of a Saeki domain retainer, Nakajima Beika was a native of Bungo, part of modern Ōita prefecture. In his mid-teens he studied with *Hirose Tansō and Kamei Shōyō (1773-1836) in northern Kyushu, making frequent visits to Kyoto and Osaka as well. When *Rai San'yō met Beika in Tansō's village of Hita in 1818, he declared him a peerless genius.[1] Three years later, Beika went to the Shōheikō college in Edo to study with Koga Tōan, rising to become the head of the school. From 1827, Beika served as a Confucian functionary in his home domain of Saeki. He also taught at Shikyōdō (Hall of the Four Teachings), the domain school. He passed away at thirty-four, leaving behind his wife and a son who died at a young age himself. Described as unaffected and openhearted, Beika was admired for his frank, straightforward manner. His poetry is fresh, elegant and flowing; as one source puts it, "his heart leaped ahead of his brush."[2] His corpus includes a posthumous collection of his poems, as well as *Aikindō shū* (A Collection of Works from the Academy of Aikin [The *Ch'in* Devotee]) and *Nihon shin gafu* (New Japanese Folk Poems).

---

[1]Andō, p. 119.

[2]Ibid.

◐ 344 Sennenji Temple

From afar I hear the chanting of sutras through the wisteria vines.
A twisting path leads over a bridge, then winds its way to the heavens.
Late spring, and the hillside barley now gives shelter to the pheasants.
Abundant rain, and by the duckweed in the stream tadpoles now are gathered.
Outside the temple the smoke from tea-fires is locked in by bamboo.
I lift the blinds and mountain scenery fills my room in abundance.
"Gentlemen, rent me, if you please, a plot of land three bows long,
That I may flee the world and build a Nest of Tranquility."

Hirano, p. 270

Line seven: "Three bows," i.e., three *kyū*, a total length of somewhere between fifteen and twenty-four feet. The actual length of a *kyū* varied over time. The gentlemen being addressed here are priests.
Line eight: "Nest of Tranquility" is an allusion to Ssu-ma Kuang's place of retirement, where he had a small farm. Ssu-ma was a renowned eleventh-century scholar and statesman who resigned from service in about 1070 and went into retirement, after which he wrote the famous history of China titled *Tzu-chih t'ung-chien* (A Comprehensive Mirror for the Aid of Government).

◐ 345 Mount Hiko

Roused from a dream in this mountain town, midnight not yet here.
A dying lamp flickers at the neighbor's house on the other side of the fence.
A conch shell sounds, bringing down the moon that shines on the central peak.
The clouds cast a chill on the temples below, thirty-eight hundred in all.

Inoguchi, pp. 263-264; Andō, p. 118

Title: Mt. Hiko (Hikosan, or alternatively, Eihikosan), twenty-five hundred meters high with three peaks, the middle one being the site of the Eihikosan Jinja shrine. Mt. Hiko was one of four sacred mountains used as training centers for *yamabushi*, itinerant monks of the Shugendō sect.
Line three: This conch would have been blown by the *yamabushi*. To the poet, its sound was so loud and penetrating that it seemed to be able to move the moon.
Line four: There were more than thirty-eight hundred temples, or temple buildings, in the village of Kamimae-chō at the base of Mt. Hiko. These declined or disappeared in the Meiji period (Andō, p. 118).

340

⏻ 346 Returning by Night

Scattered stars hang low above the mountains, their brightness nearly gone.
A deserted village lies deep in the wilderness, cut off from the world.
The solitary trees look just like men, the boulders look like tigers.
Eerie birds on the tips of the branches let out sudden squawks.

Inoguchi, p. 264

Yanagawa Kōran [née Chō], 1804-1879

A native of Mino province in what is modern Gifu prefecture, Yanagawa Kōran was the wife and second cousin of the poet *Yanagawa Seigan and a noted kanshi poet in her own right. She was also a distinguished Nanga painter. Kōran learned painting under the Nanga artist Nakabayashi Chikutō (1776-1853) and took instruction in poetry from her famous poet-husband. According to Inoguchi, certain critics speculated that Kōran's verse would no longer be worth reading once her husband died, for they assumed that he revised all her poems for her. However, following his death, she amazed her fellow poets by composing poetry that was possibly even better than what she had written during his lifetime. It was then that her skill as a poet was duly recognized by many for the first time.[1]

Seigan had married Kōran when she was seventeen—it was his second marriage—and they were an unusually fond and devoted couple, travelling everywhere together for years on end. Kōran opened her own academy in Kyoto at Kawabata Marutamachi following Seigan's death.

◙ 347 Spring Evening

Here by my window all is silent, pure the nighttime breeze.
Spring has come to the cherry-apple trees—they possess a charm of their own.
I smile to think that this house is so poor there are no candles to take outdoors.
I'll just use the moon to light my way as I wander about in the garden.

Inoguchi, *Josei to kanshi*, p. 319

Line two: This tree is also known as the aronia (*Malus micromalus*).

---

[1]Inoguchi, p. 49.

☺ 348 Getting out of Bed

A stray oriole rouses me from my dreams; I rise and lean on the railing.

The midday sun is dazzlingly bright, the water in the pond is cold.

A tiny wisp of rosy mist has landed on my mirror.

I find that the pillow has left a crease on one side of my face!

Inoguchi, *Josei to kanshi*, p. 319

☺ 349 Returning Home at Night in the Snow

I make my way along the road, supported by my maid.

Nighttime at the third watch; the ditches are frozen over.

My sandals are loose and give my feet no support at all.

The wind-driven snow makes a swishing sound,

    which I hear beneath my umbrella.

Iwanami, p. 337; Nakamura, p. 237. From *Kōran shōshū* (A Little Collection of Kōran's Works), 1841

Line two: The third watch: the period between 11:00 P.M. and 1:00 A.M.

☺ 350 Recording My Thoughts as Spring Draws to a Close

My mother now has passed away, and only Father's left.

By my solitary lamp, with the rain drizzling down, I often dream of home.

In Sekiyama spring has passed, yet still I have no news.

The sound of the cuckoo reaches my ears, scaring me half to death.

Iwanami, p. 337. From *Kōran shōshū*, 1841

Line three: Sekiyama is the poet's hometown.
Line four: Although she has no news from her father, the cuckoo seems to beckon her homeward. In the Chinese literary tradition, the call of the cuckoo sounds like the words *pu ju kuei*, "you'd better go home," hence, her alarm. The bird is also depicted in some legendary accounts as the messenger of the underworld.

◘ 351 Untitled

With sashes, I follow the common custom of wearing ones that are wide.
But in my dress I disregard fashion, mainly wearing cotton.
Cotton clothes are just the thing to keep out the winter cold,
And when you're poor you should only wear what's simple and practical, too.

Iwanami, p. 338. From *Kōran shōshū*, 1841

◘ 352 Autumn Morning

In rows of houses we happily slept, no noises could be heard.
Some idlers, though, had risen early, awakened by the crows.
Beyond my gate there stood a peddler, carrying his wares.
He'd come here selling morning glories, other flowers as well.

Nakamura, p. 240. From *Kōran shōshū*, 1841

◘ 353 Year's End

Just a few weeks left on the calendar—what an alarming thought!
I am caught in a flurry of seasonal tasks and pressed by daily affairs.
My little daughter has no idea why I'm so worn out.
All she does is question me, "When will New Year's be here?"

Nakamura, p. 241. From *Kōran shōshū*, 1841

Hirose Kyokusō, 1807-1863

Hirose Kyokusō was the son of a prosperous merchant and a native of Bungo province, in what is today Ōita prefecture. He was the younger brother of the renowned kanshi poet *Hirose Tansō, who is the better known of the two brothers. While Kyokusō's mother was pregnant with him, she once dreamed she had swallowed a large star. Someone later told her that since the star was a symbol of culture, the baby would surely grow up to be a cultured and refined individual, a prediction which proved to be accurate.[1] Kyokusō was reportedly a precocious young man who had a photographic memory. Like his brother, he studied under Kamei Shōyō in Hakata, and in 1827, he met the poet *Kan Sazan, with whom, according to one source, he was to study for about a year. Kan Sazan was evidently amazed by Kyokusō's gifts, asserting that his written and verbal abilities were "greater than those of anyone else on earth" and that he would be the leader of the next generation of scholars.[2]

In 1828, Kyokusō became a professor at the Tōmeikan academy in Hizen, and later, the head of his brother's school, which he took over following Tansō's death in 1856. Kyokusō eventually opened his own school in Osaka, but returned to his native village in 1861 to establish yet another school, called Setsuraikan. In his declining years he associated with scholars who had loyalist sentiments, and after the arrival of the American embassy ships in Uraga, in 1853, he argued for a revision of shogunal defense policy.

Kyokusō is best known for his *ku-shih* and long poems, some of which were hundreds of lines long. He was apparently able to dash off a spectacular forty- or even fifty-line verse with little effort, and his longest poem—perhaps the longest kanshi on record, titled "Sending Off Kuwabara Shika when He Returned

---

[1]Inoguchi, p. 385.

[2]Ibid.

to Amakusa"—found him a bit too eager to show off his unusual talent,[3] but his genius is nonetheless undeniable. Kyokusō's verse is unsurpassed among Edo kanshi for its mystical qualities, which the following selections demonstrate.

The first poem presents a dramatic collage of supernatural and fabulous images that convey a dark sense of menace and impending doom. The nocturnal images seen here—chilly night air, unrelieved darkness, howling wind, and disquieting visions—are reminiscent of Tu Fu, who was probably Kyokusō's model. With imaginative powers that seem to arise from a state of delirium, Kyokusō blurs the line between the real and the fantastic as the nightmare of his experience in the remote, seemingly haunted shrine unfolds. The theme of nighttime fantasy and the supernatural is seen again in the second poem. A more benign sense of mystery is found in the third and fourth verses, where the poet light-heartedly questions the identity of the "stranger" who has imposed himself upon the peaceful scene—the moon in one instance, himself in the other.

Kyokusō left behind a diary which affords remarkable insights into the mind of this accomplished scholar. Inoguchi writes that he slept for only four hours a night and upon awakening would dictate lengthy journal entries to an assistant, these sometimes running to thousands of words. He never made notes or drafts of anything to be included in the journal.[4] His diary covers a wide range of subjects including natural phenomena, strange sightings, the suppression of uprisings, and milestones in the lives of his close friends, all of which are narrated in exhaustive detail. He considered this record to be a true reflection of his innermost self and once remarked, "The person who reads it a hundred years from now will truly know me well."[5]

---

[3]Ibid.

[4]Ibid., p. 386.

[5]Ibid.

☽ 354 Staying the Night in the Usa Shrine

1 The night is quiet in this ancient shrine; my lamp casts a bluish glow.
Though nearly out it keeps on burning, smaller than a firefly its flame.
Big rats run about up in the joists, scampering like badgers.
They nibble and gnaw on the ridge beams and rafters, sending thousands of
wood shreds down.
5 Hungry mosquitoes buzz around, they've come here to bite my body.
It's as if they were intent on drilling holes—P'an Ku's seven orifices!
In a little while from a central peak a ferocious wind arises;
From the mountain cliffs there comes the sound of old cedars
splitting apart.
During the night the deities hasten to the place where Hachiman dwells,
10 The wheels of their cloud-borne chariots clacking like ornaments of jade
at the waist.
Walls fall and buildings break apart, collapsing with a clattering sound;
Dragons and serpents seem to come alive as the painted walls
tumble down.
In the shade by the shrine grow mugwort and goosefoot, tall enough to bury
a man.
As the wind arises I can just make out the backs of the carved stone horses.
15 At dawn the horned owls fly about, hooting from the tops of the trees.
A lonely silence prevails on the mountain, now that the wind has died down.
I wash my hands, then pray to the gods; the gods make no reply.
But in my bowl a lone bright star is floating on the water.

Kudō, pp. 269-70. From *Baiton shishō* (A Selection of Poems from the Plum Tree Mound), 1848

Title: This imaginative poem was written while the poet, then aged twenty-two, was spending his first night at the Usa Hachiman Shrine in Bungo province.
Line six: In Chinese mythology, P'an Ku is considered the first human being in the universe. In *Chuang Tzu*, section seven, titled "Ying Ti Wang" (Fit for Emperors and Kings), P'an Ku (also known as Hun-tun) is described as a mythical emperor of the central region, a land referred to as Chaos. *Chuang Tzu* has him dying after a seven-day ordeal during which one orifice was bored in his head each day: two nostrils, two ears, two eyes, and a mouth—a total of seven holes. See Watson, *Chuang Tzu*, p. 95.

Line twelve: Presumably the walls were painted with dragons and serpents.
Line fourteen: Horses carved from stone were common in old graveyards. The wind has parted the grass, revealing the half-buried horses.
Line fifteen: Horned owls are traditionally birds of ill omen.
Line seventeen: In the Shinto faith, ritual ablutions are performed before prayer.

☪ 355 Staying the Night in Kyōgakuin

The mountain is deserted; a chilly moon is shining.

No need to light a pinewood torch.

The papered window suddenly darkens

As a strange cloud ascends in the sky.

I know that the mountain spirits are passing,

For the sound of neighing horses fills the air.

Fujikawa, p. 309. From *Baiton shishō*, 1848

Title: Kyōgakuin (The Hall of Learning) is unidentified.
Lines four to six: The poet may have viewed the clouds and the neighing horses as an omen of his approaching death. The Chinese believed that in the mountains resided spirits of the dead.

☪ 356

Who was it who entered my house?

He graced me with his presence, I saw his shadow.

No sound of footsteps or walking stick—

He knows I love my peace and quiet.

When I went to greet him, no one was there;

The garden was bathed in cold moonlight.

Fujikawa, p. 306. From *Baiton shishō*, 1848

Line six: Here it is implied that the moon was the silent visitor.

357 Visiting Hitsuan in the Spring Rain

Through onion patches and gardens of rape I walk a slanting path.
The place where the peach trees grow in abundance is where you make
your home.
Who is it who has come this evening, knocking on your door?
It's just this poet and the rain, and the falling flowers too!

Inoguchi, p. 392; Sugano, p. 92. From *Baiton shishō*, 1848

Title: The identity of Hitsuan is unknown, but he was probably one of the poet's friends from Hita (Inoguchi, p. 392).

358 Visiting the Cherry Shrine in Early Summer

When the flowers were in bloom, thousands gathered.
But now that they're gone, there is no one left.
All I can see are two golden orioles,
Singing their song in the deep, green shade.

Hirano, p. 276; Inoguchi, p. 387

Title: Since 1758, when it was shifted from a different site, Sakuranomiya (The Cherry Shrine) has been located about a third of a kilometer from Sakuranomiya Station on the Jōtō Line in the Nakano-chō area of modern Osaka (Inoguchi, p. 387). Possessing extensive grounds, it is a famous place for viewing cherry blossoms.

Fujii Chikugai, 1807-1866

Fujii Chikugai was born in Takatsuki in the province of Settsu, part of modern Osaka-fu. He served the Takatsuki domain as an expert on weaponry, muskets in particular, and was known for his love of wine and conversation and for his magnanimous, ebullient nature. Chikugai acquired the nickname Zekku Chikugai, "Chikugai, the Quatrain Master," in reference to his special talent for writing *chüeh-chü*. He took instruction in versification from *Rai San'yō and was friendly with *Yanagawa Seigan, *Hirose Tansō, and Morita Sessai (1811-1868). Chikugai retired to Kyoto in his later years. His grave is situated in Chōrakuji temple in Kyoto next to that of San'yō and bears the humorous inscription, "Grave of Chikugai, the Drinker." The fifth poem below focusses upon this graveyard, apparently a favorite burial ground for poets.

The first poem, Chikugai's most famous, treats the theme of the demise of the Southern Court at Yoshino, a popular motif in Japanese poetry, one that is always an occasion for nostalgic recollection of the past and lamentation over the impermanence of glory. The times in which Chikugai lived were difficult and dangerous ones for many intellectuals, as is indirectly suggested in the poems titled "The Crab" and "Willows," both of which appear to contain veiled political criticism.

◑ 359 Yoshino

The pines and cedars by the old grave mound groan in the whirling wind.

I've searched for spring at this mountain temple, yet the spring seems lonely
　　and bleak.

An aged priest with snowy eyebrows puts down his broom for a while,

And where fallen flowers lie deep on the ground he talks of the Southern court.

Sugano, p. 98; Iwanami, p. 330. From *Chikugai nijūhachi ji shi* (Twenty-Eight Character Poems by Chikugai), 1858

Title: See poems 175 and 200 for historical notes on Yoshino.

◑ 360 Going Down the Silty River on a Blossom-Filled Morning

Warm waters send my boat on its way; peach blossoms are in bloom.

I turn and see a lone wild goose, vanishing into the distance.

There on the crest of Mount Hira the snow is shining white.

The winds of spring have yet to reach the province of Gōshū.

Iwanami, p. 330; Ishikawa, p. 76. From *Chikugai nijūhachi ji shi*, 1858

Title: Silty River is another name for the Yodo River (Yodogawa).
Line three: Mt. Hira (1,200 m.), one of the eight famous sights of Ōmi province, located west of Lake Biwa.
Line four: Gōshū refers to what is modern Shiga prefecture, east of Kyoto; Mt. Hira is here.

🔲 361 The Crab

Equipped by Nature with eight legs
And dressed for battle with halberd and armor,
The crab, once known as "the bellyless prince,"
Cares not that it walks in sideways fashion.

Inoguchi, p. 424. From a supplement titled *Chikugai nijū ji shi* (Twenty-Character Poems by Chikugai) appended to *Chikugai nijūhachi ji shi* (2nd ed.), 1871

Line four: Walking sideways suggests perverse and unreasonable behavior. Crabs are a symbol of tyranny in the Chinese tradition, and this poem could well have been intended as a thinly-veiled satirical comment.

🔲 362 Willows

Since first I divined a site for my home and planted willows here,
The eastern wind for twenty springs has made its presence felt.
Stop carelessly brushing the earth below with those long branches of yours:
There's far more dust on the ground right now than at any time before!

Inoguchi, p. 433

Line four: Dust in Buddhist thought connotes all affairs associated with the human realm and their tainting influence.

This poem is thought to have been written by Chikugai late in life, some time after the repressive Great Ansei Purge of 1858, which was directed against the pro-imperial anti-foreign element that actively opposed shogunal policy. Many of Chikugai's associates were imprisoned, but he himself managed to remain free, perhaps because he was able to conceal his views when necessary. The poem appears to be passing satirical comment on the instability and political decay of the times (Inoguchi, p. 433).

☻ 363

A wonderful burial ground this is, with nary a speck of dust!
On this famous hill since ancient times poets have been interred.
This body of mine shall be turned into earth, and there the flowers will grow,
Keeping their scent through wind and rain, spring after spring each year.

Hirano, p. 274

Chikugai wrote this verse after preparing his own burial plot under a plum tree one evening at Chōrakuji in Higashiyama, Kyoto (Hirano, p. 274).

Priest Kigai [Setsuan], 1809-1857

An accomplished poet and calligrapher, Priest Kigai, whose real name was Kushibuchi Hiromichi, came from Kōzuke, part of modern Gunma prefecture. He took his Buddhist vows at fourteen and spent many years travelling about the countryside, being received by important scholars and powerful lords wherever he went. In his later years Priest Kigai gained the favor of the daimyo of Himeji and was named chief priest of Ryūkōji in old Harima province. A portly, laughing man, Priest Kigai is said to have resembled the legendary Hotei, one of the Seven Gods of Good Fortune in the Japanese tradition.

◙ 364 The Old Candy Man

On his back he carries his livelihood—
Nothing else does he bear.
His flute music reaches a hamlet beyond the flowers.
Boys have gathered at a house by the willows.
The wind is warm, the spring mountains beautiful.
The sun sets in the west above a distant village.
His candy sold, he turns around and buys wine,
Then heads for home, disappearing in the mist.

Iwanami, pp. 353-354. From *Kan'un ikō* (Idle Clouds: A Posthumous Text), 1863 (date of epilogue)

Line four: The house where the boys are assembling may be an inn since willows are typically found near such establishments (Iwanami, p. 353).

☺ 365 An Impromptu Poem on Spring Rain

The rains of spring appeal to me,

For at night they fall in such fine drops.

They soak the flowers and the willow trees

And drip down, pit-a-pat, upon my robes.

Iwanami, p. 353. From *Kan'un ikō*, 1863

Line four: More literally, "upon my poetry robes," this probably being a fanciful reference to garments the poet supposedly wore when composing verse.

Murakami Butsuzan, 1810-1879

A Meiji biography of Murakami Butsuzan describes him as a man who lived for poetry.[1] A native of Buzen in modern Fukuoka prefecture, Butsuzan first studied with Hara Kosho, at the age of fifteen. The following year, when Kosho died, he became the pupil of another local scholar named Kamei Shōyō. He entered the Kyoto school of Nukina Kaioku (1778-1863) in 1830, when he was twenty, and during this period became acquainted with *Yanagawa Seigan. Butsuzan subsequently took ill with beriberi, which had plagued him periodically for years, and had to return to his village, where he opened a school. He declined to accept a domain appointment and never pursued an official career, content to lead a quiet life in his village, teaching and farming. This peaceful lifestyle is described in the first poem below. Yanagawa Seigan called this verse "a true Confucian farming poem" and said that if all the so-called Confucian teachers in the cities of Japan, who "sold their tongues" to make a living, were to read this poem, they would die of shame.[2]

---

[1]Fujikawa, p. 311.

[2]Ibid., p. 312.

☽ 366 Impromptu Recitation

Farming and Confucian studies—these are what bring me contentment.
Fame at court and profit in business do not interest me.
I've led a life of pure joy, for these eyes of mine can read.
Through good karma from a previous life, I live here in the mountains.
With my calf I try my hand at plowing—what's so tiring about this?
I summon the boys to give them their lessons—this doesn't cut into my leisure.
This morning something wonderful happened which gave me the greatest delight:
From the western fields in the misty rain I returned with some lines of verse!

Fujikawa, p. 312

☽ 367 Gazing in the Evening at the Autumn River

Returning geese mingle with returning crows in the sky above the river.
The crows are roosting in a grove by the beach, while the geese are roosting
    on the sand.
Elsewhere a fisherman upon a boat is cooking his evening meal.
Blue smoke rises up in a column from in amongst the reeds.

Fujikawa, p. 314

☽ 368 Moonlight over the Fisherman's House

He has moored his skiff at the water's edge,
Returning at dusk to a beach bathed in moonlight.
His old eyes are still fit for patching nets:
In the radiant light he sits among the reeds.

Fujikawa, p. 314

◖ 369

Vast and boundless the evening fog.

The moon has not yet risen above the pond.

A girl from the village comes carrying a jug,

Dipping into the croaking frogs just past the willows.

Fujikawa, p. 315

Line two: Literally, "above the Heng Pond," a reference to a well-known pond southwest of Nanking in China.

◖ 370 On Passing Dannoura

The huts of the fishermen and crab-catchers are enshrouded in misty rain.

I travel alone past Dannoura in straw raincoat and bamboo hat.

His spirit will not come back when called, though a thousand years have passed.

As the spring winds blow across Mimosuso River, my heart is rent by sorrow.

Sugano, p. 109; Andō, p. 165. From *Butsuzandō shishō* (A Book of Poems from the Residence of Butsuzan), 1852

Title: Dannoura, a bay near Shimonoseki in southern Honshu, was where the Heike (Taira) clan were defeated in a naval battle during the Third Month of 1185, which was the culmination of the Genpei Wars.
Line three: The spirit alluded to here is presumably that of the boy emperor Antoku (r. 1181-83), who, along with his grandmother, drowned himself at Dannoura in 1185 at the age of seven because the Taira clan, upon whom he had depended for support, had been finally defeated. His suicide occurred some seven hundred years before the poet's lifetime, not one thousand.
Line four: There are two rivers in Japan with the name Mimosusogawa. The original one, which is today called Isuzugawa, is located in Ise province and runs through the imperial Shrine of Ise. Before plunging to her death, Antoku's grandmother spoke of finding an imperial capital under the waves of this river in Ise. This anecdote is related in chapter eleven of *The Tale of the Heike*. The second Mimosusogawa, a small tributary which flows into Dannoura, is the one which was seen by the poet. It was named after the original river alluded to in the grandmother's death poem in the famous *Heike* scene.

358

☺ **371 A Rhyming Poem on the Coldness of Spring and the**
Relatively Late Blooming of the Flowers; Written
while Sitting at a Social Gathering

People are sad when the peach and plum blossoms fail to bloom on time.
But I feel glad when the spring is cold and the flowers bloom somewhat late.
Waiting for the flowers is after all just like waiting for guests:
You think of them with the greatest fondness before you actually see them!

Hirano, p. 278

☺ **372**

The old tea seller begged me for poems—I really wondered why.
So I wrote the man a book of verse and, presenting it to him, said:
"The poems I write are no different at all from the tea that you, Sir, sell.
The very best flavor, oddly enough, is found in the simple and plain!"

Fujikawa, p. 317

☺ **373**

Wild flowers of every kind, blooming and filled with dew:
Deep red and pale purple, all of them in bunches.
Poised to cut through the autumn light, a praying mantis flies past.
Quietly heading for the fragrant thicket, it has come to sharpen its axe.

Fujikawa, p. 316

Lines three and four: The raised front legs of the mantis look as though they are holding a
weapon, hence this novel description of its flight.

⬚ 374

In the secluded bamboo the wind has died down; cold the paper screens.
The first snow has started to fall, here at the lonely village.
This tiny scholar's lamp of mine casts a feeble light;
The little maid is twisting rope, the servant girl winds silk thread.

Fujikawa, p. 316

Line four: These activities occurred in the winter months after the outside farming chores had been completed for the season.

Sakuma Shōzan [Zōzan], 1811-1864

A samurai retainer and enlightened intellectual who lived in the Matsushiro domain in Shinshū, part of modern Nagano prefecture, Sakuma Shōzan went to Edo in 1839 to receive instruction from Satō Issai, an eminent scholar of the conservative Hayashi school and an adherent of Yōmeigaku. From Issai, Shōzan gained a belief in the unity of knowledge and action, which would translate into the developmental projects he pursued later, as described below.[1] In Edo, he also came to know *Yanagawa Seigan, who became a lifelong friend, and Ōtsuki Bankei (1801-1878). Together they discussed the major political issues of the day, especially the perceived mounting danger from the West. Shōzan immersed himself in the study of Western learning. Using his new-found technical knowledge from Dutch works, he learned how to make glass, refine chemicals, and cast bronze cannons and small weapons.[2] Shōzan also became an advocate of improved animal husbandry and the consumption of pork, then considered an exotic food. He is further credited with introducing potato cultivation.[3]

Shōzan's now-famous slogan, "Eastern ethics and Western science," was indicative of his belief in the indispensability of Western technology in the context of an eastern philosophical heritage. In 1842, he became an advisor to the Matsushiro domain and began receiving training in the use of firearms under the guidance of a gunnery master in Ise, obtaining his license the following year. Shōzan opened a school in Matsushiro, then another one in Edo around 1851, where he taught the classics and gunnery. He soon gained a reputation as one of Japan's foremost experts on gunnery and Western studies generally, counting among his distinguished followers Yoshida Shōin (1830-1859), Sakamoto Ryōma

---

[1]*Sources of Japanese Tradition*, vol. 2, p. 97.

[2]Ibid., p. 98.

[3]*KEJ*, vol. 7, p. 3.

(1835-1867), and Nakaoka Shintarō (1838-1867). On the importance of learning from the West he wrote:

> In the present world, the traditional knowledge of Japanese and Chinese is not sufficient....[A]fter the three great discoveries—namely, Columbus's discovery of the new world, assisted by scientific investigation; Copernicus's discovery of the true principles of the motion of the Earth; and Newton's discovery of the true principles of gravitation—the foundations of all the sciences have been firmly established and have become accurate, without any evidence of superstitious dogmas. Owing to these discoveries, conditions in Europe and the United States of America have gradually shown a remarkable improvement. Steam-ships, magnetism, telegraphs have all been invented....A truly amazing situation has come about.[4]

Shōzan advised the shogunate to establish coastal defenses, build a fleet of warships, and develop a well-supervised maritime trade, but his suggestions went unheeded. Because he felt it was important for people to go abroad and acquire first-hand knowledge of foreign lands, he laid plans for his disciple Yoshida Shōin to stow away on a Russian ship, this in violation of Japan's strict seclusionist policy, which still forbade overseas travel. The first poem below was written in the Ninth Month of 1854 to bid farewell to Shōin and give him heart upon his departure for Nagasaki, where he was to board the ship. After his attempts to assist Shōin to stow away failed, Shōzan's scheme came to light, and he was imprisoned for a year, then placed under house arrest in Matsushiro for seven more years. Once freed, he continued to campaign for the dissemination of Western knowledge, the opening of ports to foreign ships, and the strengthening of national defenses. These activities led to his assassination in August 1864 by a conservative fanatic of the pro-imperialist Chōshū faction who had campaigned for the expulsion of foreigners.

---

[4]Maruyama, p. 306, citing a letter to *Yanagawa Seigan, written in 1858.

☪ 375   Farewelling Yoshida, a Righteous Gentleman

1 This man is cut from the finest cloth;

He has long abhorred the common herd.

He has roused himself for the journey ahead,

But his plans he has told to nobody else.

5 Although he has told them to nobody else,

One can guess that perhaps he has reasons of his own.

When they see him off at the edge of town,

A lone crane will fly through the autumn sky.

The encircling seas are so vast and extensive,

10 Yet all the five continents are neighbors of ours.

You shall wander everywhere, observing things closely;

Seeing a place once beats a hundred reports.

The sage knows the value of seizing the moment,

So you must return in timely fashion.

15 If we fail to accomplish something significant,

Who will respect us after we're gone?

Inoguchi, pp. 406-407

Title: Yoshida Shōin was a samurai of the Chōshū domain and an ardent supporter of the campaign to promote an imperial restoration and keep foreign nations out of Japan.   See biographical notes on Sakuma Shōzan for information on Yoshida and the occasion of this verse.

☪ 376   Casual Musings

Slanderers, go ahead and slander me.

Sneerers, go ahead and sneer.

Heaven has always known who I am

And pays no heed to the views of others!

Sugano, p. 93. From *Shōzan sensei shishō* (A Book of Poems by Master Shōzan), 1877

Saitō Chikudō, 1815-1852

Saitō Chikudō was a native of Sendai in modern Miyagi prefecture. At sixteen, he began to read the Confucian classics under the scholar Ōtsuki Heisen (1773-1850) of the Sendai domain, but some four years later departed for Edo where he became a student of Masujima Ran'en (1769-1839). Next, he entered the Shōheikō academy in Edo, studying with Koga Tōan and becoming head of the academy at age thirty. Soon, in the fashion of the day, he opened his own private school in Edo as well. Although Chikudō was recalled by the domain to Sendai to teach, he died at the age of thirty-eight before he could take up the appointment. In addition to many volumes of his own literary writings, he left us several local histories. Also of note are such remarkable oddities as a collection of poems dealing with foreign lands, titled *Gaikoku eishi sanjūshi* ("Thirty Poems on Foreign Countries"), and a series of "barbarian" folk poems about the Ainu. Examples from both of these collections are included below.

☉ 377-379   **From a series titled "*Chikushi* (Folk Poems) on Barbarian Peoples: Ten Poems"**

(No. 1)

Spears are flying wildly about where the horizon meets the sea,
As fur seals, big as mountains, go charging through the waves.
Elsewhere, hunters have launched a volley of lances tipped with poison,
And a hundred bears drop dead on the spot without a single sound.

Fujikawa, p. 340

Title: The original order in which the three selections from this series appear is not known. The aboriginal Ainus of Hokkaido, the "barbarian peoples" in the title, are a rare subject in Edo poetry. Chikudō had never visited Hokkaido to observe the Ainu first-hand.

364

(No. 2)

Accompanying their husbands they journey afar over mountain tops and streams.
Although they wear neither stockings nor shoes, still they are not deterred.
Around their lips, dye from the petals of a thousand kinds of flowers.
Never do they allow themselves to be enjoyed by other men.

Fujikawa, p. 341; Nakamura, p. 256

Line three: Ainu women after marriage were tattooed around their mouths using dyes extracted
from various flowers. The tattoos, bluish-green in color, signified marital fidelity.

(No. 3)

A thousand pitchers of barbarian wine, poured out with abandon.
Cups now empty, vessels dry, but the effects of the wine linger on.
Upon straw mats they sing and dance, circling round and round,
Mimicking the sound of the sacred crane with heaven-rending cries.

Fujikawa, pp. 341-342

Line four: This poem describes the festivities surrounding the Bear Festival (J. Kuma Matsuri;
in Ainu, Iyomante), the biggest of the Ainu festivals.

🔊 **380-381   From a series titled "The History of
Foreign Nations: Thirty Poems"**

(No. 2)

Strange winds blew for many a month, the skies were filled with rain.

Boundless waters flooded the Earth, its mountains and its rivers.

Sadly, there was no one with divine Yu's skills to clear a channel for the waters.

All they could do was toil to build a boat that looked like a box.

Fujikawa, p. 342; Nakamura, p. 260

Poet's Note: The person in this poem was the progenitor of the Western nations. [Translators' note: Chikudō is referring to Noah here.]

Line three: Yu was a semi-legendary emperor credited with founding the Hsia dynasty (2205-1766 B.C). According to tradition, he was entrusted by Emperor Shun with controlling the great flood which had begun during the reign of the Sage Emperor Yao. The task is said to have taken nine years. Yu built dikes, dredged rivers, and led the flood waters to the sea by cutting new channels, thus, according to legend, forming the four great rivers of China (D.C. Lau, trans., *Mencius* [Penguin Classics] (Harmondsworth: Penguin Books), 1970, pp. 227-228).

Line four: The last three characters in this line ("box/like/boat") appear to follow Japanese rather than Chinese word order, as is sometimes the case in variant Chinese, and we have translated accordingly. Nakamura, p. 260, and Fujikawa, p. 342, appear to have misinterpreted the phrase as "a box that looked like a boat," as classical Chinese syntax would require.

(No. 30)

Since ancient times merit and fame have been difficult to preserve.

Before they know it, heroes end up as wood-cutters and fishermen.

What a pity it is that you who brought order to our realm,

Returned so early to your home to grow vegetables on the land.

Nakamura, p. 270

Poet's Note: "Washington was the leader of the [American] union and participated in deliberations leading to the establishment of the republic. His achievements were truly brilliant but attracted the jealousy and hatred of others. Washington therefore left politics entirely, giving up his position and going into seclusion in the countryside, where he passed the time in carefree leisure until his death. The entire nation was pained by his death and grieved for him."

George Washington (1732-1799) served as American's first president from 1789 to 1796. During his second Federalist administration, which began in 1793, he came under severe criticism from others, the Jeffersonians, in particular, and was denounced as an enemy of democracy. Washington declined to run for a third term. He was buried on his estate at Mt. Vernon.

Priest Gesshō [Seikyō], 1817-1858

Priest Gesshō came from Suō province in modern Yamaguchi prefecture and was the son of the priest in charge of the Jōdo Shinshū temple Myōenji. Gesshō took his vows at thirteen and two years later went for training at the Zenjōji temple in old Hizen province. Subsequently he went to Hasedera temple in Yamato province for further instruction but eventually tired of Buddhism, becoming interested in Chinese textual exegesis instead. At twenty, he entered the school of *Sakai Kozan in Hiroshima, later studying with *Kusaba Haisen in Saga (Kyushu) and with Shinozaki Shōchiku in Osaka.

At age thirty-two, Gesshō returned to his home town to open a private academy, which he named Seikyōsōdō (The Pure and Crazy Grass Hut), after his style name Seikyō (The Pure and Crazy [One]). Later he became the abbot of a subtemple in Kiyomizudera in Kyoto, but resigned in 1854, thereafter devoting himself to pro-imperial activities aimed at toppling the Tokugawa shogunate and restoring imperial rule. His anti-foreign sentiments come through clearly in the second verse below, where he speaks of the "rancid, frowzy odor" of the "dogs and goats," terms of opprobrium for foreigners.

Gesshō travelled a great deal, falling in with such imperial loyalists as Umeda Unpin, Yoshida Shōin, and *Yanagawa Seigan. In 1858, at the time of the political persecutions of the Great Ansei Purge, he fled with Saigō Takamori (1827-1877) to the domain of Satsuma, but their request for asylum was denied by local officials. Unable to gain entry into the province, the two men thereupon resolved to drown themselves in Kagoshima Bay. Takamori was rescued, but Priest Gesshō drowned, perishing at the age of forty-two.

◐ 382 Inscribed on a Wall before Departing on a Journey to the East

Young men who wish to make their mark leave their village behind.

If they don't succeed in their studies, they never come home again.

Why aspire to have your bones buried in the family plot,

When all throughout this world of ours green hills can be found?

Sugano, p. 84; Inoguchi, p. 332. From *Seikyō ginkō* (A Draft of Poems by Seikyō)

Title: Gesshō wrote this poem in 1843, when he was twenty-seven, around the time he was preparing to go east to study with *Shinozaki Shōchiku in Osaka (Inoguchi, p. 332). Gesshō appears to have been trying to encourage his fellows to overcome their parochialism.

◐ 383 Hearing that the Port of Shimoda Had Been Opened

The mountains and rivers of Shichiri were handed over to those dogs and goats.

After the earthquake the spring landscape was a scene of desolation.

The cherry blossoms don't bear the taint of that rancid, frowzy odor:

Alone they shine in the morning sun, their scent our nation's finest!

Inoguchi, p. 335

Title: This poem was written on the first anniversary of the opening of Shimoda and Hakodate to American commerce. These ports were opened on the third day of the Third Month of 1854 through the Treaty of Kanagawa which was concluded by the U.S. envoy Commodore Matthew C. Perry (1794-1858) and the Japanese shogunate. This agreement was vehemently opposed by many among the Japanese elite who wanted Japan to remain closed to the outside world. Shimoda is a port city on the Izu Peninsula south of Tokyo in Shizuoka prefecture.
Line one: Shichiri is a coastal area near Shimoda. "Dogs and goats" is a derogatory reference to foreigners.
Line two: A massive earthquake occurred on the fourth day of the Eleventh Month of 1854 in eastern Japan, some eight months after the opening of the ports. It caused extensive and serious damage in Shimoda, and the death toll was said to be around three hundred thousand. Gesshō seems to have taken the earthquake to be a sign of the gods' displeasure over the opening of the ports.
Line three: The rancid, frowzy odor is a reference to the smell of foreigners, who, because they ate red meat, unlike the Japanese of the time, were believed to have an unpleasant body odor.

Takasugi Tōgyō [Tōkō, Shinsaku], 1839-1867

Takasugi Tōgyō, whom historians generally refer to by his other name, Shinsaku, was a native of Hagi, a castle town, and a retainer of Chōshū domain in what is today Yamaguchi prefecture. He is known today less for his kanshi than for his political activities as a leading figure in the movement to topple the shogunate in the mid-nineteenth century. As a youth, he was educated at the domain school, Meirinkan, and at nineteen, he was tutored by the pro-imperial activist and intellectual Yoshida Shōin, who ran Shōka Sonjuku (The Village School under the Pines) located in the Matsumoto neighborhood of Haga. Shinsaku and Kusaka Genzui (1840-1864) were called the "Two Jewels" of the school, and Shinsaku was appointed as head of Meirinkan in 1860, when he was only twenty-two.

Shōin introduced Shinsaku to *Sakuma Shōzan, the well-known loyalist and advocate of Western learning. Shinsaku visited Shanghai briefly in 1862 on a shogunal ship, this after mastering the art of marine navigation at the shogunal training school. Witnessing the Taiping Rebellion and the foreign presence in China strengthened his resolve to work for the overthrow of the shogunate to prevent a similar fate from befalling Japan. Rallying his supporters to "revere the emperor and repel the foreigners," Shinsaku became a key player in the campaign to overthrow the shogunate and restore imperial rule, unifying his entire domain behind this cause.

After Chōshū artillery attacked foreign ships in the Shimonoseki Straits in the Sixth Month of 1863, Shinsaku organized a defense force to protect the domain from retaliation. This all-volunteer force, the Kiheitai, became the core militia which supported his later political activities. Shinsaku left his domain without permission in 1864, for which offense he was imprisoned for five months. Two of the poems which follow were written during his incarceration. Chōshū suffered a heavy bombardment from foreign ships in 1864 and was the object of a punitive expedition mounted by the shogunate. Shinsaku, once out of prison, led a coup against the newly-installed conservative Chōshū faction and together with Kido Takayoshi (1833-1877) took over leadership of the domain. In 1866, he successfully repelled another punitive force, paving the way for unified action on the part of a group of anti-shogunal domains which finally brought down the Tokugawa shogunate.

Shinsaku died of tuberculosis a year before the Meiji Restoration, never living to see the ensuing transformation of Japan which he had worked so hard to bring about. While primarily known for his political activism, Shinsaku was also a Yōmeigaku scholar and had a sensuous, aesthetic side which comes through in his poem "Spring Dawn," immediately below.

◔ 384 Spring Dawn

The courtyard is bathed in dawn colors: a scene from a scroll-painting poem.
Through the window and over to my pillow steals the light of the waning moon.
Last night, unbeknownst to me, there was a passing shower of rain.
Now apricot flowers have come into bloom on several of the branches!

Sugano, p. 103. From *Tōgyō shibun shū* (The Collected Writings and Poems of Tōgyō), 1893

◔ 385 Seeing My Aged Father in a Dream One Night
while Moored at Murotsu

I saw my father, clear as can be, in the middle of the night.
It thrilled me to see his kindly face, just as it used to be.
Although I've woken from the dream, my mind keeps dreaming on,
And here aboard this very boat I feel his presence still.

Sugano, p. 105. From *Tōgyō shibun shū*, 1893

☪ 386 A Poem Written while in Prison

Grieving for our country, distressed by the times, I sigh and lament alone.

The solitary prisoner's thoughts are in turmoil, tangled up like hemp.

If perchance I should lose my life in these dark and murky depths,

My loyal spirit will return to heaven to protect this nation of ours.

Inoguchi, p. 458

☪ 387 Written in Prison

1   All alone and bound in shackles,

    A hundred cares within my breast.

    I only know that there is today,

    And know not if there'll be a tomorrow.

5   The evening crows caw from the rooftop;

    The dawn sun shines through the prison window.

    I pray to the sun, shedding useless tears.

    I listen to the crows and it breaks my heart.

    Though heart-broken, I feel no righteous indignation;

10   Though tears I shed, I care not for my life.

    Perils from abroad threaten my Lord.

    What will be our nation's fate?

Inoguchi, p.458

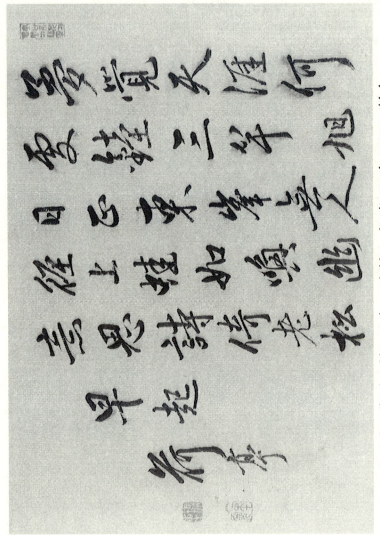

5. A four-line kanshi quatrain, probably early-nineteenth century, titled "Rising Early," by an unidentified poet named Katei.

KYŌSHI (HUMOROUS VERSE)

The genre known as kyōshi (crazy poems) is believed to be quite ancient, possibly dating back as far as early Heian times. It is considered unique to Japanese culture, distinct from any known Chinese forms. Few pre-Edo examples survive, because most such poems were not routinely recorded, being considered a passing amusement rather than literary gems worth preserving for posterity. One of the earliest known examples is by Minamoto Shitagō (911-983), but only the title is known to us, being mentioned in the eleventh-century Japanese anthology of Chinese poetry and letters, *Honchō monzui*.

The first recorded examples of such poetry, while not yet called kyōshi, were written by the Gozan priests of the fourteenth to sixteenth centuries and are found in such collections as *Kokkei shibun* (Comic Literature) and *Baika mujinzō* (The Inexhaustible Storehouse of Plum Blossoms).[1] The following verse, titled "The Flea," by the poet Priest Ikkyū (1394-1481), is a representative example from this period, although the kyōshi scholar Sakauchi Yasuko observes that Ikkyū's humorous poetry does not display the irregularity of rhyme typical of kyōshi.[2]

Could it be dirt? Or is it dust? Just what is this thing?
All my life I've thought of you as just a worthless wretch.
Feeding off the blood of others made you very fat,
But now this skinny priest has crushed you, snuffing out your life![3]

*Priest Bunshi Genshō (also known as Nanpo, 1555-1620) is credited with being the first poet to possess a consciousness of kyōshi as a distinct genre. Indeed, he is the first poet ever to use the term, which occurs in the posthumous

---

[1]Sakauchi Yasuko, "Kyōshi," in Ōsone, p. 115.

[2]Ibid.

[3]From *Ikkyū shokoku monogatari* (The Story of Ikkyū's Travels through the Provinces), comp, ca. 1670; text follows Iwanami, pp. 371-372.

collection titled *Nanpo bunshū* (The Collected Writings of Nanpo, 1625).[4] Other early examples from the Edo period are found in the collection titled *Jūban kyōshi-ai* (A Kyōshi Competition in Ten Rounds, 1668).[5] Genshō and his colleagues wrote comic verse as a diversion from their more serious kanshi pursuits, employing pseudonyms, as if to adopt an entirely separate persona for this less dignified poetic activity. The kyōshi genre fell into disuse during the strictly moralistic Kyōhō reform period (1716-1735) and was not revived until the 1760s, when it finally gained a firm footing "above ground" in Japanese literary society.

From this time, the genre began to display certain literary features beyond the mere treatment of plebeian and vulgar subject matter, these including irony, caricature, satire, and social criticism, which were to characterize kyōshi thereafter. Kyōshi were typically occasional in nature, written on the spur of the moment. Slang, dialect, and puns are found in abundance, and, while possessing rhyme, kyōshi usually do not adhere to the strict Chinese tonal rules governing kanshi.

---

[4]Sakuchi, in Ōsone, p. 115.

[5]Ibid.

Priest Bunshi Genshō [Nanpo], 1555-1620

A native of Hyūga in modern Miyazaki prefecture, Bunshi Genshō, also known simply as Nanpo, was a Buddhist priest and Neo-Confucian scholar. He is perhaps best known for his gloss annotations appended to Neo-Confucian commentaries accompanying *The Four Books*. At age six he entered a local temple where he underwent training in *The Lotus Sutra*. There he was known by the nickname Monjudō (The Child Manjushiri), in allusion to the Bodhisattva of Wisdom and Intellect. Nanpo went on to study at Ryūgenji temple with a priest named Genshin. Under Genshin's guidance, he read Chinese religious texts and learned the mechanics of kanshi versification, adopting the clerical name Genshō after he received the tonsure. In 1569 Nanpo entered the Tōfukuji temple for further research into the Japanese and Chinese classics, remaining there for five years. Four years later, he accompanied his earlier teacher Genshin to Shingoji temple in Ōsumi (modern Kagoshima prefecture), before taking up residence in two other temples in the same area.

After becoming known to the feudal lord Shimazu Yoshihisa (1533-1611), Nanpo was appointed Chief Priest of the Ankokuji and Shōkōji temples in southern Kyushu, also lecturing on the classics in Hyūga province. Later, he offered instruction on *The Great Learning* at Tōfukuji temple, having followed his lord to his residence at Fushimi in Kyoto, in 1599. Emperor Go-Mizunoo had him lecture on the Sung Neo-Confucianist commentaries attached to *The Four Books*, a distinct honor. In 1601, Nanpo returned to Satsuma in southern Kyushu to take up residence at the Shōkōji temple and in 1611 established the Dairyūji temple at Kagoshima. The verse which follows is one of the earliest known Edo kyōshi. It may seem unexpected coming from the brush of such a serious priest and scholar.

◉ 388

At the village assembly the men and women are wearing clothes that are new.
Together they raise their cups of wine, drinking until sundown.
Their shoulders droop from their heavy loads: what could they have bought?
They're carrying home upon their backs the people who are drunk!

Quoted in Yamagishi Tokuhei, "Kyōshi to sono sakuhin," in Yamagishi Tokuhei, ed., *Nihon kanbungaku shiron kō* (Tokyo: Iwanami Shoten, 1974), pp. 574-575. Orig. verse from *Nanpo bunshū* (The Collected Writings of Nanpo), vol. 2, dated 1625.

Meppōkai [Dōmyaku Sensei, Hatanaka Kansai], 1752-1801

The poet who called himself Meppōkai and, more commonly, Dōmyaku Sensei (Master Copper Vein), was a Kyoto native and one of the most prominent kyōshi poets of the Edo period. In his youth, he studied with Naba Rodō (1727-1789). A Teishugaku scholar and colleague of *Ōta Nanpo, with whom he is often compared, his real name was Hatanaka Kansai (Tanomo). In 1769, when he was eighteen years old, Dōmyaku published a kyōshi collection titled *Taihei gafu* (Folk Poems for a Nation at Peace), whose sharp, satirical commentaries on contemporary society won him wide popular acclaim.

◎ 389 To a Beggar

Your hem is ripped, your rush-mat torn, and though it's daytime you're cold.
This morning you got no alms at all, and so your stomach's empty.
You turn your head and from it fall some "goddesses of a thousand arms,"
Then taking your time you study them, off in a sunny spot.

Iwanami, p. 374. From *Taihei gafu* (Folk Poems for a Nation at Peace), 1769

Line three: "Goddesses of a thousand arms" is a colloquial term for head lice.

◐ 390 Going to an Outhouse in the Bush

I went to the outhouse, feeling the urge,
But someone else was already there.
I coughed a few times, but he wouldn't come out,
So my body trembled and trembled.

Iwanami, pp. 374-375. From *Seta no karahashi* (The Chinese-Style Bridge at Seta), 1771 (date of preface)

Chōsaibō, b. ca. 1765

Chōsaibō was a minor kyōshi poet about whom little is known, except that he was a native of Kyoto and in all likelihood rather poor, judging from the verse that follows. This poem, with its wry, self-deprecatory humor that can be readily appreciated even today, is the only selection from his corpus included in the Iwanami anthology.

◐ 391 The Misery of Poverty

I'm poorer than anyone else alive
But I hate work nonetheless.
Regrets come after, never before;
And now that I'm old it's all such a shame!

Iwanami, p. 383. From *Kyōshi baka shū* (A Collection of Verse by the Kyōshi Idiot)

Sūkatan, ?-?

Nothing is known about the life of the kyōshi poet known as Sūkatan. The Iwanami commentators speculate, based on certain textual evidence, that he was none other than *Nakajima Sōin, who commonly wrote his comic Chinese verse under the penname Ankutsu Sensei.[1]

◖ 392 A Poem Written Impromptu during a Big Storm

The roof is buffeted by the wind, the rain keeps leaking in.
He crouches and hastily hides himself in a corner of the closet.
The children, speaking in hushed tones, inquire of their father:
"Is the bill-collector going to come to our house again tonight?"

Iwanami, p. 380. From *Taihei sankyoku* (Three Compositions Written in Peaceful Times), 1821 (date of preface)

---

[1]Iwanami, p. 488.

Gubutsu [Osokusai], 1797?-1828

A kyōshi poet of some distinction, Gubutsu (The Foolish Buddha) was also
known by the pseudonym Osokusai (Studio of Muddy Feet). His real name is not
known. Few details concerning his life have emerged, except that he was a
student of *Nakajima Sōin and that his works were published by Hachimonjiya
(The Figure-of-Eight Shop) in Kyoto. He was probably in his early thirties at the
time of his death.

◐ 393 In Praise of a Picture of Someone Extinguishing a
Lantern Light by Breaking Wind

Pssss! Pssss! Pssss! Pssss!—his bottom's open wide!
An onlooker meanwhile holds his nose, and then he laughs out loud.
Bowels out of gas, their force now lost; that flame's so hard to put out!
Tomorrow night he'll eat plenty of yams, and then he'll try again!

Iwanami 379. From *Shoku Taihei gafu* (More Folk Poems for a Nation at Peace), 1820

382

◐ **394-397   From a series titled "Suffering from Scabies: Seven Poems"**
(No. 1)

My wrists and the skin between my fingers keep on itching and itching.

As I rub and scratch myself, little welts pop up.

I haven't asked the doctor yet just what is ailing me,

But everybody says to me, "You must be a daimyo!"

Miura, p. 462; Iwanami, p. 377.   From *Taihei shishū* (A Collection of Poetry for a Nation at Peace)

Line four: There is a play on words being exploited here. The words for scabies, *hizen*, happens to be homophonous with the name of the province Hizen (in Kyushu), over which a daimyo ruled. The pun is that both the poet and the daimyo "possess Hizen."

(No. 5)

Pox, pox, and still more pox!

Scars, scars, and still more scars!

Scabies I've had for three whole years, I've three years' scars to boot!

Praying and scratching for three long years, a horrible nuisance it is!!

Miura, p. 463

(No. 6)

Nearly half my skin has now come off.

I'm afraid to do anything or appear in public.

I want it to end, the sooner the better,

So I'm off to Koyama to buy some medicine!

Miura, p. 463

(No. 7)

Although I abstain from eating meat and avoid strong tasting foods,
There are still so many things right now that I really must avoid.
A pity it is that morning and night I cannot give up eating,
For old, pickled radishes are all that I can eat!

Miura, p. 463

◖ **398   The Flea**

Jumpety jumpety jumpety jump, jumpety jump went the flea,
Wandering around in the seam of my robe, so cramped its bones might break!
I searched and searched for him with my hand and finally I got him.
But once he was killed I took a look and found only a bit of thread!

Iwanami, p. 378. From *Taihei fūga* (Peacetime Refinements), 1828

◖ **399   The Dogfight**

Bow-wow-wow and a bow-wow-wow
And a bow-wow-wow-wow, wow-wow-wow!
The night was dark, and I was unaware
    just how many dogs there were out there.
From first to last, all that I could hear was
    bow-wow-wow-wow, wow-wow-wow!

Iwanami, pp. 378-379. From *Shoku Taihei gafu*, 1820

Hōgai Dōjin, ?-?

Hōgai Dōjin (The Transcendental Priest) was also known by the style name Baian (Plum Retreat). His real name was Fukui Ken and, as a youth, he trained as a doctor. Beyond this, few facts are known, other than that he achieved a reputation for himself as a stylishly unconventional kyōshi poet and was the author of several collections of such verse. The poem which follows has a surprisingly modern tone, reminding us that housewives chafing against their burdensome lot in life are by no means just a recent phenomenon.

☪ 400 Housewife's Lament

At night I'm plagued by mosquitoes and fleas, by day I'm plagued by the kids.
Half an hour of peace and quiet is very hard to find.
Washing the cotton summer robes and starching all the clothes,
Fetching the water, cooking the meals—all of this falls on me!

Iwanami, p. 381. Originally from a collection called *Shōchū higashi* (Humorously Annotated Poetic Confectionery). *Shōchū*, meaning "humorously annotated," is a pun on a more common homophonous compound meaning "copiously annotated," typically seen in book titles.

BIBLIOGRAPHY

Addiss, Stephen, trans. *Tall Mountains and Flowing Water: The Arts of Uragami Gyokudō*. Honolulu: University of Hawaii Press, 1987.

Andō Hideo. *Rai San'yō den*. Tokyo: Kondō Shuppansha, 1982.

----------, comp. *[Shintei] Nihon kanshi hyakusen*. Tokyo: Sōdōsha, 1983.

Arai Hakuseki. Trans. by Joyce Ackroyd. *Tales Around a Brushwood Fire: The Autobiography of Arai Hakuseki*. Tokyo: University of Tokyo Press, 1979.

Arntzen, Sonja, trans. and annot. *Ikkyū and the Crazy Cloud Anthology*. Tokyo: University of Tokyo Press, 1986.

Bitō Jishū. Ed. with introd. by Rai Tsutomu. *Seikiken shū [Kinsei juka bunshū shūsei*, vol. 10]. Tokyo: Perikansha, 1991.

Bitō Masahide. *Nihon bunka to Chūgoku [Chūgoku bunka sōsho*, vol. 10]. Tokyo: Taishūan, 1968.

Bodman, Richard Wainwright. *Prose and Poetry in Early Medieval China: A Study and Translation of Kūkai's Bunkyō Hifuron*. Ann Arbor, Michigan: University Microfilms, 1984.

Brower, Robert, and Earl Miner. *Japanese Court Poetry*. Stanford: Stanford University Press, 1961.

Chang, Kang-i Sun. *The Evolution of Chinese Tz'u Poetry from Late T'ang to Northern Sung*. Princeton: Princeton University Press, 1980.

-----------------. *Six Dynasties Poetry*. Princeton: Princeton University Press, 1986.

Davis, A. R. *T'ao Yuan-ming (A.D. 365-427): His Works and Their Meaning*. 2 vols. Cambridge: Cambridge University Press, 1976.

Dazai Shundai. Ed. with introd. by Kojima Yasunori. *Shundai sensei Shishienkō [Kinsei juka bunshū shūsei*, vol. 6]. Tokyo: Perikansha, 1986.

Endō Tetsuo. *Kanshi*. 3 vols. [*Shinshaku kanbun taikei*, vols. 42-43, 52]. Tokyo: Meiji Shoin, 1989-1992.

Fairbank, John K., Edwin O. Reischauer, and Albert O. Craig. *East Asia: Tradition and Transformation*. Boston: Houghton-Mifflin Company, 1973.

Frankel, Hans H. *The Flowering Plum and the Palace Lady: Interpretations of Chinese Poetry*. New Haven: Yale University Press, 1976.

Fujikawa Hideo. *Kan Sazan to Rai San'yō* [*Tōyō Bunko series*]. Tokyo: Heibonsha, 1971.

--------------. *Edo kōki no shijintachi* [*Chikuma Shobō sōsho*, vol. 208]. Tokyo: Mugi Shobō, 1973.

--------------, comp. *Kan Sazan* [*Nihon shijin sen*, vol. 30]. Tokyo: Chikuma Shobō, 1981.

--------------, Matsushita Tadashi, and Sano Masami, eds. *Shikashū Nihon kanshi*. 11 vols. Tokyo: Kyūko Shoin, 1983-1984.

--------------, Matsushita Tadashi, and Sano Masami, eds. *Shishū Nihon kanshi*. 20 vols. Tokyo: Kyūko Shoin, 1985-1990.

Graham, A.C. *Poems of the Late T'ang*. Harmondsworth: Penguin Books, 1965.

Harada Kenyū, comp. *Nihon kanshi sen*. Kyoto: Jinbun Shoin, 1974.

Hattori Nankaku. Ed. with introd. by Hino Tatsuo. *Nankaku sensei bunshū* [*Kinsei juka bunshū shūsei*, vol. 7]. Tokyo: Perikansha, 1986.

Hightower, James R. *Topics in Chinese Literature: Outlines and Bibliographies* [*Harvard-Yenching Institute Studies*, vol. 3] Cambridge: Harvard University Press, 1966.

------------------. *The Poetry of T'ao Ch'ien*. Oxford: Clarendon Press, 1970.

Hino Tatsuo, annot. *Narushima Ryūhoku, Ōnuma Chinzan* [*Edo shijin senshū*, vol. 10]. Tokyo: Iwanani Shoten, 1990.

Hirano Hikojirō, et al., comp. *Kanshi meishi hyōshaku shūsei*. Tokyo: Meichō Fukyūkai, 1936.

Hung, William. *Tu Fu: China's Greatest Poet*. Cambridge: Harvard University Press, 1952.

Ibi Takashi, annot. *Ichikawa Kansai, Okubō Shibutsu* [*Edo shijin senshū*, vol. 5]. Tokyo: Iwanami Shoten, 1990.

Imanaka Kanshi and Naramoto Tatsuya, eds. *Ogyū Sorai zenshū*. 5 vols. Tokyo: Kawade Shobō Shinsha, 1973-1978.

Inoguchi Atsushi, comp. and annot. *Nihon kanshi*. 2 vols. (jō, ge; continuous pagination) [*Shinshaku kanbun taikei*, vols. 45 & 46]. Tokyo: Meiji Shoin, 1972.

--------------, comp. and annot. *Josei to kanshi: wakan joryū shi shi* [*Kazama sensho*, vol. 103]. Tokyo: Kazama Shoin, 1978.

--------------. *Nihon kanshi kanshō jiten*. Tokyo: Kadokawa Shoten, 1980.

-------------- and Matano Tarō. *Fujiwara Seika, Matsunaga Sekigo* [*Sōsho Nihon no shisōka*, vol. 1]. Tokyo: Meitoku Shuppansha, 1982.

--------------. *Nihon kanbungaku shi*. Tokyo: Kadokawa Shoten, 1984.

Inoue Tetsujirō. *Nihon shushigakuha no tetsugaku*. Tokyo: Fuzanbō, 1905.

--------------. *Nihon kogaku-ha no tetsugaku*. Tokyo: Fuzanbō, 1923.

Iritani Sensuke. *Kindai bungaku to shite no Meiji kanshi* [*Kanbun sensho*, vol. 42]. Tokyo: Kenbun Shuppan, 1989.

--------------, annot. *Rai San'yō, Yanagawa Seigan* [*Edo shijin senshū*, vol. 8]. Tokyo: Iwanami Shoten, 1990.

Iriya Yoshitaka. *Nihonjin bunjin shisen*. Tokyo: Chūō Kōronsha, 1983.

Ishida Kazuo. *Asami Keisai, Wakabayashi Kyōsai* [*Sōsho Nihon no shisōka*, vol. 13]. Tokyo: Meitoku Shuppansha, 1990.

Ishikawa Tadahisa, comp. *Kanshi no sekai*. Tokyo: Taishūkan Shoten, 1989.

Itō Tamoatsu. *Itō Jinsai tsuketari Itō Tōgai* [*Sōsho Nihon no shisōka*, vol. 10]. Tokyo: Meitoku Shuppansha, 1983.

Itō Tōgai. Ed. with introd. by Miyake Masahiko. *Shōjutsu sensei bunshū* [*Kinsei juka bunshū shūsei*, vol. 4]. Tokyo: Perikansha, 1988.

Kageki Hideo. *Gozan shishi no kenkyū*. Tokyo: Kazama Shobō, 1977.

Kanda Kiichirō, ed. *Meiji kanshi bunshū* [*Meiji bungaku zenshū*, vol. 62]. Tokyo: Chikuma Shobō, 1983.

Kato, Shuichi. *A History of Japanese Literature*. vol. 2. New York: Kodansha International, 1990 [paperback ed.]

Keene, Donald. *World Within Walls*. New York: Holt, Reinhart and Winston, 1976.

------------. *Some Japanese Portraits*. Tokyo, New York and San Francisco: Kodansha International, Ltd., 1983.

------------. *Seeds in the Heart: Japanese Literature from the Earliest Times to the Late Sixteenth Century*. New York: Henry Holt and Company, 1993.

Kimura Mitsunori and Ushio Haruo. *Nakae Tōju, Kumazawa Banzan [Sōsho Nihon no shisōka*, vol. 4]. Tokyo: Meitoku Shuppansha, 1978.

Kitō Yūichi. *Hosoi Heishū tsuketari Nakanishi Tan'en [Sōsho Nihon no shisōka*, vol. 21]. Tokyo: Meitoku Shuppansha, 1988.

Kobayashi Nobuaki, Ichiki Takeo, et al., eds. *Kanbun binran*. Tokyo: Hyōronsha, 1973.

Kodansha Encyclopedia of Japan. 9 vols. + supp. vol. Tokyo and New York: Kodansha, 1983.

Kokushi daijiten. 15 vols. [ref. supplements forthcoming]. Ed. by *Kokushi daijiten* Iinkai. Tokyo: Yoshikawa Kōbunkan, 1979-1993.

Konishi Jinichi, annot. *Bunkyō hifuron kō*. 3 vols. Kyoto: Ōyashima Shuppan, 1948-1952.

---------------. Trans. by Aileen Gatten and Mark Harbison. *A History of Japanese Literature*. vol. 3. Princeton: Princeton University Press, 1991.

Koschmann, J. Victor. *The Mito Ideology: Discourse, Reform, and Insurrection in Late Tokugawa Japan, 1790-1864*. Berkeley, Los Angeles and London: University of California Press, 1987.

Kose Susumu and Okada Takehiko. *Yamazaki Ansai [Sōsho Nihon no shisōka*, vol. 6]. Tokyo: Meitoku Shuppansha, 1985.

Kudō Toyohiko. *Hirose Tansō, Hirose Kyokusō [Sōsho Nihon no shisōka*, vol. 35]. Tokyo: Meitoku Shuppansha, 1978.

Kurokawa Yōichi, annot. *Kan Sazan, Rikunyo [Edo shijin senshū*, vol. 4]. Tokyo: Iwanami Shoten, 1990.

Lau, D.C., trans. *Mencius [Penguin Classics]*. Harmondsworth: Penguin Books, 1970.

Liu, James J.Y. *The Art of Chinese Poetry*. Chicago: University of Chicago Press, 1962 (paperback 1966).

--------------. *Major Lyricists of the Northern Sung*. Princeton: Princeton University Press, 1974.

Liu, Wu-chi, and Irving Yucheng Lo, eds. *Sunflower Splendor: Three Thousand Years of Chinese Poetry*. Bloomington and Indianapolis: Indiana University Press, 1975.

McCraw, David R. *Du Fu's Laments from the South*. Honolulu: University of Hawaii Press, 1992.

McCullough, Helen Craig. *Brocade by Night: 'Kokin Wakashū' and the Court Style in Japanese Classical Poetry*. Stanford: Stanford University Press, 1985.

Maruyama Masao. Trans. by Mikiso Hane. *Studies in the Intellectual History of Tokugawa Japan*. Tokyo: Tokyo University Press, 1974.

Matsumoto Shigeru. *Motoori Norinaga*. Cambridge: Harvard University Press, 1970.

Matsushita Tadashi. *Edo jidai no shifū shiron*. Tokyo: Meiji Shoin, 1957.

Minagawa Kien. Ed. with introd. by Takahashi Hiromi. *Kien bunshū [Kinsei juka bunshū shūsei*, vol. 9]. Tokyo: Perikansha, 1986.

Miura Osamu, comp. *[Shinsen] Senryū kyōshi shū*. Tokyo: Yūhōdō, 1914.

Mizuta Norihisa, annot. *Katsu Shikin, Nakajima Sōin [Edo shijin senshū*, vol. 6]. Tokyo: Iwanami Shoten, 1993.

Najita, Tetsuo, and Irwin Scheiner, eds. *Japanese Thought in the Tokugawa Period (1600-1868)*. Chicago and London: The University of Chicago Press, 1978.

Nakamura Shinichirō, comp. *Edo kanshi [Koten o yomu*, vol. 20]. Tokyo: Iwanami Shoten, 1985.

Nakamura Shunsaku, et al. *Minagawa Kien, Ōta Kinjō [Sōsho Nihon no shisōka*, vol. 26]. Tokyo: Meitoku Shuppansha, 1986.

Nakamura Yukihiko, ed. *Kinsei no kanshi*. Tokyo: Kyūko Shoin, 1986.

Naoki Kōjirō. *Kanshi kindai meishi kenkyū shūsei: kanshi no enkaku; Meiji Taishō meishisen kenkyū oyobi kanshō*. Tokyo: Meicho Fukyūkai, 1981.

Nienhauser, William H., Jr., ed. and comp. *The Indiana Companion to Traditional Chinese Literature*. Bloomington: Indiana University Press, 1986.

Nihon jinmei daijiten. 7 vols. Shimonaka Kunihiko, ed. Tokyo: Heibonsha, 1979.

Nihon kanbungaku daijiten. 1 vol. Kondō Haruo, comp. Tokyo: Meiji Shoin, 1985.

Nosco, Peter, ed. *Confucianism and Tokugawa Culture*. Princeton: Princeton University Press, 1984.

------------. *Remembering Paradise: Nativism and Nostalgia in Eighteenth-Century Japan* [*Harvard-Yenching Monograph Series*, no. 31]. Cambridge: Harvard University Press, 1990.

Ogawa Tsuramichi. *Kangakusha denki oyobi chojutsu shūran*. Tokyo: Meicho Kankōkai, 1977 (rpt. of orig. pub. 1925).

Okamura Shigeru, annot. *Hirose Tansō, Hirose Kyokusō* [*Edo shijin senshū*, vol. 9]. Tokyo: Iwanami Shoten, 1991.

Ōoka Makoto. Trans. by Takako U. Lento and Thomas V. Lento. *The Colors of Poetry* [*Reflections series*]. Rochester, Michigan: Katydid Books, 1991.

Ooms, Herman. *Tokugawa Ideology: Early Constructs, 1570-1680*. Princeton: Princeton University Press, 1985.

Ōsone Shōsuke, et al., eds. *Kanshi, kanbun, hyōron* [*Kenkyū shiryō Nihon koten bungaku*, vol. 11]. Tokyo: Meiji Shoin, 1984.

Owen, Stephen. *The Poetry of the Early T'ang*. New Haven: Yale University Press, 1977.

------------. *The Great Age of Chinese Poetry: The High T'ang*. New Haven: Yale University Press, 1981.

------------. *Remembrances: The Experience of the Past in Classical Chinese Literature*. Cambridge: Harvard University Press, 1986.

Pollack, David. "Kyōshi: Japanese 'Wild Poetry.'" *Journal of Asian Studies* 38, no. 3 (May 1979): 499-517.

------------. *The Fracture of Meaning: Japan's Synthesis of China from the Eighth Through the Eighteenth Century*. Princeton: Princeton University Press, 1986.

The Princeton Companion to Classical Japanese Literature. Earl Miner, Hiroko Odagiri, and Robert E. Morrell, comps. Princeton: Princeton University Press, 1985.

Rabinovitch, Judith N., with Akira Minegishi. "Some Literary Aspects of Four *Kambun* Diaries of the Japanese Court: Translation with Commentaries on Excerpts from *Uda Tennō Gyoki, Murakami Tennō Gyoki, Gonki,* and *Gyokuyō,*" in *The Humanities* [*Journal of the Yokohama National University,* Section II, Language and Literature] 39 (Oct. 1992): 1-37.

Reischauer, Edwin O., and Albert M. Craig. *Japan: Tradition and Transformation*. Boston: Houghton Mifflin Company, 1978.

Rickett, Adele Austin R., ed. *Chinese Approaches to Literature from Confucius to Liang Ch'i-ch'ao*. Princeton: Princeton University Press, 1978.

Roberts, Laurance P., comp. *A Dictionary of Japanese Artists*. Tokyo: Weatherhill, 1976.

Rubinger, Richard. *Private Academies in Tokugawa Japan*. Princeton: Princeton University Press, 1982.

Sansom, George. *A History of Japan, 1615-1867*. Stanford: Stanford University Press, 1963.

Satō Tsutomu. *Kanshi no imēji*. Tokyo: Taishūkan Shoten, 1992.

Shindō Hideyuki. *Miyake Kanran, Arai Hakuseki* [*Sōsho Nihon no shisōka*, vol. 14]. Tokyo: Meitoku Shuppansha, 1984.

Spae, Joseph John. *Itō Jinsai: A Philosopher, Educator and Sinologist of the Tokugawa Period* [*Monumenta Serica Monograph Series*]. Peiping: Catholic University of Peking, 1948.

Stevens, John. *Three Zen Masters: Ikkyū, Hakuin, Ryōkan*. Tokyo: Kodansha International, 1993.

Sugano Hiroyuki and Kunikane Kaiji, comp. *Nihon kanbun* [*Kanbun meisakusen*, vol. 5]. Tokyo: Taishūkan Shoten, 1984.

Takasu Yoshijirō, ed. *Mitogaku taikei*. 8 vols. Tokyo: Mitōgaku Taikei Kankōkai, 1941.

Taninaka Shinichi, ed. *Nihon Chūgoku kanshi kankei ronbun sōmoku sakuin*. Tokyo: Waseda University, 1989.

Toda Hiroaki. *Nihon kanbungaku tsūshi*. Tokyo: Musashino Shoin, 1957.

Tōgō Toyoharu. *Ryōkan shishū*. Tokyo: Sōgensha, 1962.

Tokuda Takeshi, annot. *Nomura Kōen, Tachi Ryūwan [Edo shijin senshū*, vol. 7]. Tokyo: Iwanami Shoten, 1990.

--------------, annot. *Yanada Zeigan, Akiyama Gyokuzan [Edo shijin senshū*, vol. 2]. Tokyo: Iwanami Shoten, 1992.

Tsunoda Ryusaku, William Theodore de Bary, and Donald Keene, eds. *Sources of Japanese Tradition*. vol. 2. New York and London: Columbia University Press, 1958.

Uemura Kankō, ed. *Nihon gozan bungaku zenshū*. 5 vols. Tokyo: Gozan Bungaku Zenshū Kankōkai, 1936. Reprinted Kyoto: Shibunkaku, 1979.

Ueno Yōzō, annot. *Ishikawa Jōzan, Gensei [Edo shijin senshū*, vol. 1]. Tokyo: Iwanami Shoten, 1991.

Uete Michinari, annot. *Rai San'yō [Nihon shisō taikei*, vol. 49]. Tokyo: Iwanami Shoten, 1977.

Uno Shigehiko. *Hayashi Razan tsuketari Hayashi Gahō [Sōsho Nihon no shisōka*, vol. 2]. Tokyo: Meitoku Shuppansha, 1992.

Ury, Marian, trans. *Poems of the Five Mountains*. Tokyo: Mushinsha, 1977.

Waley, Arthur. *The Life and Times of Po Chü-i*. London: G. Allen and Unwin, 1951.

Watson, Burton. *Early Chinese Literature*. New York: Columbia University Press, 1962.

--------------, trans. *Chuang Tzu: Basic Writings*. New York and London: Columbia University Press, 1964.

--------------. "Some Remarks on the *Kanshi*." *Journal-Newsletter of the Association of Teachers of Japanese* 5, no. 2 (July 1968).

--------------, trans. *Cold Mountain: 100 Poems by the T'ang Poet Han-shan [Translations from the Oriental Classics]*. New York: Columbia University Press, 1970.

--------------. *Chinese Lyricism: Shih Poetry from the Second to the Twelfth Century*. New York and London: Columbia University Press, 1971.

--------------, trans. *Japanese Literature in Chinese*. vol. 2. New York: Columbia University Press, 1976.

-------------, trans. *Grass Hill: Poems and Prose by the Japanese Monk Gensei* [*Translations from the Oriental Classics*]. New York: Columbia University Press, 1983.

-------------, trans. *Kanshi: The Poetry of Ishikawa Jōzan and Other Edo-Period Poets*. San Francisco: North Point Press, 1990.

Yamagishi Tokuhei, ed. and annot. *Gozan bungaku shū Edo kanshi shū* [*Iwanami koten bungaku taikei*, vol. 89]. Tokyo: Iwanami Shoten, 1966.

-----------------, ed. *Nihon kanbungaku shiron kō*. Tokyo: Iwanami Shoten, 1974.

Yamamoto Kazuyoshi and Yokoyama Hiroshi, annot. *Hattori Nankaku, Gion Nankai* [*Edo shijin senshū*, vol. 3]. Tokyo: Iwanami Shoten, 1991.

Yamashita, Samuel Hideo. "Compasses and Carpenters' Squares: A Study of Itō Jinsai and Ogyū Sorai." Ph.D diss., University of Michigan, 1981.

Yanada Zeigan. Ed. with introd. by Tokuda Takeshi. *Zeigan shū* [*Kinsei juka bunshū shūsei*, vol. 5]. Tokyo: Perikansha, 1985.

Yang, Xiaoshan. "Having It Both Ways: Manors and Manners in Bai Juyi's Poetry." *Harvard Journal of Asiatic Studies* 56, no. 1 (June 1996): 123-149.

Yip, Wai-lim. *Chinese Poetry: Major Modes and Genres*. Berkeley: University of California Press, 1976.

Yoshikawa Hatsuki. *Kanshi to haiku: Bashō, Buson, Issa, Shiki*. Tokyo: Kyōiku Shuppan Sentā, 1985 (first ed.).

Yoshikawa Kōjirō. "Chinese Poetry in Japan: Influence and Reaction." In *Cahiers d'Histoire Mondiale* 2, no. 4 (1955).

-----------------. Trans. by Burton Watson. *An Introduction to Sung Poetry*. Cambridge: Harvard University Press, 1967.

Yu, Pauline. *The Reading of Imagery in the Chinese Poetic Tradition*. Princeton: Princeton University Press, 1987.

JAPANESE STUDIES